FERGUSON

CAREER COACH

MANAGING YOUR CAREER IN THE

Computer Industry

The Ferguson Career Coach Series

Managing Your Career in the Art Industry
Managing Your Career in the Computer Industry
Managing Your Career in Education
Managing Your Career in the Health Care Industry
Managing Your Career in Law Enforcement
Managing Your Career in the Music Industry
Managing Your Career in the Sports Industry
Managing Your Career in Theater and the Performing Arts

FERGUSON

CAREER COACH

MANAGING YOUR CAREER IN THE

Computer Industry

Shelly Field

Checkmark Books®
An imprint of Infobase Publishing

Ferguson Career Coach: Managing Your Career in the Computer Industry

Checkmark Books
An imprint of Infobase Publishing, Inc.
132 West 31st Street
New York NY 10001

Library of Congress Cataloging-in-Publication Data

Field, Shelly.
  Ferguson career coach : managing your career in the computer industry / Shelly Field.
     p. cm. — (The Ferguson career coach series)
  Includes bibliographical references and index.
  ISBN-13: 978-0-8160-5358-2 (hardcover : alk. paper)
  ISBN-10: 0-8160-5358-8 (hardcover : alk. paper)
  ISBN-13: 978-0-8160-5359-9 (pbk. : alk. paper)
  ISBN-10: 0-8160-5359-6 (pbk. : alk. paper)
 1. Computer science—Vocational guidance—United States. 2. Computer industry—
Vocational guidance—United States. I. Title.
  QA76.25.F54 2008
  004.023—dc20   2008031738

Checkmark Books are available at special discounts when purchased in bulk quantities for businesses, associations, institutions, or sales promotions. Please call our Special Sales Department in New York at (212) 967-8800 or (800) 322-8755.

You can find Facts On File on the World Wide Web at http://www.factsonfile.com

Text design by Kerry Casey
Cover design by Takeshi Takahashi

Printed in the United States of America

VB Hermitage 10 9 8 7 6 5 4 3 2 1

This book is printed on acid-free paper and contains 30% post-consumer recycled content.

Disclaimer: The examples and practices described in this book are based on the author's experience as a professional career coach. No guarantee of success for individuals who follow them is stated or implied. Readers should bear in mind that techniques described might be inappropriate in some professional settings, and that changes in industry trends, practices, and technology may affect the activities discussed here. The author and publisher bear no responsibility for the outcome of any reader's use of the information and advice provided herein.

CONTENTS

1

INTRODUCING YOUR CAREER COACH

In the 1940s, when the first electronic computer was built and completed, no one could have possibly known the importance that machine would have. No one could have known the tremendous innovation it would become. No one could have imagined that some 60-plus years later, computers would become things most of us couldn't live without.

For most of us today, it's difficult to envision a world without computers. We use them to communicate, to write, to research, to learn, and to work. We use them to play, to shop, to pass the time, and even to find new relationships.

Computers have revolutionized not only the way we live our lives, but our world. Our phone system is computerized; banking is computerized; our cars are computerized; street lights are computerized; medical records are computerized; travel is revolutionized; and the list goes on.

And computers aren't just used for personal and business computing purposes. New technology, for the most part, is based on computers in some manner. The importance of computers and computer technology in our world is clear. Without them, our world would be a very different place.

Do you want a career in this exciting field? Do you want to be part of this important industry? If so, the options are vast and varied. One of them might be for you.

A career in the computer industry can be exciting, challenging, and fulfilling. And most importantly, a career in the computer industry just might be the career you have been dreaming about.

When you think of working in the computer industry, what professions come to mind? Computer programmer? Software developer? Webmaster?

The computer industry is a very diverse field. There are hundreds of job possibilities in a variety of areas. What do you want to do? What is your dream?

Is it your dream to work with some aspect of the Web? The explosion of the Internet has created myriad new job opportunities. Do you want to work in Web development? Web design? How about e-commerce? Perhaps you want to be a Web site editor. Maybe you want to sell advertising for Web sites. What about some other facet of the Web? The possibilities are limitless.

Is it your dream instead to work in some aspect of computer design? What about the manufacturing end of computers? How about the marketing end of the industry? What about a career in the wholesale end of the industry?

What about the retail segment? Are you hoping to work in some aspect of computer service or repair?

Are you interested in developing additional uses for computerized machinery? Do you want to invent the next Ipod? What about a new type of cell phone? How about some innovative new medical machinery that can help change people's lives? The choice is yours.

Is it your dream to be a systems analyst? Do you want to work in programming? Do you want to work in some aspect of computer operations?

Do you want to work in support? Do you want to be the one who helps people use their computer or software? Do you want to be the one who saves the day by troubleshooting and coming up with a solution?

Do you want to work in some area of database management? What about database storage? The possibilities are endless.

Do you aspire for a career in some area of information services? What about teaching? Do you want to write about computers? How about writing the documentation for computers or their peripherals?

Is it your dream to develop software? Do you want a career working in computer graphics? What about animation?

Are you looking for a job? Would you rather be an independent consultant? Are you an entrepreneur seeking to start a new business?

Do you want to be the next Michael Dell? What about Steve Jobs? How about Bill Gates? Do you want to blaze your own successful path in some aspect of the computer industry? Your career is waiting for you. You just need to go after it!

While many choose to work hands on in one of the various segments of the computer industry, there are also other opportunities in the peripheral areas.

Depending on the area you choose to work, there are opportunities in the business and administration segments of the industry as well as support services. There are opportunities for accountants, public relations people, marketing specialists, attorneys, paralegals, journalists, and more.

There are so many opportunities in this industry that for some it is hard to choose. Where will you fit? What will be your contribution? No matter which segment of the industry you choose, your career can be exciting and rewarding. Every day will be different. Every day will be full of new challenges and new experiences. Are you ready? The dream is yours. You just have to identify exactly what it is.

Some parts of the industry are easier to enter. Some are more competitive. Can you make it? Can you succeed? Can you make your dreams come true?

I'm betting you can and, if you let me, I want to help you get where you want to be. Whether you've just decided that you want to work in some aspect of the computer industry, it's been your dream for some time, or you already work in the industry and you want to move up the career ladder, this book is for you.

Whether you want a career working hands on in the computer industry; in the business, administration, or support segments of the industry; in the peripherals; or anywhere in between, this book can be your guide to success.

I know what it's like to have a dream. I know what it is like to want to have the career of your dreams so badly you can taste it. I know what it is like to want to experience success.

It doesn't matter if your dream is exactly like my dream or my dream is like yours. It doesn't even really matter exactly what you want to do. What matters is that if you have a dream, whatever it is, I want you to know you can find a way to attain it.

While I would love to tell you that working in the computer industry was my dream, it was not. But that doesn't mean I don't know how badly you want to experience success.

When I was beginning my career I had a dream and I was not about to give it up. Although it wasn't related to the computer industry in any way, I'm going to share it with you for a number of reasons.

Why? To begin with, I want to illustrate to you that dreams can come true. I want to show you how perseverance in your career (or anything else for that matter) can help you achieve your dreams and goals. Furthermore, you also might find it interesting to see how sometimes things you do in your career are stepping-stones to the career of your dreams, even if they don't seem so at the time.

I've done a lot of things in my life in pursuing my own dreams. Some worked out and some didn't. What I can say, however, is that I never will have to look back at my life and say, "I wish I had done this" or "I wish I had done that," because when I wanted to try something I always did. My hope is that you will be able to do the same thing.

Do I work in some aspect of the computer industry now? While I don't work in the front lines of the industry, part of my career has touched the peripherals. As a career expert, through seminars, workshops, and classes, I often teach people how to find, enter, and succeed in their perfect career. Some of those careers are in the computer industry.

As a stress management specialist, I also have worked with those in various aspects of

the computer industry as well as the peripherals to help them learn how to deal with stress, how to manage stress, and reduce stress in their work and life. I also teach people how to use humor to feel better and how to find ways to laugh both in their career and life.

These segments of my career came after I had done a lot of other things and lived a lot of dreams. They might not have occurred had I not done other things along the way. This type of thing might happen to you as well.

It's important to remember that dreams can change, but as long as you keep going toward your goals you're on the right road. With that in mind, here's my story of one of my career dreams.

For as long as I can remember, I wanted to be in the music industry, probably more than anything else in the world. I struggled to get in. Could I find anyone to help me? No. Did I know anyone in the business? No. Did I live in one of the music capitals? No. The only thing I had going for me was a burning desire to be in the industry and the knowledge that I wasn't going to quit until it happened.

At the time I was trying to enter the industry, I wished there was a book to give me advice on how to move ahead, to guide me toward my goals, and to give me insider tips. Unfortunately, there wasn't. I wished that I had a mentor or a coach or someone who really knew what I should be doing and could tell me what it was. Unfortunately, I didn't have that either.

Did anyone ever help me? It wasn't that no one wanted to help, but most of the people in my network just didn't have a clue about the music industry. Did they know that the music industry was a multibillion dollar business? Did they know that it offered countless opportunities? It really didn't matter, because no one I knew could give me an edge on getting in anyway.

A couple of times I did run into some music industry professionals who did try to help. In one instance, a few months after I had started job hunting, I finally landed an interview at a large booking agency. I arrived for my appointment and sat waiting for the owner of the agency to meet with me. I sat and sat and sat.

A recording artist who was a client of the agency walked over to me after his meeting with the agent and asked how long I had been there. "Close to three hours," I replied. My appointment was for 1:00 p.m. and it was almost 4:00 p.m. "What are you here for?" he asked. "I want to be in the music industry," was my answer. "I want to be a tour manager."

"Someday," he said, "you'll make it and this joker [the agency owner] will want something from you and you can make him wait. Mark my words, it will happen." He then stuck his head inside the agency owner's door and said, "This woman has been sitting out here for hours, bring her in already." As I walked into the office I had a glimmer of hope. It was short lived, but it was hope just the same.

The agency owner was very nice. During our meeting he told me something to the effect of, if he ever needed someone with my skills and talents, he would be glad to give me a call, and I should keep plugging away. In other words, "Thanks for coming in. I talked to you now please leave. Don't call me I'll call you."

He then explained in a hushed voice, "Anyway, you know how it is. Most managers don't want girls on the road with their acts." Not only was I being rejected because of my skills and talents, but now it was because I was a girl. (Because my name is Shelly, evidently many people incorrectly assumed I was male instead of female when their secretaries were setting up appointments. The good news is that this got me

Tip from the Top

During that interview I learned two important lessons. One, use what you have to get your foot in the door. If someone thought I was a man because of my name, well, my idea was not to correct them until I got in the door. At least that way I could have a chance at selling myself.

The second lesson I learned was to choose your battles wisely. Had I complained about sexual discrimination at the point, I might have won the battle, but I would have lost the war.

into a lot of places I probably wouldn't have had a chance to get in. The bad news, once I got there they realized I was not a man.)

I smiled, thanked the agent for meeting with me, and left wondering if I would ever get a job doing what I wanted. Was it sexual discrimination? Probably it was, but in reality the agent was just telling me the way it was at that time. He actually believed he was being nice. Was it worth complaining about? I didn't think so. I was new to the industry and I wasn't about to make waves before I even got in. The problem was, I just couldn't find a way to get in.

On another occasion, I met a road manager at a concert and told him about how I wanted to be a tour manager. He told me he knew how hard it was to get into the industry so he was going to help me. "Call me on Monday," he told me on Saturday. I did. "I'm working on it," he said. "Call me Wednesday." On Wednesday he said, "Call me Friday." This went on for a couple of weeks before I realized that while he was trying to be nice, but he really wasn't going to do anything for me.

I decided that if I were ever lucky enough to break into the music industry, I would help as many people as I possibly could to fulfill their dream, whatever job they wanted. I wasn't sure when I'd make it, but I knew I would get there eventually.

While like many others I dreamed about standing on a stage in front of thousands of adoring fans singing my number one song, in reality I knew that was not where my real talent was. I knew that I did have the talent to make it in the business end of the industry.

I did all the traditional things to try to get a job. I sent my resume, I searched out employment agencies that specialized in the music industry, I made cold calls, and I read the classifieds.

And guess what? I still couldn't land a job. Imagine that? A college degree and a burning desire still couldn't get me the job I wanted. I had some offers, but the problem was they weren't offers to work in the music industry. I had offers for jobs as a social worker, a newspaper reporter, a teacher, and a number of other positions I have since forgotten. Were any of these jobs that I wanted? No! I wanted to work in the music business, period, end of story.

Like many of you might experience when you share your dreams, I had people telling me why my dreams were a bad idea. I had people tell me that I was pipe dreaming. "The music industry," I was told, "is for the other people. You know, the lucky ones." I was also consistently told how difficult the music industry was to get into and once in, how difficult it was to succeed. In essence, I was being told not to get my hopes up.

Want to hear the good news? I eventually did get into the music industry. I had to "think outside of the box" to get there, but the important thing was I found a way to get in. Want to hear some more good news? If I could find a way to

---

⭐ **Tip from the Coach**

As big as the world is, it really is small. Always leave a good impression. Remember what the recording artist at the agency told me? A number of years after I broke into the industry, his words actually did come true. At the time I was working on a project booking the talent for a big music festival overseas and the booking agent heard about it. He put in a call to me to see if I'd consider using his talent for the show. "Hi, Shelly, it's Dave. It's been a long time," said the voice mail. "I heard you were booking a new show and I wanted to talk to you about having some of my acts appearing on the show. Give me a call." As soon as I heard his name, the words of that recording artist came flooding back into my mind. This was a true "mark my words" moment.

I was busy, so I couldn't call him right away. He kept calling back. He really wanted his acts on the show. I finally took his call and told him I'd get back to him. He must have called 25 times in a two-day period to see if I had made up my mind. He finally said, "How long do you expect me to wait?"

I then reminded him of the day I sat in his office and waited and waited for him to see me. He, of course, didn't even remember the moment, but to his credit, he apologized profusely and promised never to have me wait again. I accepted his apology and told him, he'd only have to wait a little bit longer.

---

break into the industry of my dreams and create a wonderful career, you can find a way to break into the industry of your dreams and create a wonderful career too! As a matter of fact, not only can you get in, but you can succeed.

Coming full circle, remember when I said that if I got into the music business, I would help every single person who ever wanted a job doing anything?

> ### ⭐ Tip from the Coach
> In addition to not leaving a bad impression, try not to burn bridges. The bridge you burn today might just be the bridge you need to cross tomorrow.

Well I did get into the business I dreamed about and was successful in having a career I loved. You want to work in some aspect of the computer industry and I want to help you get there. I want to help you succeed. And I want to help you live your dreams, whatever they are.

How can I help? I am a career expert and have written numerous books on a wide array of different career-oriented subjects. I give seminars, presentations, and workshops around the country on entering and succeeding in the career of your dreams. I'm a personal coach and stress management specialist to people in various walks of life, including celebrities, corporate executives, and people just like you who want a great career and a great life. Unfortunately, much as I wish I could, I can't be there in person for each and every one of you.

So with that in mind, through the pages of this book, I'm going to be your personal coach, your cheerleader, and your inside source for not only finding your dream career, but getting in and succeeding as well.

A Personal Coach—What's That?

The actual job title of "personal coach" is relatively new, but coaches are not. Athletes and others in the sports industry have always used coaches to help improve their game and their performance. Over the past few years, coaches have sprung up in many other fields.

There are those who coach people toward better fitness or nutrition, vocal coaches to help people improve their voices, acting coaches to help people with acting skills, and etiquette coaches to help people learn how to act in every situation. There are parenting coaches to help people parent better, retirement coaches to help people be successful in retirement, and time management coaches to help people better manage their time.

There are stress management coaches to help people better manage their stress, executive business coaches to help catapult people to the top, life coaches to help people attain a happier, more satisfying life, and career coaches to help people create a great career. Personal coaches often help people become more successful and satisfied in a combination of areas.

"I don't understand," you might be saying. "Exactly what does a coach do and what can he or she do for me?" Well, there are a number of things.

Basically, a coach can help you find your way to success faster. He or she can help motivate you, help you find what really makes you happy, get you on track, and help you focus your energies on what you really want to do. Unlike some family members or friends who may be skeptical of your dreams, coaches aren't judgmental. You, therefore, have the ability to freely explore ideas with your coach without fear of them being rejected. Instead of accepting your self-imposed limitations, coaches encourage you to reach to your full potential and improve your performance.

Coaches are objective, and one of the important things he or she can do for you is to point out things that you might not see yourself. Most of all, a coach helps you find the best in you and then shows you ways to bring it out. This in turn will make you more successful.

As your coach, what do I hope to do for you? I want to help you find your passion and then help you go after it. If a career in some segment of the computer industry is what you want, I want to help you get in and I want you to be successful.

Whichever sector of the industry you aspire to work in, we'll work on finding ways to get you in and catapult you to the top. If you're already in, we'll work on ways to help you climb the career ladder to your dream position.

Whatever your career vision, we'll work together to find a way to help you get in and achieve your dreams. Whether we use traditional methods or think outside of the box, the possibilities are endless!

Look at me as your personal cheerleader and this book as your guide. I want you to succeed and will do as much as possible to make that happen. No matter what anyone tells you, it is possible to not only get the job of your dreams, but also succeed at levels higher than you dare to dream. Thousands of people have done so and now one of them can be you!

Did you ever notice that some people just seem to attract success? They seem to get all the breaks, are always at the right place at the right time, and have what you want? It's not that you're jealous, but you just want to get a piece of the pie too.

"They're so lucky," you say.

Well, here's the deal. You can be that lucky too. Want to know why? While a little bit of luck is always helpful, it's not just chance. Some people work to attract success. They work to get what they want. They follow a plan, keep a positive attitude, and they know that they're worthy of the prize. Others just wait for success to come. The problem is, often when all you do is wait success may just pass you by.

The good news here is you can be one of the lucky ones who attract success if you take the right steps. This book will give you some of the keys to control your destiny; it will hand you the keys to success in your career and your life.

Through the pages of this book, you'll find the answers to many of your questions about a career in the computer industry. You'll get the inside scoop on how the industry works, key employment issues, and finding opportunities.

You'll find insider tips, tricks, and techniques that have worked for others who have succeeded in the industry. You'll discover secrets to help get you get in the door and up the ladder of success as well as the lowdown on things others wish they had known when they were first beginning their quest for success.

If you haven't attended any of my career seminars, my workshops on climbing the career ladder and succeeding in your dream career, my stress management seminars, or any of the other presentations I offer, you will get the benefit of being there. If you have attended one, here is the book you've been asking for!

Change Your Thinking, Change Your Life

Sometimes, the first step in getting what you want is just changing the way you think. Did you know that if you think you don't deserve something, you usually don't get it? Did you know that if you think you aren't good enough, neither will anyone else? Did you know that if you think you deserve something, you have a much better chance of getting it? Or, if you think you are good enough, your confidence will shine through?

When you have confidence in yourself, you start to find ways to get what you want and guess what? You succeed!

And while changing your thinking can change your life, this book is not just about a positive attitude. It's a book of actions you can take.

While a positive attitude is always helpful in order to succeed in whatever part of the industry you're interested in pursuing, you need to take positive actions, too.

If all it took for you to be successful was for me to tell you what you needed to do or even me doing it for you, I would. I love what I do and my career, and I truly want to help everyone live their dream, too.

Here's the reality of the situation. I can only offer advice, suggestions, and tell you what you need to do. You have to do the rest. Talking about what you can do or should do is fine, but without you taking action it's difficult to get where you want to go.

This is your chance to finally get what you want. You've already taken one positive step to getting your dream career simply by picking up this book. As you read through the various sections, you'll find other actions to take that will help get you closer to the great career you deserve.

One of the things we'll talk about is creating your own personal action plan. This is a plan which can help you focus on exactly what you want and then show you the actions needed to get what you want.

Your personal action plan is a checklist of sorts. Done correctly it can be one of the main keys to your career success. It will put you in the driver's seat and give you an edge over others who haven't prepared a plan themselves.

We'll also discuss putting together a number of different kinds of journals to help you be more successful in your career and life. For example, one of the problems many people ex-perience when they're trying to get a new job, move up the career ladder, or accomplish a goal is that they often start feeling like they aren't accomplishing anything. A career journal is a handy tool to help you track exactly what you've done to accomplish your goals. Once that is in place, you know what else needs to be done.

Is This the Right Career for Me?

Unsure about exactly what part the computer industry in which you want to become involved? As you read through the book, you'll get some ideas.

"But what if I'm already working at a job in another industry?" you ask. "Is it too late? Am I stuck there forever? Is it too late to go after a career in the computer industry?"

Here's the deal. It is never too late to change careers, and going after something you're passionate about can drastically improve the quality of your life.

Thousands of people stay in jobs because it's easier than going after what they want. You don't have to be one of them.

We all know people who are in jobs or careers that they don't love. They get up every day, waiting for the workweek to be over. They go through the day, waiting for it to be over. They waste their life waiting and waiting. Is this the life you want to lead? I'm guessing you don't.

⭐ Tip from the Coach

Don't procrastinate. Every day you wait to get the career you are passionate about is another day you're not living your dream. Start today!

Tip from the Coach

Contrary to what many people think, it is possible to love your job. Do not listen to the people who tell you work is called *work* for a reason. If you love what you do, even if there are challenges, for the most part, you will enjoy going to your job and creating a great career.

You now have the opportunity to get what you want. Are you ready to go after it? I'm hoping you are.

As we've discussed, there are countless opportunities in the various segments of the computer industry and its peripherals. In addition to the traditional jobs most people think of, there are an array of others for you to explore. No matter what your skills or talents, you can almost always find a way to parlay them into some aspect of a career in the computer industry if you think creatively.

Don't be afraid to put your dreams together. "Like what?" you ask.

Let's say you want to work in the entertainment industry and you also aspire to work in Web design or Web development. What about seeking a position doing Web design for a record label? What about finding a job handling Web development for a recording artist? How about looking for a position handling Web development for a film company?

Words from the Wise

Always carry business or networking cards with your phone number and other contact information. Make it easy for people to find you when an opportunity presents itself.

Putting together your dreams gives you even more options for creating a great career you will love and be excited about.

A Job versus a Career: What's the Difference?

What do you want in life? Would you rather just have a job or do you want a career? What's the difference? A job is just that. It's something you do to earn a living. It's a means to an end. A career, on the other hand, is a series of related jobs. It's a progressive path of achievement, a long-term journey. A career is something you build using your skills, talents, and passions.

You might have many jobs in your career. You might even follow more than one career path. The question is what do you want?

If all you want is to go to work day after day, week after week just to get paid, a job is all you need, and there is nothing wrong with that. On the other hand, if you would like to fill your life with excitement and passion while getting paid, you are a prime candidate for a great career.

How can you get that? Start planning now to get what you want. Define your goals and then start working toward them.

Not everyone starts off with a dream job. If you just sit and wait for your dream job to come to you, you could be sitting forever. What you can do, however, is take what you have and make it work for you until you get what you want. What does that mean?

It means that you can make whatever you do better, at least for the time being. The trick in this whole process is finding ways to give the job you have some meaning. Find a way to get some passion from what you're doing. If you get that mind-set you'll never have a bad job. Focus on your ultimate career goal and then look at each job as a benchmark along the way to what you want.

Using This Book to Help You Succeed in the Computer Industry

While ideally I would love for you to read this book from beginning to end, I know from experience that's probably not the way it's going to happen. You might browse the contents and look for something that can help you now, you might see a subject that catches your eye, or you might be looking for an area of the book that solves a particular problem or challenge you have.

For this reason, as you read the book, you might see what appears to be some duplication of information. In this manner, I can be assured that when I suggest something that may be helpful to you in a certain area you will get all the information you need, even if you didn't read a prior section.

You might have heard the saying that knowledge is power. This is very true. The more you know about the various aspects of the computer industry and how it works, the better your chances are of succeeding. This book is full of information to help you learn things you need to know about the industry and how it works. I'm betting that you will refer back to information in this book long after you've attained success.

As you read through the various sections you'll find a variety of suggestions and ideas to help you succeed. Keep in mind that every idea and suggestion might not work in every situation and for every person. The idea is to keep trying things until one of them works. Use the book as a springboard to get you started. Just because something is not written here doesn't mean that it's not a good idea. Brainstorm to find solutions to barriers you might encounter in your career, even if you have to brainstorm with yourself.

My job is to lead you on your journey to success in whatever area of the computer industry you aspire to work. Along the way you'll find exercises, tasks, and assignments that will help get you where you want to be faster. No one is going to be standing over your shoulder to make you do these tasks. You alone can make the decision on the amount time and work you want to put into your career. While no one can guarantee you success, what you should know is that the more you put into your career, the better your chances of having the success you probably are dreaming about.

Are you worth the time and effort? I think you are! Is a great career in the computer industry worth it? I believe it is! If you have the passion and desire to work in this industry, it can be one of the hottest industries in the world in which to work. Not only will you have the opportunity to make a good living, but you also will be doing something you love and fulfilling your dreams.

No matter what level you're currently at in your career and whatever capacity, this book is for you. You might not need every section or every page, but I can guarantee that there are parts of this book that can and will help you.

Whether you're just starting to think about a career in the computer industry or have been in the industry for a while; whether you're still in high school, attending college, or have already finished your education; whether you are working directly in the industry, in the business segment, support services, or a peripheral area, this book can help you experience more success in your career and a help you have a happier, more satisfying, and stress-free life.

A Sampling of What This Book Covers

This informative guide to success in the computer industry is written in a friendly, easy to read style. Let it be your everyday guide to success. Do you want to learn how to focus on what your really want to do? Want to learn how to plan and prepare for your dream career? Do you want to focus on job search strategies geared especially for the computer industry? Check out the book!

How about tips for making those important industry contacts? Need some ideas on how to network? How about ways to create the ideal resume or cover letter specifically geared toward a specific segment of the computer industry? Check out the book!

Do you need to know how to develop your action plan? Do you want to get your portfolio together? Want to know what business or networking cards can do for you and your career? Check out the book!

Do you want to learn how to get your foot in the door? How about checking out tried and true methods to get people to call you back? Do you want to learn the best way to market yourself and why it's so important? Do you want to learn how to succeed in the workplace, deal with workplace politics, keep an eye out for opportunities, and climb the career ladder? You know what you have to do, check out the book!

Do you want to know how a press release can help you in your career? Want to know the basics of writing one? What about how to get your press release to the media? You know what you have to do! Read the book!

Want to know about different types of interviews? What about how to break the ice when you walk in the door? Want to know how to make yourself stand out in a positive way at an interview? Check out the book.

Want to know how to succeed in your chosen field? How to move up the ladder? You got it. You need to read this book.

Do you need important contact information so you can move your career forward? Check out the listings of important organizations, unions, and associations in the appendix. Want some Web sites where you can start looking for a great career? Check out the appendix of the book. Want to read some books or check out some trade magazines? The appendix is chock full of ideas.

While this book won't teach you how to do programming, develop software, or build a computer, it will help you to find ways to garner success no matter where your passion lies.

Anyone can apply for a job and hope they get it. Many people do just that. But I'm guessing, you do not just want a job. You want a career you can be passionate about. You want a career you love. You want a career that gives you joy! Take charge of your career now and you can have all that and more.

If your dream is not only working in the computer industry but having a successful career as well, this book can help turn your dream into a reality. Have fun reading it. Know that if your heart is in it, you can achieve anything.

Now let's get started.

2

FOCUSING ON A GREAT CAREER IN THE COMPUTER INDUSTRY

Focusing on What You Really Want to Do

Do you know what you want to do with your life? Do you wish you could have a career doing something you truly love? Do you daydream about working in some aspect of the computer industry? Do you wonder how you're going get in? Do you wonder how you can succeed?

Unless you're independently wealthy or just won the megamillion-dollar lottery, you, like most people, have to work. Just in case you're wondering, life is not supposed to be miserable. Neither is your job.

Life is supposed to have a purpose. That purpose is not sleeping, getting up, going to a job that you don't particularly care about, coming home, making dinner, and watching TV, only to do it all over again the next day.

In order to be happy and fulfilled you need to enjoy life. You need to do things that give you pleasure. As a good part of your life is spent working, the trick is to find a career that you love and that you're passionate about—the career of your dreams.

This is not something everyone does. Many people just fall into a career without thinking about what it will entail ahead of time. Someone may need a job, hear of an opening, answer an ad, and then go for it without thinking about the consequences of working at something for which he or she really has no passion. Once hired, it's either difficult to give up the money, just too hard to start job hunting again, or they don't know what else to do, and so they stay. That person may wind up with a career that is okay but one he or she is not really passionate about.

Then there are the other people. The ones who have jobs they love, the lucky people. You've seen them. They're the people who have the jobs and life you wish you had.

Have you noticed that the people who love their jobs are usually successful, not only in their career but also in other aspects of their life? They almost seem to have an aura around them

---

⭐ **Tip from the Coach**

Okay is just that—it's okay. Just so you know, you don't want just okay, you don't want to settle, you want GREAT! That's what you deserve and that's what you should go after.

---

of success, happiness, and prosperity. Do you want to be one of them? Well you can!

Finding a career that you want and love is challenging but it is possible. You are in a better position than most people. If you're reading this book, you've probably at least zeroed in on a career path. You likely decided that you are passionate about some segment of the computer industry. Now all you have to do is determine exactly what you want to do within the industry.

What's your dream career? What do you really want to do? This is an important question to ask yourself? Once you know the answer, you can work toward achieving your goal.

If someone asked you right now, what do you really want to do, could you answer the question? Okay, one, two, three: "What do you want to do with your life?"

If you're saying, "Uh, um, well . . . What I really want to do is . . . Well it's hard to explain," then it's time to focus on the subject. Sometimes the easiest way to figure out what you want to do is to focus in on what you don't want to do.

Most people can easily answer what they don't want to do. "I don't want to be a doctor. I don't want to be a nurse. I don't want to work in a factory. I don't to work in a store. I don't want to sell. I don't want to be a teacher. I don't want to work with numbers. I don't want to work in a job where I have to travel. I don't want to have to do a lot of writing," and the list goes on. The problem is that just saying what you don't like or don't want to do doesn't necessarily get you what you want to do. You can, however, use this information to your advantage.

It may seem simple, but sometimes just looking at a list of what you don't like will help you see more clearly what you do like.

Sit down with a sheet of paper or fill in the "Things I Dislike Doing/Things I Don't Want To Do" worksheet and make a list of work-related things you don't like to do. Remember that this list is really just for you. While you can show it to someone if you want, no one else really has to see it, so try to be honest with yourself.

Here's an example to get your started. When you make your list, add in things you don't want to do. Add in your own personal dislikes.

◎ I hate the idea of being cooped up in an office all day.
◎ I don't want to be bored in my job.
◎ I don't want to do the same thing every day.
◎ I hate the idea of having to work with numbers.
◎ I don't want to have to do a lot of reports.
◎ I don't want to have to go to work early in the morning.
◎ I don't want to have to work evenings.
◎ I don't want to have to travel for my job.
◎ I hate having to explain how to do things to others.
◎ I don't want to have to speak in front of large groups of people.
◎ I don't want to have to commute for an hour each way every day.
◎ I don't want to work in sales.
◎ I don't like being under constant deadlines.
◎ I don't like not having challenges.
◎ I don't like someone telling me what to do every minute of the day.
◎ I don't like working where I don't make a difference.
◎ I don't like working for someone.
◎ I don't like working where I'm not appreciated.
◎ I don't like working in situations where I don't interact with a lot of people.
◎ I don't like working in stressful situations.
◎ I don't want to have to live in a city.
◎ I don't want to live in a rural area.

Things I Don't Like Doing/Things I Don't Want to Do

◎ I don't want to relocate.

◎ I don't like working outdoors.

◎ I don't want to work in a cubicle.

◎ I don't like making decisions.

◎ I don't like being in charge.

◎ I don't like taking risks.

◎ I don't like working under constant pressure.

◎ I don't like not knowing where my next paycheck is coming from.

◎ I don't like having a boss working right on top of me.

We now know what you don't like. We know what you don't want to do. Use this list as a beginning to see what you do like. If you look closely, you'll find that the things you enjoy are the opposite of the things you don't want to do.

Here are some examples to get you started. You might make another list as well as using the "Things I Enjoy Doing/Things I Want To Do" worksheet. Remember that the reason you're writing everything down is so you can look at it, remember it, and focus in on getting exactly what you want.

◎ I hate the idea of having to work with numbers
  ▫ But I really like writing and creating with words. And I can explain things easily. I think I would really enjoy writing technical documentation or maybe even computer or software support manuals. I might also enjoy a career as a publicist, public relations director, or marketing director for a computer or software company.

◎ I don't want to have to do a lot of reports. The thought of it bothers me.
  ▫ I don't want to do reports because I'm not confident in my writing skills. Perhaps if I take some writing

classes I'll begin to feel more confident. Then I can go after the job I really want in administration.

◎ I don't want to have to go to work early in the morning.
  ▫ I really want to work in some sort of computer or Web support position. Maybe I can find a job working the afternoon or night shift. Maybe I can start a consulting business.

◎ I don't want to have to commute for an hour each way every day.
  ▫ I'm going to focus my job search on companies within 20 minutes from where I live. If that doesn't work, I'm going to consider moving closer to where I find my job.

◎ I don't like not knowing where my next paycheck is coming from.
  ▫ Although I could work as a consultant, I'm going to look for a job.

◎ I don't like having a boss working right on top of me.
  ▫ I think I'm going to look for a position where I am out on the road some of the workday. Maybe I'll see if I can find a position telecommuting.

◎ I don't want to work in the computer hardware segment of the industry.
  ▫ But I am really interested in working in software development.

◎ I don't like having to explain things to laypeople.
  ▫ But I really want to teach professionals more about computers and software. Perhaps I'll look for a position giving IT professionals support.

◎ I don't like not having challenges.
- □ Whatever job I have, I will challenge myself to do better. I will push the limits. I can't wait to finish college and start my career!

◎ I don't like someone telling me what to do every minute of the day.
- □ Perhaps instead of looking for a job, I would be better off becoming a consultant or having my own business of some sort. I know you still have clients telling you what to do, but I think I would be happier. I'm going to have to look into some possibilities.

◎ I don't like being in charge.
- □ I don't have to be the director of a department to be successful. If I'm doing something I love, in my eyes, I will be successful.

◎ I don't like working under constant pressure.
- □ But I realize that we all make a lot of our own pressure. I think I'm going to take a class or seminar on dealing with stress and pressure.

As you can see, once you've determined what you don't like doing, it's much easier to get ideas on what you'd like to do. It's kind of like brainstorming with yourself.

You probably know some people who don't like their job. There are tons of people in this world who don't like what they do or are dissatisfied with their career. Here's the good news. You don't have to be one of them.

You and you alone are in charge of your career. Not your mother, father, sister, brother, girlfriend, boyfriend, spouse, or best friend. Others can care, others can help, and others can offer you advice, but in essence, you need to be in control. What this means is that the path you

---

Tip from the Coach

Try to associate with positive people who like what they do. Otherwise, the negativity of others may begin to rub off on you.

---

take for your career is largely determined by the choices you make.

The fastest way to get the career you want is by choosing to take actions now and going after it! You can have a career you love and you can have it in some aspect of the computer industry. And when you're doing something that you love, you'll be on the road to not only a great career but also a satisfied and fulfilled life.

The next section will discuss how to develop your career plan. This plan will be your road map to success. It will be full of actions you can take not only to get the career in the computer industry you want, but to succeed in it as well. Before you get too involved in the plan however, you need to zero in on exactly what you want your career to be.

At this point you might be in a number of different employment situations. You might still be in school planning your career; just out of school beginning your career; or in a job that you don't really care for. You might be in your late teens, 20s, 30's 40s, 50s, or even older.

"Older? Did you say older?" you ask. "Can I start a career in the computer industry even if I'm older?"

Yes! If you have a dream, it is never too late not only to pursue it, but also to succeed at it. And it doesn't matter what segment of the computer industry interests you.

As a matter of fact, if you're interested in working in one of the areas of the industry in

Things I Enjoy Doing/Things I Want to Do

_____

_____

_____

_____

_____

_____

_____

_____

_____

_____

_____

_____

_____

> ### ⭐ Tip from the Coach
>
> If you give up your dream because you think you are too old or it's too late to start, the success you are wishing for might never come your way.

which there is a shortage, you will be an attractive candidate.

You might also be interested to know that the Age Discrimination In Employment Act of 1967 specifically prohibits discrimination against people who are 40 years of age or older.

What does that mean to you? If you are a career changer, it means that you have just as much chance of getting a job as anyone else. Of course, you need to make yourself the best candidate possible, but we're going to cover that later in the book.

Whether you start off choosing a career in some segment of the computer industry, you're a career change, or you are into your second career, it's never too late to go after your dreams.

We already know how huge and far reaching the computer industry is. Perhaps you always wanted to work in some segment of the computer industry or maybe you've done some research on various career areas and decided the computer industry is for you. With so many options to choose from, do you know what your dream career is?

There are hundreds and hundreds of exciting career choices. Some are working directly in the computer industry. Others are working with computers in another industry. Some are on the peripherals. The choice is yours.

Do you want to work with hardware or software? Do you want to work with PCs or mainframes? Do you want to work with application software or system software?

Do you want to work in networking? How about the manufacturing of computer systems

and peripherals? What about system integration? How about in customer support?

Do you want to work in teaching? What about training? Are you interested in working in customer service? What about in the support area? Are you interested in writing technical documentation for hardware or software?

Is it your passion to work in animation? What about some area of game creation? Do you want to work in computer graphics? Do you want to work in desktop publishing? How about one of the other multimedia services?

Are you instead interested in a career in some aspect of CAD (computer-aided design)? Do you want to work in fashion design? What about architecture? What about equipment design? Your options are endless.

Is it your dream to work in some area of e-commerce? Is your interest in the business-to-business segment or the business-to-consumer sector?

Do you think you might be interested in a career in call center management? What about call center training? What about database management? Do you want a career as a Webmaster? Is your passion Web design? Are your skills and talents in Web programming? What about Web development? Do you see yourself selling advertising for Web sites? How about developing or writing copy for a Web site? What about Web site marketing? The sky is the limit. You just need to find your passion.

Are you interested in a career in some segment of computer science? Do you aspire to a career in computer engineering? Do you want to work in the public sector? What about the private sector? Once again the choice is yours.

Are you interested in a career in some facet of IT (information technology)? Do you want to work in programming? Are you interested in a career as a database analyst? Are you interested in a career as a software engineer?

Do you think you might like working as a computer operator? What about a database administrator? How about a network administrator? Do you want to work in the retail sector of the industry selling computers, peripherals, or software? Are you interested in a career in some area of the wholesale segment of the industry?

Do you want to work in the business end of the industry? What about a career in the marketing area? How about in some aspect of public relations or publicity? What about in advertising?

Do you think you might like a career writing about some facet of the computer industry? Would you like to write textbooks? How about a career as a reporter for a trade magazine or consumer publication?

Opportunities are available in the business segment of the industry, technology, consulting, sales, and communications. Opportunities are available in administration and management as well as research and development. There are additional options in peripherals and more. It's up to you to decide which one you want to pursue.

So let's focus a bit on exactly what you want to do.

What's Your Dream?

I bet that you already have an idea of what your dream job is and I'm sure that you have an idea of what it should be like. I'm also betting that you don't have that job yet or if you do, you're not at the level you want to be. So what can we do to make that dream a reality?

One of the challenges many people often have in getting their dream job is that they just don't think they deserve it. They feel that dream jobs are something many people talk about and wish they had, but just don't. Many people think that dream jobs are for the lucky ones.

Well, I'm here to tell you that you are the lucky one. You can get your dream job, a job

you'll love. And it can be in the area of the computer industry you choose!

If I had a magic wand and could get you any job you wanted what would it be? What is your dream? What is your passion? What is your vision? What do you daydream about? Your dream job can be a reality if you prepare.

Not sure what you want to do? Then read on!

Determining what you really want to do is not always easy. Take some time to think about it. Throughout this process, try to be as honest with yourself as possible Otherwise you stand the chance of not going after the career you really want.

Let's get started with another writing exercise. While you might think these are a pain now, if you follow through, you will find it easier to attain your dream.

Get a pad of paper and a pen and find a place where you can get comfortable. Maybe it's your living room chair. Perhaps it's your couch or even your bed. Now all you have to do is sit down and daydream for a bit about what you wish you could be and what you wish you were doing.

"Why daydream?" you ask.

When you daydream your thinking becomes freer. You stop thinking about what you can't do and start thinking about what you can do. What is your dream? What is your passion? What do you really want to do? Admit it now or forever hold your peace!

Many people are embarrassed to admit when they want something because if they don't get it they fear looking stupid. They worry people are

---

⭐ **Tip from the Coach**

What are your dreams? Are you ready to turn them into reality? You increase your chances of success if you have a deep belief in yourself, your vision, and your ideas.

going to talk badly about them or call them a failure. Is this what you worry about?

Do you really want to be a chief information officer, but you're afraid you'll fail. Is your dream to be the director of an IT department of a large corporation, but you're not sure you'll make it? Do you want your own call-in radio show focusing on all aspects of personal computing, but you're worried everyone will think it's a stupid idea? Do you want to be a corporate software trainer, but you're not sure anyone will think you're good enough? Do you want to start your own computer company and be the next Michael Dell but you're afraid people will tell you that it can never happen? Do you want to create the next big social networking site, but are frightened that you just don't have what it takes to make it?

First of all, don't ever let fear of failure stop you from going after something you want. While no one can guarantee you success, what I can guarantee is that if you don't go after what you want, it is going to be very difficult to get it.

One thing you never want to do is get to the end of your life and say with regret, "I wish I had done this or I wish I had done that." Will you get each and every thing you want? While I would like to give you a definitive "Yes," that probably wouldn't be true.

The truth of the matter is you might not succeed at everything. But—and this is a major *but*—even if you fail when you try to do something, it usually is a stepping-stone to something else. And that something else can be the turning point in your career.

"How so?" you ask. "What do you mean?"

There are often things you do in your life and your career that, while at the time, you can't see their importance, end up impacting the career of your dreams in a very positive way.

At one point in my life, I wanted to become a comedienne and do stand-up comedy on a professional basis. Wanting to at least give something I wanted to do a shot, I overcame my fear and, for a short while, did stand-up. The reason I bring it up is to illustrate the point that while I certainly didn't turn into a megastar stand-up comedienne, performing comedy was a major stepping-stone for me to do other things I wanted to accomplish in my career. Had I not done stand-up, I probably would never have ended up teaching stress management, becoming a motivational speaker, doing corporate training, or even coming up with ideas about doing something in those areas.

Had I been too scared to try it or not wanted to take the risk for fear I would fail, I would have missed out on important opportunities that helped shape my career. I also would have always looked back and said, "I wish I had."

And while your dreams are probably totally different from mine, what you need to take from the story is the concept that taking risks and pursuing your dreams can lead to wonderful things.

Let's get started. Think about things that make you happy. Think about things that make you smile. Continue to indulge your passions as you daydream. As ideas come to you, jot them down on your pad. Remember, nothing is foolish, so write down all the ideas you have for what you want to do. You're going to fine-tune them later. Here's an example to get you started.

◎ I want to be the CIO of a major corporation.
◎ I want to be an animator. As a matter of fact, I want to be one of the head animators at Disney!

Words from the Wise
The only thing we have to fear is fear itself.

—Franklin Delano Roosevelt

Tip from the Coach

If there is something that you want to do or something that you want to try in your career or your life, my advice is go for it. No matter what the risk, no matter how scared you are, no matter what. Your life and career will benefit more than you can imagine and you'll never look back with regrets. Even if it doesn't work out, you'll feel successful because you tried.

◎ I want to be a graphics designer and animator. I want to design exciting and unique computer games.

◎ I want to be a software development engineer.

◎ I want to be CEO of my own computer company. (Okay, I really want to be bigger than Michael Dell and Steve Jobs.)

◎ I want to teach computer technology to kids.

◎ I want to develop a method of easily teaching older people how to use computers. I also want to write a book on the subject and become an expert in the field.

◎ I want to have a Web site dedicated to everything computers and computer technology. As a matter of fact, I want the most successful computer technology Web site in the world.

◎ I want to be a systems analyst for a large company.

◎ I want to be a security expert for a major corporation.

◎ I want to be the Webmaster for a network or major cable television station.

◎ I want to work as the public relations director of a large software company. Then I want to be promoted to marketing director.

◎ I want to be a corporate software trainer.

Do you need some help focusing on what you really want to do in the computer industry? In order to choose just the right career you should pinpoint your interests and what you really love doing. What are your skills? What are your personality traits? What are your interests? Fill in the following worksheet to help you zero in even more. After you have completed it, see what types of things you enjoy doing and how you might possibly find ways these things can relate to a career you will love.

Focusing on the Job of Your Dreams

Finish the following sentences to help you pinpoint your interests and find the job of your dreams.

In my free time I enjoy

_____

In my free time I enjoy going

_____

(continues)

Focusing on the Job of Your Dreams (continued)

My hobbies are

_____

Activities I enjoy include

_____

When I volunteer, the types of projects I enjoy most are

_____

When I was younger I always dreamed of being a

_____

My skills are

_____

My talents are

_____

My best personality traits include

_____

My current job is

_____

What I like about my current job is

_____

Prior types of jobs have been

_____

Things I like about prior jobs were

_____

The subjects I liked best in school

_____

If I didn't have to worry about any obstacles, the three jobs I would want are

_____

What steps can I take to get one of those jobs?

_____

The Inside Scoop

When you write down your ideas you are giving them power. Once they are written down on paper, it makes it easier to go over them, look at them rationally, and fine-tune them.

What Is Stopping You from Getting What You Want?

Now that you have some ideas written down about what you want to do, go down the list. What has stopped you from attaining your goal?

Is it that you told people what you wanted to do and they told you that you couldn't do it? Did they tell you it was too difficult and your chances of making it were slim? Did they tell you that you were too old to go after your dreams?

Is it that you don't have the confidence in yourself to get what you want? Is it that you need some sort of certification? Or is it that you need more education or training?

Perhaps it's because you aren't in the location most conducive to your dream career? If you can identify the obstacle, you usually can find a way to overcome it, but you need to identify the problem first.

Do you know exactly what you want to do but can't find an opening? Do you, for example, want a career as a marketing director of a large software company, but can't find a job? Do you

Tip from the Coach

Start training yourself to practice finding ways to turn cant's in your life into cans.

want to be an animator but can't find a position? Do you want to teach computer technology to high school students, but can't find a job?

Sometimes, while you know what type of job you want, you just can't find a job like that which is available. Don't give up. Keep looking. Remember, you may have to think outside of the box to get what you want, but if you're creative, you can succeed. Try to find ways to get your foot in the door and then once it is in, don't let it out until you get what you want.

Have you found the perfect job and interviewed for it, but then the job wasn't offered to you? While at the time you probably felt awful about this, there is some good news. Generally, when one door closes, another one opens.

Hard to believe? It may be, but if you think about it, you'll see it's true. Things work out for the best. If you lost what you thought was the job of your dreams, a better one is out there waiting for you. You just have to find it!

Perhaps you're just missing the skills necessary for the type of job you're seeking. This is a relatively easy thing to fix. Once you know the skills that are necessary for a specific job, if you don't have them, take steps to get them. Take classes, go to workshops, attend seminars, or become an apprentice or intern.

Maybe you're missing the certification needed for a specific job. This is easily fixed to. Once you know which certifications might give you the edge over other job candidates, take the steps needed to get them.

"But," you say, "I'm missing the education necessary for the job I want. The ad I read said I needed a minimum of a bachelor's degree and I don't have one."

Here's the deal. In certain cases, educational requirements may be negotiable. Just because an ad states that a job has a specific educational requirement doesn't mean you should just pass it by if your education doesn't meet the requirement. First of all, advertisements for jobs generally contain the highest hopes of the people placing the ads, not necessarily the reality of what they will settle for. Second of all, organizations will often accept experience in lieu of education. Lastly, if you're a good candidate in other respects, many organizations will hire you while you're finishing the required education.

Is a lack of experience what's stopping you from your dream career? Depending on the career area you're pursuing, this can be easily fixed.

If you can't get experience in the workplace, volunteering is one of the best ways to get experience for any type of job. How do you get experience? Take every opportunity that presents itself to get the experience you need. Depending on what you want to do and where you live, you might need to get creative, but you can definitely find a way to do it.

For example, do you need experience doing publicity for a career in the public relations department of a software company? Experience is transferable. What about getting some experience by volunteering to do publicity for a community or civic organization? What if that doesn't pan out? See if you can find an internship with a business or organization.

Do you need experience as a computer graphics designer? What about volunteering to do a project for the local hospital or other not-for-profit organization? Do you need experience teaching or as a trainer? Offer to run a class in computer and software training at a local library.

Is one of the obstacles you're facing that you just aren't in the geographic location of the opportunities you're looking for? Do you, for

example, want to work for one of the large Internet companies, yet you don't live any where near even one of them? Do you want to work for a large software firm but don't live in the area where any software firms are located?

There's no question that living in an area that doesn't have the opportunities you're looking for makes your job more difficult. If this obstacle is what is holding you back, put some time into developing a solution and find a way to move forward. If you're not prepared to move and don't want to give up your career dreams, you might want to start your career working in a smaller company, closer to where you live. After a year or two, you might be ready to move on. You might also see if you can find a position telecommuting. Think outside the box until you find a way to get past every obstacle you encounter.

Is what's holding you back that you don't have any contacts? Here's the deal. You have to find ways to make contacts. Take classes, seminars, and workshops in subject areas related to the segment of the computer industry in which you're interested.

Volunteer. Make cold calls. Network, network, and network some more. Put yourself in situations where you can meet people in the industry and sooner or later you will meet them.

What else is standing between you and success? "The only thing between me and success," you say, "is a big break." Getting your big break may take time. Keep plugging away. Most of all, don't give up. Your break will come when you least expect it.

Are you just frightened about going after what you want? Are you not sure you have the talent or the skills. Are you not sure you can make it? If you start doubting yourself, other people might do the same. As we just discussed,

Tip from the Coach

While you're working on your day-dreaming exercise, don't get caught up in thinking any of your ideas are foolish or stupid. Let your imagination run freely. If these negative ideas come into your head, consciously push them way.

do not let fear stop you from doing what you want.

Most importantly, don't let anyone chip away at your dream, and whatever you do, don't let anyone burst your bubble. What does that mean?

You know how it is when you get excited about doing something that you just can't keep it to yourself. You might share your ideas of what you want to do with your family and friends. And while you want them to be excited too, they may try to destroy your dream by pointing out all the possible problems you might encounter.

It's not that they're not trying to be supportive, but for some people it seems to be their nature to try to shoot other people's dreams apart.

Why? There are a number of reasons. Let's look at a few scenarios.

Scenario 1—Sometimes people are just negative. "Oh," they might say to you, "you don't want to get involved in that industry. It keeps changing. It's not stable. You don't want to get involved."

"Well," you tell them, "I think it's a great industry. It is one of the fastest growing industries in the country. I can keep learning and advancing. This industry is our future. I'm excited to be part of it."

Their response? "It's hard work. You don't really want to do that. You're going to be competing with a lot of other people."

Scenario 2—Sometimes people are jealous. They might hate their job and be jealous that you are working toward finding a great career. They might have similar dreams to yours and be jealous that you have a plan and they don't. Some might just be jealous that you might make it before them.

Scenario 3—Sometimes people are just scared of change. In many cases friends or family are concerned about your well-being and are just scared of change. "You have a job," your girlfriend may say, "why do you want to go back to school? Why don't you think about it for a while?"

Scenario 4—Sometimes people just think you're pipe dreaming. "You're a pipe dreamer," your family may say, "what you need is a dose of reality. You never are going to make the kind of money you think you are. The odds are not good."

Scenario 5—Sometimes people really think it's not realistic for you to believe you should make a living doing something you love. "Nobody likes their job, " a family member may tell you, "work is just something you have to do."

Scenario 6—Sometimes people think that you are too old to change careers or go after your dream. "You're 45 years old," your friend says. "Who is going to hire a 45-year-old for a job in the computer industry? The industry is for young people. You might just as well give up before you fail."

Whatever the scenario, there you sit, starting to question yourself. Well, stop! Do not let anyone burst your bubble. No matter what anyone says, at least you are trying to get the career you want. At least you are following your dream.

While I can't promise you that you will definitely achieve every one of your dreams, I can promise you if that if you don't go after your dream, it will be very difficult to achieve. What I want you to do is not listen to anyone negative and keep working toward what you want.

What Gives You Joy? What Makes You Happy?

Let's zero in further on what you want to do. Let's talk about what gives you joy. Let's talk about what makes you happy. Did you ever notice that when you're doing something you love, you smile? It's probably subconscious, but you're smiling. You're happy inside. And it's not only that you're happy, you make others around you happy.

Let's think about it for a few minutes. What makes you happy. What gives you joy? Is it helping others? Is it teaching others? Is it writing? Is it organizing things? Is it developing things? Is it problem solving? Is it coming up with solutions? Is it a combination of things?

Does the thought of developing a new software program make you smile? When you close your eyes can you see yourself as the CIO of a prestigious corporation? Can you almost hear yourself giving a lecture to students on some aspect of computer technology?

Can you see yourself standing at the podium at a major conference delivering a paper on database security? Are you smiling as you read your byline in one of the top computer trade magazines? Would it give you joy to see your name on the cover as the author of a series of books on using various computer software programs?

Would it make you smile to see yourself finally figuring out what was wrong with a computer? What about helping a frustrated customer on the phone deal with his or her computer issues? Then maybe that's your dream. That is what would make you happy.

Keep dreaming. Keep asking yourself what makes you happy. What gives you joy? Are you having a hard time figuring it out? Many of us do. Here's an idea to help get your juices flowing.

Take out your pad and a pen again. Make a list of any jobs or volunteer activities you've done, things you do on your "off time," and hobbies. If you're still in school, you might add in extra-curricular activities in which you've participated. Note what aspects of each you like and what you didn't like. This will help you see what type of job you're going to enjoy. What are your special talents, skills, and personality traits? What gives you joy and makes you happy?

Do you truly enjoy teaching someone something new? Are you patient? What about creative? A career where you are working hands on teaching people how to use hardware or software might be just what you should look for.

Have you always been good at motivating others? Are you inspiring? Are you a good teacher? Perhaps a career in corporate training might be for you.

Are you creative? Do you have computer skills? What about using your skills and talents for a career as a desktop publisher? What about a career as a graphic artist or designer? The choice is yours.

Do you have problem-solving skills? Do you like helping people? Do you love the challenge of determining what causes operating errors in computer systems and then finding a solution? Maybe you would like a career as a network and computer systems administrator? Would you rather do similar work on databases? Perhaps you would like a job as a database administrator, a database analyst, database programmer, or systems manager. What is going to give you joy? What are your aspirations?

Is your special talent writing and crafting words? Does writing give you joy? Do you enjoy explaining things? There are dozens of ways you can parlay these talents into a wonderful career in the computer industry. Perhaps you want to handle the public relations or marketing at a hardware or software company. Perhaps you want to write textbooks. Maybe you want to be a technical writer. How about developing the content for a computer-oriented Web site? There are traditional options as well as less traditional ones. The choice is yours.

Do you love spending every waking minute on the Internet? There are a ton of choices for you, depending on your passions. What about a career as a researcher? What about a career as a Web designer? How about a career as a Web developer? How about a career as a Web administrator? What about a career in some type of support? The trick to finding a career you love is finding work you are passionate about.

Are your special skills in administration? You need only decide what area of the industry you want to pursue. Perhaps it would give you joy to work in a large corporation. Maybe your passion is to use your skills and talents in a smaller company. Maybe you want to manage the IT department of a noncomputer-oriented organization. Perhaps you would prefer work-

> ## Words from the Wise
> The first requisite for success is the ability to apply your physical and mental energies to one problem incessantly without growing weary.
>
> –Thomas Edison

ing directly in the industry. What would get you excited about going to work every day?

What Are Your Talents?

It's important to define what your talents are. Sometimes we're so good at something that we just don't even think twice about it. The problem with this is that often we don't see the value in our talent. What does this mean? It means that we may overlook the possibilities associated with our talents.

It is also important to know that you can have more than one talent. Just because you are an inspirational teacher doesn't mean you can't be a talented artist. Just because you're a talented writer doesn't mean you can't be a great speaker. Just because you are great working with numbers doesn't mean you're not good at organizing. Just because you're creative doesn't mean you can't make people laugh. Most of us have more than one talent. The trick is making sure you know what your talents are and using them to your advantage.

Do you know your talents? Can you identify them? This is another time you're going to have to sit down with a pad of paper and start writing. Write down everything that you're good at. Write down all of your talents, not just the ones you think are related to the area of the computer industry in which you're interested. This is not the time to be modest. Remember that this list is for you, so be honest with yourself.

> ## Tip from the Coach
> If you dream large and reach high you can have a life and career that are better than you can ever imagine. If, on the other hand, you just settle, you will never feel fulfilled.

Can you finish this sentence? "I am a talented (fill in the blank)." You might be a talented systems analyst, problem solver, Web designer, graphic artist, teacher, administrator, writer, publicist, caregiver, photographer, salesperson, etc.

Now finish the sentence, "I am talented in _____." You might be talented in organizing, supervising, cooking, or baking. You might be talented at negotiating, problem solving, teaching, making people feel better about themselves, writing, persuasion, painting, drawing, decorating, or public speaking. Whatever your talents, there usually is a way you can use them to help your career.

How? Let's say you want to be a marketing or public relations director for a hardware or software company. Your talents, among others, are creativity and writing. You also are very persuasive and a great negotiator. While creativity and writing are the talents that can help you become a successful marketing or public relations director, having the talent to persuade the media to give stories a certain spin or the talent to negotiate to get your press release in the paper or reporters to your press conference can be priceless.

Let's say you want to work in some area of computer repair or customer support. In addition to having the technical skills necessary for a career in this area, your talents include creativity, organization, and leadership. You also are very good at problem solving and are a very talented gourmet cook. In addition, you have a natural ability to relate to people and are a great listener. While having a natural ability to deal well with people is paramount to working in customer support, being creative and organized helps a lot as well. The ability to listen so you can actually hear what a client is saying is essential. Leadership skills help you move your career to the top.

"But how can being a great cook help me in my career?" you ask.

Well that depends on how creative you are. I've seen people use cooking in business to build teamwork. I've seen people use cooking analogies to explain how a computer or software program works. What else? I have seen people in various careers in an array of industries use their gourmet cooking skills to network and move their career ahead. How? Some volunteer to bring a gourmet dish to an event for a not-for-profit fund-raiser. Others volunteer to teach a gourmet cooking class, give a workshop in preparing healthy gourmet meals quickly, or give cooking lessons at a local community center.

How can any of those activities help your career in the computer industry? It can help make you visible. It can help bring your name to the powers that be in a positive way. It can help give you exposure. Even if you are volunteering in a capacity totally out of the realm of your career, you can never tell who is out there looking for someone with your professional talents.

Use every talent you have to catapult you to the top. Don't discount those talents you feel are not "job" related. Whether your extra talents get you in the door, help you stand out, or climb the career ladder, they will be useful tools in your career.

Getting What You Want

You hear opportunity knocking. How do you get what you want? How do you turn your dream into reality? One of the most important things you need to do is have faith in yourself and your dream. It is essential that you believe you can make it happen in order for it to happen.

As we've discussed, you need to focus on exactly what you really want; otherwise you'll be going in a million different directions. Remember that things may not always come as fast as you want. No matter how it appears, most people are not overnight successes.

Generally, in life you have to "pay your dues." What does that mean? On the most basic level, it means you probably have to start small to get to the big time. Before you get to ride in the limo, you're going to have to drive a lot of Chevys. (There's nothing wrong with a Chevy; it's just not the same as having a chauffeured limo.)

Depending on your situation, it might mean working in a smaller organization before getting a job in a larger, more prestigious company. It might mean being assigned the less desirable time slots instead of the more desirable shift. It might mean working as a coordinator before you become a director.

Paying your dues means you may have to pound on a lot of doors before the right one opens. It means you may have to take jobs that are not your perfect choice to get experience so you can move up the career ladder and get the job of your dreams. You may have to do a lot of the grunt work and stay in the background while others get the credit. While all this is going on you have to be patient with the knowledge that everything you do is getting you closer to your goal.

If you look at every experience as a stepping-stone to get you to the next level of your career, it's a lot easier to get through the difficult things or trying times you may have to go through.

Setting Goals

Throughout this whole process it's essential to set goals. Why? Because if you don't have goals,

Tip from the Top
   Successful people continue setting goals throughout their career. That ensures their career doesn't get stagnant and they always feel passion for what they do.

it's hard to know where you want to end up. It's hard to know where you're going. If you don't know where you're going, it's very difficult to get there. It is sometimes easier to look at goals as the place you arrive at the end of a trip. You can also look at your actions as the trips you take along the way to your destinations.

What's the best way to set goals? To start with, be as specific as you can. Instead of your goal being, "I want to work in computers," your goal might be, "I want a career as a software developer for a major company." Instead of your goal being, "I want a career working in some aspect of the Web," your goal might be, "I want to be the director of Web design for a large, prestigious entertainment company." Instead of your goal being, "I want to be involved in e-commerce," your goal might be, "I want to be the Web developer for a large television shopping network. I want develop a site that will help increase business."

You should also try to make sure your goals are clear and concise. You'll find it easier to focus on your goals if you write them down. Writing down your goals will help you see them more clearly. Writing down your goals will also give them power and power is what can make it happen.

Take out your pad of paper or notebook and get started. As you think of new ideas and goals, jot them down. Some people find it easier to work toward one main goal. Others find it

> ## ★ Tip from the Top
> Goals are not written in stone. Just because you have something written down does not mean that you can't change it. As you change, your goals might change as well. This is normal.

easier to develop a series of goals leading up to their main goal.

To help you do this exercise, first develop a number of long-term goals. Where do you think you want to be in your career in the next year? How about the next two years, three years, five years, and even 10 years?

Need some help? Here is an example of the goals for someone who is still in school and pursuing a career as a software engineer.

First-Year Goals

◎ I want to complete my bachelor's degree, majoring in computer science with an emphasis in software engineering.

◎ I want to get some practical experience while I'm still in school. I want to do an internship with a large company so I can make some important contacts and learn a variety of things from a variety of people.

Second-Year Goals

◎ In order to get experience, I am going to look for a job in programming with a large company where I will have more opportunities to move up the career ladder.

◎ I want to continue my education and begin working on my master's degree in software engineering.

◎ I expect to be promoted to a better job as a computer software engineer within the year.

◎ I want to network and start getting known in my field.

◎ I want to join and get involved in some trade associations.

Third-Year Goals

◎ I want to be working as a project manager in a large corporation.

◎ I want to continue my education and training, constantly honing my skills.

◎ I want to be known and respected in my field.

Long-Term Goals

◎ I want to have my master's degree completed.

◎ I want to become the chief information officer of a company so I can fully use my experience, skills, talents, and expertise.

◎ I want to be recognized as a talented and innovative professional by my peers.

◎ Eventually I want to begin my own computer consulting firm, specializing in system design.

Once you've zeroed in on your main goals, you can develop short-range goals you might want or need to accomplish to reach your long-range goals. Feel free to add details. Don't concern yourself with situations changing. You can always adjust your goals.

When focusing on your goals, remember that there are general work-related goals and specific work-related goals. What's the difference? Specific goals are just that. See the following examples.

◎ General goal: I want to get a promotion.
  ▫ Specific goal: I want to become the project manager in my department.

◎ General goal: I want to work in some segment of information technology.

- ▫ Specific goal: I want to be the chief information officer of a large, well-known entertainment company.
- ◎ General goal: I want to work with Web sites.
  - ▫ Specific goal: I want to be a Webmaster for a large newspaper.
- ◎ General goal: I want to own my own computer company.
  - ▫ Specific goal: I want to own my computer repair business. I also want to provide classes for using computers and various software programs. I also want to provide crisis phone support, so when people have a problem using their computer we can deal with it on the phone when possible. I also want to volunteer to teach senior citizens how to use computers.

Visualization Can Help Make It Happen

Visualization is a powerful tool that can help you succeed in all aspects of your career and your life. Visualization is "seeing" or "visualizing" a situation the way you want it. It's setting up a picture in your mind of the way you would like a situation to unfold.

How do you do it? It's simple. Close your eyes and visualize what you want. Visualize the situation that you long for. Think about each step you need to take to get where you want to go in your career and then see the end result in your mind. Want to see how it's done?

What do you want to be? How do you want your career to unfold? Do you want to be the CIO of a large company? Want to be a software engineer? How about the director of information services for a large retail chain?

Want to have your own Web site? Want to be a Webmaster? How about starting your own Web store? Do you want to develop new software programs? How about becoming an animator? What about becoming a game designer? Do you want to design computer systems?

Perhaps you want to be the technology expert for a newspaper or magazine. Maybe you want to write a book about how to create Web sites. Perhaps you want to write a book about teaching kids to use computers. Maybe you want to create the next MySpace, Facebook, YouTube, or Google.

Do you want to teach people how to use computers? Do you want to train people how to use software programs? Do you want to design an entire computer system for new businesses?

Do you want to be the director of marketing for a software company? Do you want to be the director of sales of a computer company? What about the director of public relations? How about the director of product research? Do you think you might want to be the brand manager of a computer company?

The options are endless. The decision is yours. Whatever your dream career is, visualization can help you get there!

How so? No matter what type of career you are aspiring to, start by visualizing having it. Visualize driving up to a company parking lot in the morning and parking in the space which says, "*Reserved for _____,*" with your name on the sign. Visualize walking into the building and getting on the elevator. As you're walking down the hall to your office, imagine hearing your colleagues greeting you.

You get to a door and see a sign outside your office. Do you see your name? "Sharon Adams, IT Director." Wow! You can hardly believe you are living your dream.

Now visualize yourself standing at the front of a large meeting room giving a PowerPoint presentation. Visualize looking at your colleagues in the room. Imagine telling them about an exciting new project on which the company is embarking. Everyone is discussing what a great idea it is. When you finish with your presentation, the people in the room break into applause.

Your heart is pounding because you are so excited. You are doing what you prepared for and trained to do. What a feeling. It's a good day and it's only one of many. You're living your dream. Got the picture? That's visualization!

Are you getting the idea? You need to visualize your life and your career the way you want it to be. Visualize yourself as you would like others to see you.

No matter what you want to do you can visualize it to help make it happen. Visualize the career you want. Visualize the career you deserve. See yourself going for the interview, getting the job, and then sitting at your desk. Visualize speaking to coworkers, going to meetings, and doing your work.

The more details you can put into your visualization, the better. Add in the colors of things around you; the fragrance of the flowers on your desk; the aroma of the coffee in your mug; the color of the suit you're wearing; even the bright blue sky outside. Details will help bring your visualization to life.

Whatever your dreams, concentrate on them, think about them, and then visualize

The Inside Scoop
Visualization works for more than your career. Use it to help you make all your dreams come true in all facets of your life.

Tip from the Coach
Make a commitment to your dream and stick to it. Without this commitment, your dream will turn into a bubble that will fly away and burst in mid air.

them. Here's the great news. If you can visualize it, you can make it happen! No one really knows why, but it does seem to work, and it works well. Perhaps it's positive energy. Perhaps you're just concentrating more on what you want.

One of the tricks in visualizing to get what you want is actually visualizing all the actions you need to take to achieve your goal. If you don't know what these actions are or should be, an easy exercise that might help is called reverse visualization. In essence what you're going to do is play the scenes in reverse.

Start by visualizing the point in your life where you want to be and then go back to the point where you are currently. So what this means is if your dream is to be the senior director of Web site development for a major retail chain, that's where you're going to start. If you're currently a Webmaster, that's where you're going to end up.

If your dream is to be a software engineer, that's where you're going to start. If you have just graduated from college and you're looking for a job, that's where you're going to end up.

In the same vein, if your dream is to teach computer science to high school students, that's where you are going to start. If you are student teaching, that is where you're going to end up.

Let me show you how it works. Go back to your dream of being a teacher. As we just did a moment ago, start visualizing that you have what you want. You have a great job as a computer science teacher. Now visualize the school you work in; its location, what it looks like from the outside, what it looks once you walk in the door. Now visualize your classroom. Think about what it looks like. Visualize the computer lab. Visualize your desk and the setup of the room, the books, and other learning materials. Even the blackboard with the chalk dust!

Now visualize the students in your class. Imagine saying, "Good morning class," and then interacting with them. Imagine them asking you questions about your current lesson. Imagine their excitement when you teach them something new. (Imagine your excitement when they teach you something you didn't know!)

Now, take one step back. Right before you got to that point in your career, what did you do? There were probably a number of things. Let's make a list of how events might have unfolded in reverse.

◎ You answered the phone. You got the job! You will be working in the Big City High School teaching computer science.
◎ You interviewed for the job. The hiring committee asked hard questions, but you knew all the right answers. It seems like a good match.
◎ You drove to the interview.
◎ You got dressed in your blue suit for the interview and made sure your resume and supporting materials were perfect.
◎ You prepared for the interview.
◎ You went to the school's Web site, downloaded an application, filled it in, wrote a cover letter, and forwarded it all with your resume via e-mail.
◎ You saw an advertisement in the newspaper for a job teaching computer science.

◎ You took and passed your state's test and fulfilled the requirements necessary to get a provisional teaching license.
◎ You graduated from college with a bachelor's degree.
◎ You love absolutely everything about student teaching. Every day is like an adventure.
◎ You decided that you wanted to fulfill your dream of becoming a computer science teacher and finished your student teaching. (This is the point where you are now.)

Here's a different example of the same type of reverse visualization exercise you might do. It's the same concept, just a slightly different way of doing it.

Let's say you want to work in information technology. As a matter of fact, your goal is to become the CIO of a major corporation. Think about where you'd like to work. Think about your job title. Visualize that you are the CIO of the corporation of your choice.

Add in your office environment, the office décor. Now add in your coworkers. Next put yourself in the picture. Remember to visualize what you're wearing, your accessories, even the color of your suit.

Visualize yourself speaking to colleagues, supervisors, and even the board of directors. Create a picture in your mind of some of the projects you'll be working on. Visualize the day you see the cover story in *CIO* magazine about your rise to fame. Feel the excitement of the day.

Now go backward. Visualize yourself in the other jobs you've held at the company. Keep visualizing. Now see yourself driving to work at that same company on your first day. Keep visualizing. Now you're thinking about getting dressed that morning. Keep going. Remember hearing the alarm buzzing and how you just couldn't wait to get up to go to work.

Keep visualizing in reverse. Hear your cell phone ringing and remember the feeling you had when the voice at the other end told you that you got the job. Going back, visualize the feeling that you had waiting for that call. Visualize the thank-you note you wrote to the human resources director after your interview. See the letter in your mind. Now, remember leaving the interview. Visualize in detail what you wore, what the experience was like, the questions that you were asked, and the feelings you had at that moment. Remember how much you hoped you would be hired.

Visualize filling out the application and developing and sending in your resume with your perfectly tailored cover letter. Now visualize seeing the job advertised and the excited feeling you had.

Recall all the preparation you did to find that job. The skills you updated. The people you spoke to; the networking. Visualize the internship you went through.

Words from the Wise

I have learned this at least by my experiment: that if one advances confidently in the direction of his dreams, and endeavors to live the life which he has imagined, he will meet with a success unexpected in common hours.

–Henry David Thoreau

You are now back at the position in the visualization process where you currently are in your career. You now have an idea of the steps needed to get where you want to go. This might not be the exact way your situation unfolds, but hopefully, it can get you started on the visualization process.

Paint a picture in your mind of what you want to achieve detail by detail. Whether you're using a reverse visualization or a traditional visualization technique, this powerful tool can help you get what you want. Give it a try. You'll be glad you did.

3

PLAN FOR SUCCESS IN THE COMPUTER INDUSTRY

Take Control and Be Your Own Career Manager

You might have heard the old adage that if you want something done right, you need to do it yourself. While this might not always hold true for everything, there's a shred of accuracy in relation to your career.

It's important to realize that no one cares about your career as much as you do. Not your mother, your father, your sister, or your brother. Not your best friend, girlfriend, boyfriend, or spouse. Not your colleagues, your supervisor, or even your mentor. It's not that these people don't care, because in most situations they probably not only care, but want you to be successful. It just is that no one really cares as much as you do.

If you want more control over success in your career, a key strategy to incorporate is becoming your own career manager. What does this mean? It means that you won't be leaving your career to chance. You won't be leaving your career in someone else's hands. You will be in the driver's seat! You will have control and you can make your dream career happen!

Will it take a lot of work? Yes, being your own career manager can be a job in itself. The payoff, however, will be worth it.

If you look at successful people in almost any industry, you will notice that most have a tremendous dedication to their career. Of course, they may have friends, colleagues, professionals, and others who advise them, but when it comes to the final decision-making, they are the ones who take the ultimate responsibility for their career.

Now that you've decided to be your own career manager you have some work to do. Next on the list is putting together an action plan. Let's get started!

What Is an Action Plan?

Let's look at success a little closer. What's the one thing successful people, successful businesses, and successful events all have in common? Is it money? Luck? Talent? While money, luck, and talent all certainly are part of the mix, generally the common thread most share is a well-developed plan for success. Whatever your goal, be it short range or long range, if you have a plan to achieve it, you have a better chance of succeeding. With that in mind, let's discuss how you can create your

> ### ★ Voice of Experience
> Once you get the knack of creating action plans, you can use them for everything in your life, not just your career. You'll find everything goes smoother with a plan in place.

own plan for success. What can you do with your plan? The possibilities are endless.

People utilize all types of plans to help ensure success. Everyone has his or her own version of what is best. To some, just going over what they're going to do and how they're going to do it in their mind is plan enough. Some, especially those working on a new business, create formal business plans. Some people develop action plans. That's what we're going to talk about now.

What exactly is an action plan? In a nutshell, an action plan is a written plan detailing all the actions you need to take to successfully accomplish your ultimate goal. In this case that goal is success in your chosen career.

Frequently during seminars, while going over the section on action plans, there are always some people who ask if they really need them.

"Why do I need a plan?" someone inevitably asks. "All I want is a job."

The answer is simple. You don't just want a job. You want to craft a great career. An action plan can help you do that.

How an Action Plan Can Help You Succeed

Success is never easy but you can stack the deck in your favor by creating your own personal action plan. Why is this so critical? To begin with, there are many different things you might want to accomplish to succeed in your career. If you go about them in a haphazard manner, however, your efforts might not be as effective as they could be. An action plan helps define the direction to go

and the steps needed to get the job done. It helps increase your efficiency in your quest for success.

Another reason to develop an action plan is that sometimes actually seeing your plan in writing helps you to see a major shortcoming, or simply makes you notice something minor that may be missing. At that point, you can add the actions you need to take and the situation will be easily rectified.

With an action plan, you know exactly what you're going to be doing to reach your goals. It helps you focus and be sure that everything you need to do is organized.

Many of us have had the experience of looking in a closet where everything is just jumbled up. If you need a jacket or a pair of pants from the closet, you can probably find it, but it may be frustrating and take you a long time. If you organize your closet, however, when you need that jacket or pair of pants, you can reach for them and find them in a second with no problem.

One of the main reasons you develop a plan is to have something organized to follow. When you have something to follow things are easier to accomplish, and far less frustrating. In essence, what you're creating with your action plan is a method of finding and succeeding in your dream career no matter what segment of the computer industry you are interested in pursuing. When you put that plan into writing, you're going to have something to follow and something to refer to making it easier to track your progress.

"Okay," you say. "How do I know what goes into the plan? How do I do this?"

Well, that depends a lot on what you want to do and what type of action plan you're putting together. Basically, your action plan is going to consist of a lot of the little, detailed steps you're going to have to accomplish to reach your goal.

Some people make very specific and lengthy action plans. Others develop general ones. You might just create a single plan that details everything you're going to need to do from the point where you are now up to the career of your dreams, or you might create a separate action plan for each job you pursue or a plan for your next goal. As long as you have some type of plan to follow, the choice is yours.

Your Personal Action Plan for Success in the Computer Industry

Now that you've decided to be your own career manager, it's up to you to develop your personal action plan for success in your career in the computer industry. Are you ready to get started?

A great deal of your action plan will depend on what area of the industry you're interested in and exactly what you want to do. Let's start with some basics.

Take a notebook, sit down, and start thinking about your career and the direction you want it to go. Begin by doing some research.

What do you want to find out? Almost any information can be useful in your career. Let's look at some of the things that might help you.

Your Market

One of the first things to research is your market. What does that mean? Basically, it means that you need to determine what jobs and employment situations are available and where they are located. Who will your potential employers be? If you are interested in working for yourself, as a consultant, or having your own business, who will be your clients? Where will they be located?

While jobs in the computer industry can be located throughout the country, in some situations you might have to relocate to find the perfect job. Where are the best opportunities for the area you're interested in pursuing? With a bit of research, you can start to find the answers.

Remember that the clearer you are in your goals, the easier it will be to reach them, so it's important when identifying your goals, to clarify them as much as possible.

Let's say, for example, you've decided you want to be a computer programmer. What type of programmer do you want to be? Where are the opportunities? Do you want to work in a large company or a smaller company? Do you want to work directly in the computer industry or in a non-computer industry? Are you looking for a traditional job or do you want to be a consultant? If you do some research you'll find a variety of options.

Are your aspirations to become a Webmaster? What kind of company do you want to work for? Do you want to work for a company that handles the Web needs of others? Do you want to work for an Internet Service Provider (ISP)? Do you want to work as a Webmaster for a company in the retail industry? What about working as a Webmaster for a health care facility? How about for a casino? What about for a governmental agency? How about for a military entity? In which part of the country would you prefer to work? Do you want to do contract work? Do you want to have your own company? What are your goals? What are your aspirations? Where can you find these opportunities? These are your markets.

Tip from the Top

With a bit of creativity, you can weave your passions together in your career. If you want to be around the music industry, for example, and you also want to work in the computer industry, depending on your skills and talents there might be a variety of options. You might locate a position as a Webmaster for a recording group or even an entire record label. You might find a position handling the online street marketing for a recording artist. Depending on your talents, you might even create and record music via computers and computerized programs.

If you are interested in working around the casino gaming industry you might weave together your love for both computers and gaming with a career creating the slot machine or video terminal games. You might seek out a career handling database management of a casino's clients. You might also look for a position handling a casino gaming company's information security (IS).

If you enjoy teaching and also love computers you can weave your interests together as well. You might seek out a traditional teaching job teaching computer science or technology in an elementary school, junior high, or high school. You might seek out a position teaching one or more of the computer science or technology courses in a college or university. You might decide you want to do corporate training or even offer private classes in some aspect of computers or software. You might even want to consider teaching online classes. Get creative. Think outside of the box and you might just find the career of your dreams.

Let's say you want your own computer consulting business. Who will your potential clients be? Who will your clients be if you want to pursue your own desktop publishing business?

Are you going to pursue a career in some area of the computer industry within another industry? What industry are you interested in working in? The choice is yours.

No matter what type of career you are choosing, where, specifically, could your markets be located? Who might your potential employers be? Who might your clients be?

Why do you have to research your market now? Why do you need this information at all? Because information is power! The more you think about your potential options and markets now, the more opportunities you may find down the line.

What Do You Need to Do to Get What You Want?

Next, research what you need to do to get the career you want. Do you need additional skills? Training? Education? Experience? Do you need to move to a different location? Make new contacts? Get an internship? Do you need to get certified? Licensed? Do you need to take exams? What do you need?

Do you need to get your bachelor's degree? What about your master's degree? Do you need your doctorate? Would additional continuing education help you get where you want to go?

Do you need to take a class or seminar to learn new skills? Do you need to get a book to help you learn something you need to help you get that promotion you want?

Do you need to join a union? Would joining a trade association help you? Do you need to find new ways to network? Do you need more contacts?

What you need to determine is what is standing in between you and the career you want. What obstacles do you face?

If you are already working in the computer industry in some capacity, you need to determine what is standing in between you and the success you are looking for. How can you climb the career ladder of success and perhaps even skip a few rungs to get where you want to go?

Take some time thinking about this. If you can determine exactly what skills, qualifications, training, education, licensing, certification, or experience you're missing or what you need to do, you're halfway there.

It often helps to look at exactly what is standing between you and what you want on paper. What barriers do you face? Here's a sample to give you an idea.

What Stands Between Me and What I Want?	Possible Solution
I need my degree.	I'm going to finish college.
I need to get certified.	I'm going to contact the organizations that offer certifications and get information on how to obtain the certifications that can help me in my career.
I can't find a job opening doing what I want where I live.	I'm going to check out Web sites and online newspapers to see if there are opportunities available in other locations. Maybe there are some jobs I haven't seen yet.
I don't know how to find a job as a Webmaster for a recording group (entertainer, sports personality, business, etc.).	I'm going to cold call and send out letters to see if there are jobs available or if I can create my own job. I'm going to check out the Web and browse to find some possibilities. Perhaps I'll put a small ad in *Billboard* (or other trade publication, depending on my specific interest).
It would help me to be bilingual.	I'm going to look into an immersion course to see if I can learn another language quickly.
I need to find a way to advance my career and can't get a promotion because my supervisor isn't going anyplace.	I'm going to start actively looking for a better job.
I want to start my own computer repair and training consulting business and I don't know how to begin.	I'm going to check out a book on beginning a new business. I am also going to contact the county offices bu and local community college to see if there are any programs to give assistance on starting new businesses. I also am going to see if I need a business permit and get one if necessary.
I need to learn a new programming language.	I am going to find a course or workshop and take it ASAP.
I am not up to date on my skills.	I am going to look for some classes and workshops to pick up new skills.
I need some experience to get a decent job.	I am going to find a way to volunteer in my area of interest to get some experience or see if I can find an internship.

Use this form to help you clarify each situation and the possible solution you feel is standing between you and the career success you want.

What Stands Between Me and What I Want?	Possible Solution

How Can You Differentiate Yourself?

No matter what area you want to be involved in the computer industry, I can almost guarantee that there are other people who want the same type of job.

There are thousands of people who want to be programmers; thousands who want to be systems analysts; thousands who want to be software engineers; and thousands who want to be network administrators. There are thousands who want to work as computer scientists; thousands who want to be computer engineers; and thousands who want to design or create other peripherals.

There are thousands who want to work in both the wholesale and retail sales segment of computers, peripherals, and software; and thousands who want careers in service, support, and repair.

There are thousands who want to be Webmasters; thousands who want to be Web developers; thousands who want to be Web designers; thousands who want to write and edit Web content; and thousands who want to work in various segments of IP hosting, sales, and support.

There are thousands who want to be computer graphic artists and designers, thousands who want to be animators, and thousands who want to be game developers.

There are thousands who want to work in the various segments of e-commerce, thousands who want to work in computerized call centers, and thousands who want to come up with the next best Internet business.

There are thousands who want careers in one of the various segments of social networking; thousands who want to be technical writers; and thousands who want careers writing about computers, peripherals, software, and technology.

There are thousands who want to be in teaching and training, thousands who want to work in computer and peripheral repairs, and thousands who want to work in the computer and software support and service.

There are thousands who want to work in computer security and thousands who want to work in information. There are thousands who want to work as data entry operator and thousands who want to work in the area of quality assurance.

There are thousands who want to be project managers, department directors, and CIOs. And don't forget all the people who want to work in the peripheral segments of the computer industry handling the business, marketing, sales, publicity, advertising, human resources, and more.

I can almost hear you say, "That is a lot of competition. Can I make it? Can I succeed?"

To that I answer a definitive, "Yes!" Lots of people succeed in all aspects of the computer industry. Why shouldn't one of them be you?

Here's the challenge. How can you stand out in a positive way? What attributes do you have or what can you do so people choose you over others?

"I don't like calling attention to myself," many people tell me. "I just want to blend into the crowd."

Unfortunately, that isn't the best thing to do if you want to make it. Why? Because the people who get the jobs, who succeed, who make it, are the ones who have found a way to set themselves apart from others. And if you want success, you are going to have to find a way to stand out too.

How? Perhaps it's your personality or the energy you exude. Maybe it's your sense of humor or the way you organize things. Perhaps it's your calm demeanor in the face of a storm. Maybe it's your smile or the twinkle in your eye. Some people just have a presence about them.

It might be the special way you have of dealing with others. Perhaps you have a way of explaining something difficult in an easy-to-understand manner. Maybe it's the way you defuse a difficult situation or make people feel better. Possibly it is the way you make others feel special themselves.

Perhaps it's the way you can look at an accounting ledger and see the error while everyone else has been trying to find. Maybe it's the way you see exactly what is wrong with a software program. Perhaps it is the creative way you look at things.

Maybe it's the way you motivate people or inspire them. Maybe it's the way you can take a complicated project and can just make it easier to understand. Perhaps it is that you are not only a visionary, but have the ability to bring your visions to fruition.

Maybe it's the way you can calm an irate customer. Perhaps it's the way you can negotiate so that both sides feel they are getting what they want.

The Inside Scoop

Successful people usually have something special about them, something that sets them apart from others. Sometimes it is related to their career, sometimes it isn't. If you don't take advantage of what makes you stand out in a positive way and your expertise, whatever it is, you might not gain the success you deserve.

Tip from the Coach

If you don't know what makes you special, take a cue from what others tell you. You know those conversations where someone says something in passing such as, "You're so funny, I love being around you." "You always know just what to say to make me feel better." "You have such a beautiful voice that I love listening to you sing." "You always are so helpful." "You are a great negotiator. Even when people don't get everything they want, they're happy." Or, "You make it so easy to understand, the most difficult things." Listen to what people say and always take compliments graciously.

Everyone is special in some way. Everyone has a special something they do or say that makes them stand out in some manner. Most people have more than one trait that makes them special. Spend some time determining what makes you special in a positive way so you can use it to your advantage in your career.

How to Get Noticed

Catching the eye of people important to your career is another challenge. How are you going to bring your special talents and skills to the attention of the people who can make a difference to your career? This is the time to brainstorm.

First of all, instead of waiting for opportunities to perform to present themselves, I want you to actively seek them out. You are also going to want to actively market yourself. We're going to discuss different ways to market yourself later, but at this point you need to take some time to try and figure out how to make yourself and your accomplishments known to others.

Consider joining a not-for-profit or civic organization whose mission you believe in. And don't just join, get involved. How? That depends what your passion is and where your talents lie. You might, for example, offer to do the marketing, publicity, or public relations for a civic group, not-for-profit organization, or one of their events. You might volunteer to do fund-raising for a nonprofit or even suggest a fund-raising idea and then chair the project.

You might offer to computerize the records for a community group you're working with or even set up their Web site. You might volunteer to teach people how to use a computer or simple software in a library.

Why volunteer when you're trying to get a job or climb the career ladder? What does this have to do with your career in the computer industry? Aside from doing something for someone else, it can help you get noticed.

"I can see volunteering in something related to some area of the computer industry," you say, "but what will volunteering for an unrelated industry do for my career?"

It will give you experience. It will give you exposure. And maybe someone else involved in the nonprofit or civic group for which you're volunteering may have some contacts in the area of the computer industry you are seeking a job.

Just keep coming up with ideas and writing them down as you go. You can fine-tune them later. Think creatively. Don't forget to send out a press release about your activities if you do something noteworthy.

Why are you doing this? You want to get your name out there. You want to call attention to yourself in a positive manner. You want to set yourself apart from others. You want people in the position to hire you to not only know you exist, but also to think of you and remember you when opportunities for employment or promotions arise.

Have you won any awards? Have you been nominated for an award (even if you didn't win)? Honors and awards always set you apart from others and help you get noticed. Have you presented a paper or spoken at a conference or convention? These events can help set you apart from others as well.

What have you done to set yourself apart? What can you do to accomplish this goal? Think about these possibilities. Can you come up with any more? As you come up with answers, jot them down in a notebook. That way you'll have something to refer back to later. Once you determine the answers, it's easier to move on to the next step of writing your plan.

What Should Your Basic Action Plan Include?

Now that you've done some research and brainstormed some great ideas, you are on your way. It's time to start developing your action plan. What should your basic action plan include?

Career Goals

One of the most important parts of your action plan will be defining your career goals. Are you just starting your career? Are you looking for a new job or career? Are you already in the industry and want to climb the career ladder? Are you interested in exploring a different career in the computer industry, other than the one you're in now?

What is your dream? The sky is the limit once you know what your goals are.

When defining your goals try to make them as specific as possible. So, for example, instead of writing in your action plan that your goal is to be a Web site developer, you might want to refine your goal to be a successful, Web content developer working for a large, retail E-commerce site. Instead of writing that your goal is to be an animator, you might refine your goal to be a successful animator working for one of the top studios. Instead of writing that your goal is to be involved in some aspect of programming, you might refine your goal to be a computer systems software engineer working in a large company in the New York metropolitan area. Instead of defining your goal to be involved in some aspect of marketing, you might want to define your goal to being the director of marketing for a large, prestigious software company. .

When thinking about goals, you might include your short-range goals as well as your long-range ones. You might even want to include mid-range goals. That way you'll be able to track your progress, which gives you inspiration to slowly but surely meet your goals.

For example, let's say you're interested in pursuing a career in software engineering. Your short-range goals might be to go to college and get your bachelor's degree with a major in computer science or computer technology. Your mid-range goals might be to get a job as a software engineer in a large financial institution and after some experience become a project manager. Your long-range goals might be to become the CIO of the institution.

Keep in mind that goals are not written in stone and that it is okay to be flexible and change them along the way. The idea is that no matter what you want, moving forward is the best way to get somewhere.

What You Need to Reach Your Goals

The next step in your action plan is to put in writing exactly what you need to reach your goals. Do you need some sort of training or more education? Do you need to learn new skills or brush up on old ones? Do you need to move to a different geographic location? Do you need to network more? Do you need to make more contacts?

Your Actions

This is the crux of your action plan. What actions do you need to attain your goals?

◎ Do you need to get a bachelor's degree?
  ▫ Your actions would be to identify colleges and universities that offer the degree you are looking for, apply and get accepted to the school, complete the coursework, and gradate with the degree you need.
◎ Do you need to take some classes or attend some workshops to learn new skills?
  ▫ Your actions would be to identify, locate, and take classes and workshops.
◎ Do you need to learn new programming languages?
  ▫ Your actions would to determine what languages you need to learn and find and take classes to teach you those languages.
◎ Do you need to move to another geographic location?
  ▫ Your actions would be to find a way to relocate.

◎ Do you need to attend industry events, conferences, and conventions?
  ▫ Your actions would be to locate and investigate events, conferences, and conventions, and then attend them.

◎ Do you need to find more ways to network or just network more?
  ▫ Your actions would be to develop opportunities and activities to network and follow through with those activities and opportunities

◎ Do you need more experience?
  ▫ Your actions might include becoming an intern, volunteering, or finding other ways to get experience by working at one job until you get the experience you need to go after another job you want.

◎ Do you need to determine exactly what area of the computer industry in which you want to work?
  ▫ Your actions would be to locate people working in various segments of the industry and talk to them about their job. Your actions might also include doing research on various career options.

Your Timetable

Your timetable is essential to your action plan. In this section you're going to include what you're going to do (your actions) and when you're going to do them. The idea is to make sure you have a deadline for getting things done so your actions don't fall through the cracks. Just saying, "I have to do this or I have to do that," is not effective.

Remember, there is no right or wrong way to assemble your action plan. It's what you are comfortable with. You might want your plan to look different in some manner, have different items, or even have things in a different order. That's okay. The whole purpose of action plans is to help you achieve your career goals. Choose the one that works for you.

Let's look at a couple of examples. The first is a sample of what a basic action plan might look like. The others are samples that are partially partly filled in by someone with specific career goals.

Here's a different type of action plan.

After reviewing these samples, use the blank plan provided to help you create your own personal action plan. Feel free to change the chart or add in sections to better suit your needs.Remember, you can start your action plan at whatever point you currently are in your career.

Example 1

My Basic Action Plan

Career Goals

Long-range goals:
Mid-range goals:
Short-range goals:

My market:

What do I need to reach my goals?

How can I differentiate myself from others?

How can I catch the eye of people important to my career?

What actions can I take to reach my goals?

What actions do I absolutely need to take now?

What's my timetable?
  Short-range goals:
  Mid-range goals:
  Long-range goals:

Actions I've taken: Date completed:

Example 2

My Basic Action Plan

Career Goals

Long-range goals: To become the CIO of a large, prestigious casino gaming company. To be known and respected in my field. To be earning a high six-figure salary.

Mid-range goals: To have a position as the director of database management for a casino gaming company. To continue my education, obtaining master's degrees in information systems and business.

Short-range goals: Complete my education and obtain my bachelor's degree with a double major in business and computer science. Secure a position in a casino or gaming company in the IT department.

My Market (short term): Gaming companies, casinos, etc.

My Market (long term): Gaming companies, casinos, etc.

Possibilities for employment (short term): Casinos or gaming companies located in Las Vegas or Atlantic City.

Possibilities for employment (long range): Gaming companies located in Las Vegas. (I would love to work for Caesars or Trump.)

What do I need to reach my goals?
Get internship in casino or gaming company.
Graduate from college.
Network.
Get experience.
Keep networking.
Look for mentor.
Join trade associations.
Search out opportunities.
Get certified.
Get a job.

(continues)

Example 2, continued

Get promotions.
Get master's degree.
Continue getting experience.
Seek out headhunter.
Be recruited for position as CIO.
Get the job!

How can I differentiate myself from others? I attend the major casino conventions and go to all the networking events. I was a student panelist at one breakout session at a gaming convention and received great ratings from participants. I was just accepted to be on another panel speaking about increasing business at casinos via technology. I've networked and have a number of good contacts. I interview well. I'm continuing my education.

How can I catch the eye of people important to my career? Network at industry events, join industry associations, volunteer.

What actions can I take to reach my goals? Look for industry specific seminars and workshops, continue my education, find a mentor.

What actions do I absolutely need to take now? See if I can find and participate in an internship. Graduate from college with my undergraduate degree. Go to industry events; network. Continue finding opportunities to speak at conferences.

What's my timetable?
Short-range goals: Within the next 3 years
Mid-range goals: Within the next 5 years
Long-range goals: Within the next 7 years (I want it sooner, but I want to be realistic.)

Actions I've Taken
Finished two years of college toward my bachelors degree.
Spoken to my adviser about my goals.
Talked to Professor Jones about internship at a couple of different casinos.
Spoken to a number of people in different capacities working in IT in gaming companies.
    (This is the industry for me!)
Continue on with actions.

Example 3

My Personal Action Plan

CAREER GOALS (Long-range): Vice president of marketing, computer hardware or software company

CAREER GOALS (Short-range): Marketing specialist, computer hardware or software company

ACTION TO BE TAKEN	COMMENTS	TIMETABLE/ DEADLINE	DATE ACCOMPLISHED
SHORT RANGE			
Start looking for job.		ASAP	
Contact ABS Computers.	Informational interview on May 19.	ASAP	May 10
Attended informational interview.	People were nice and company makes great computers.		May 19
Checked out trade magazines for job possibilities and to keep up with industry trends.	Found them at college library. Will look through each issue for job openings.	ASAP	May 12
Surfed Web to check out job openings.	Noticed Green Software had opening in marketing department advertised on their Web site.	Now	May 14
E-mailed an application to Green Software.	Received an e-mail back that I will be getting a call next week regarding an interview.		May 15
Start working on resume.		Finish first draft by end of next month.	
MID RANGE			
LONG RANGE			

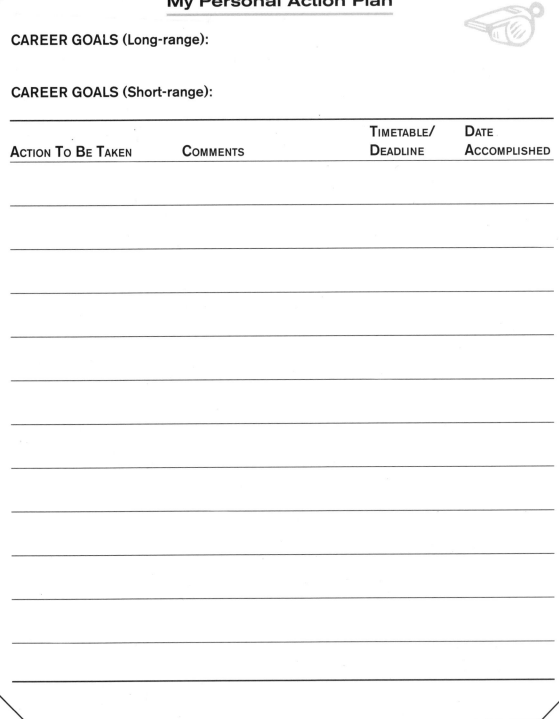

My Personal Action Plan

CAREER GOALS (Long-range):

CAREER GOALS (Short-range):

ACTION TO BE TAKEN	COMMENTS	TIMETABLE/ DEADLINE	DATE ACCOMPLISHED

Specialized Action Plans

What things might be in your specialized action plan? Once again, that depends on the area in which you're interested in working and the level you currently are in your career.

Let's first look at some general actions you might take. Remember, these are just to get you started. When you sit down and think about it, you'll find tons of actions you're going to need to take.

◎ Identify your skills.
◎ Identify your talents.
◎ Identify your passions.
◎ Look for internships.
◎ Develop different drafts of your resume.
◎ Develop cover letters tailored to each position.
◎ Network.
◎ Go to industry events.
◎ Make contacts.
◎ Volunteer to get experience.
◎ Obtain reference letters.
◎ Get permission to use people's names as references.
◎ Develop your career portfolio.
◎ Attend career fairs.
◎ Look for seminars, workshops, etc., in your area of interest.
◎ Take seminars, workshops, and classes.
◎ Get a college degree.
◎ Make business cards.
◎ Perform research online.
◎ Learn about industry trends.
◎ Make cold calls to obtain job interviews.

Depending on the particular area of the industry you are pursuing, you will find additional actions you might take to help you succeed. Here are a couple of career-specific actions to give you some ideas. After you look them over, start thinking about what actions you need to take for your specific career area.

Let's say your aspirations are to become a programmer or systems analyst. What other actions might you add in?

◎ Get certified in one or more areas.
◎ Take classes and learn specific programming languages.
◎ Look for and take part in internship.
◎ Read trade publications.

What actions could you add if your career aspirations are to become a game programmer?

◎ Get certified in one or more areas.
◎ Learn specific programming languages.
◎ Create one or more demo games for your portfolio.
◎ Surf the net to locate newsgroups or forums on gaming development.
◎ Read trade publications.

What actions might you add if your career aspirations are in Web design?

◎ Design one or more Web sites to use for your portfolio.
◎ Volunteer to design a Web site for a local nonprofit or civic organization.
◎ Join trade associations.

What actions could you add if your career aspirations are to work in some area of e-commerce?

◎ Look for and take seminars or classes in basic business.
◎ Find books on the segment of e-commerce in which you're interested.
◎ Look for and take seminars or workshops in online promotion.
◎ Check out other e-commerce sites on the Web.

◎ Join chamber of commerce for networking opportunities.

What other actions might you add if your career aspirations are to work in training and/or support?

◎ Take seminar in public speaking and facilitating.
◎ Look for seminar on improving presentation skills.
◎ Look for industry-specific conferences to attend.
◎ Join trade associations.
◎ Take courses, seminars, and workshops in training and techniques.
◎ Get experience training.

When developing your own action plan, just keep adding new actions as you think of them.

Using Action Plans for Specific Jobs

Action plans can be useful in a number of ways. In addition to developing a plan for your career, you might also utilize action plans when looking for specific jobs. Let's look at an example.

Copy the blank plan provided on page 60 to use when you find specific jobs in which you're interested to keep track of your actions. Feel free to change the chart or add sections to better suit your needs.

How to Use Your Action Plan

Creating your dream career takes time, patience, and a lot of work. In order for your action plan to be useful, you're going to have to use it. It's important to set aside some time every day to work on your career. During this time you're going to be taking actions. The number of actions you take, of course, will depend on your situa-

tion. If you are currently employed and looking for a new job, you may not be able to tackle as many actions as someone who is unemployed and has more time available every day. Keep in mind that some actions take may take longer than others.

For example, putting together your career portfolio will take longer than making a phone call. So if you're working on your portfolio you might not accomplish more than one action in a day.

Try to make a commitment to yourself to take at least one positive action each day toward getting your dream career or becoming more successful in the one you currently have. Do more if you can. Whatever your situation, just make sure you take some action every day.

In addition to an action plan, you'll find it helpful to keep an action journal recording all the career-related activities and actions you take on a daily basis Use the journal to write down all the things that you do on a daily basis do to help you attain your career goals. You then have a record of all the actions you have taken in one place. Like your action plan, your action journal can help you track your progress.

I can hear you telling me, "I don't remember hearing about anyone else looking for a job in any aspect of the computer industry going through all this. Why am I doing it?"

Here's the answer. First of all, just because you didn't hear that someone was doing all this

---

★ The Inside Scoop

Once you start writing in your daily action journal, you'll be even more motivated to fulfill your career goals.

Action Plan Looking for Specific Job

Job Title: Tech Support Rep for Internet service provider (ISP)

Job Description: Handling incoming customer support calls regarding Internet service and e-mail, provide customers with accurate technical solutions.

Company Name: Some Town Internet

Contact Name: Mark Jenkins

Secondary Contact Name: None

Company Address: Some Town Internet, 322 Broad Street, Some Town, NY 11111

Company Phone Number: (123) 333-5555

Company Fax Number: (123) 222-1111

Company Web site Address: http://www.sometowninternet.com

Company e-mail: e-mail@sometowninternet.com

Secondary e-mail: None

Where I heard about job: Saw ad in The Record

Actions Taken: Asked for application. Filled in application. Tailored resume and cover letter to job. Spoke to references to tell them I was applying for job and make sure I could still use them as references. Faxed application, resume, and cover letter. E-mailed application, resume, and cover letter.

Actions Needed To Follow Up: Review career portfolio, make extra copies of my resume, call if I don't hear back within three weeks.

Interview Time, Date, and Location: Received call on 6/11 asking me to come in for interview, interview set for 2:00 p.m. on 6/17 with Mark Jenkins.

More actions to follow up on: Get directions to office, pick out clothes for interview, try everything on to make sure it looks good, rehearse giving answers to questions most likely to be asked during interview.

Comments: Went to interview, very nice people working there. I would like the job. Mr. Jenkins seemed impressed with my resume and career portfolio. He told me that there is a lot of room for career advancement. He said he was conducting interviews for the next week and would get back to me one way or another in a couple of weeks.

Extra Actions: Write note thanking Mr. Jenkins for interview.

Results: 6/30—Mr. Jenkins called and asked me to come back for another interview to meet with some other people. He is interested in me working as a level one supervisor because of my background.
6/31—Mr. Jenkins called and asked if I would be interested in the job! He asked me to come in next week to discuss salary and benefits!

Action Plan for Specific Job

Job Title:

Job Description:

Company Name:

Contact Name:

Secondary Contact Name:

Company Address:

Company Phone Number:

Company Fax Number:

Company Web site Address:

Company E-mail:

Secondary E-mail:

Where I Heard about Job:

Actions Taken:

Actions Needed To Follow Up:

Interview Time, Date, and Location:

Comments:

Results:

doesn't mean they aren't doing it. Secondly, as we have discussed previously, chances are you don't just want a job. You are trying to craft a career. If it takes a little longer or you have to do a little more, in the long run, it will be worth it.

How do you do this? Here's a sample to get you started.

Daily Action Journal

Sunday, May 9

Read Sunday papers.
Checked papers for interesting stories and articles on Web design, Web sites, etc.
Read through classifieds. Found four openings I was interested in.
Surfed Internet looking for job openings in other areas.

Monday, May 10

Refined resume for specific jobs.
Wrote cover letter for each job.
Downloaded applications.
Mailed resumes, cover letters, and application.

Tuesday, May 11

Read daily newspapers and checked out classifieds.
E-mailed Adam Johnson, of Zalazon.com, telling him I was interested in volunteering for projects he discussed on TV news yesterday regarding helping seniors learn to use the Internet and build simple Web sites. Sent to adamj@zalazon.com.
Surfed Internet looking for stories about interesting Web sites. Also looked for unique sites.

Wednesday, May 12

Read daily paper and scanned classified section.
Read employment section of a couple of Sunday papers online.
Called ZBA Corporation to see if I could set up meeting to possibly redesign their Web site. Spoke to Dan Hines (321-1111). He asked for a resume or background sheet. Will e-mail tomorrow.

Thursday, May 13

Worked on my career portfolio.
E-mailed Dan Hines letter and resume.
Called Literacy Helps To Read program and volunteered to design and develop a Web site for them.
Set up lunch date with Maria Evans for Monday, May 18, at noon at Michaels Restaurant.
Continue actions.

With your daily action journal, you can look back and see exactly what you've done, who you've called, who you've written to, and what the result was. Additionally you have the names, phone numbers, times, dates, and other information at your fingertips. As an added bonus, as you review your daily action journal, instead of feeling like you're not doing enough, you are often motivated to do more.

Your Personal Career Success Book

In this section, we've discussed being your own career manager, and we've talked about developing action plans and putting together a daily action journal. The next step is to discuss your personal career success book.

What is your personal career success book? It's a folder, scrapbook, notebook, binder, or group of notebooks where you keep all your career information. Eventually, you might have so much that you'll need to put everything in a file drawer or cabinet, and that's okay too. That means your career is progressing.

You will find your personal career success book useful no matter what segment of the computer industry you are pursuing.

What can go in your personal success career book? You can keep your action plans, your daily action journals, and all of the information you have and need to get your career to the level you want to reach.

What else can go into your personal success career book? What about career related correspondence? It's always a good idea to keep copies of all the letters you send out for your career, as well as the ones that you receive which are career related. Don't forget copies of e-mail.

Why do you want to keep correspondence? First of all, it gives you a record of people you wrote to as well as people who wrote to you. You might also find ways to make use of letters people send you. For example, instead of getting a rejection letter, reading it, crumpling it up, and throwing it in the trash, take the name of the person who signed it, wait a period of time and see if you can pitch another idea, another job possibility, anything that might further your career or get you closer to where you want to be. Call that person and ask if he or she can point you in another direction. Ask what you could have done better or differently. Take the advice constructively (whatever it is) and then use it for next time.

Will the person at the other end always help? Probably not. But they might, and all you need is one good idea or suggestion to get you where you want to go. It's definitely worth the call or the letter.

What else can go in your book? Keep copies of advertisements for jobs that you might want or be interested in now and even in the future. Keep copies of information on potential companies you might want to work for or that may offer employment opportunities. Keep copies of advertisements of jobs you might aspire to in your long-range plans or even interesting job opportunities you might not have thought of.

"I don't need to write it down," you say, "I'll remember it when I need it."

Maybe you will and maybe you won't. Haven't you ever been in a situation where you do something and then say to yourself, "Oh, I forgot about that. If I had only remembered whatever it was, I wouldn't have done it like that." Or, "It slipped my mind." Writing things down means you're not leaving things to chance.

Keep lists in this book of potential support staff or other people who might be helpful in your career. Keep names and addresses of recruiters, headhunters, etc. You might not need an attorney now, but if you needed one quickly who would you call? If you need an accountant, who would you use? As you hear of professionals who others think are good, write down their names. That way you'll have information when you need it.

What else? You might keep lists of media possibilities, names, addresses, phone and fax numbers, and e-mail addresses. Let's say you're watching television and see an interesting interview about something in the area of the computer industry in which you're interested. It might be an interview with a programmer, a game developer, the CEO of a Web site, an author, or a CIO. At the time you think you're going to remember exactly what you saw, when you saw it, and who the reporter or producer was. Unfortunately, you will probably forget some of the details. You now have a place to jot down the information in a section of your book. When you need it, you know where to look!

Don't forget to clip out interesting interviews, articles, and feature stories. Instead of having them floating all over your house or office, file them in this book. Want to network a bit? Write the reporter a note saying you enjoyed his or her piece and mentioning why you found it so interesting. Everyone likes to be recognized, even people in the media. You can never tell when you might make a contact or even a friend.

It goes without saying you should also clip and make copies of all articles, stories, and features that appear in the print media about you. Having all this information together will make it easier later to put together your career portfolio.

What else is going into your personal career success book? Copies of letters of recommendation, notes that supervisors and colleagues have sent you, even letters from students thanking you for doing such a good job.

As your career progresses, you will have various resumes, background sheets, CV, etc. Keep copies of them all in your book as well (even after you've replaced them with new ones). What about your Networking and Contact Worksheets? They now have a place too.

We've discussed the importance of determining your markets and possible employers. This is where you can keep these lists as well. Then, when you find new possibilities, just jot them down in your book. With your personal career success book everything will be at your fingertips.

If you are like most people, you may attend seminars or workshops and get handouts or take notes. You now know where to keep them so you can refer back to them when needed. The same goes for conference and convention material. Keep everything in your personal career success book.

You know how sometimes you just happen to see a place where you would love to work? You just know you would fit right in. Until you have a chance to brainstorm and get your foot in the door there, jot down your ideas. You'll be able to come back to them later and perhaps find a way to bring that job to fruition.

You'll find success is easier to come by if you're more organized, and having everything you need in one place is key.

If you're now asking yourself, isn't there a lot of work involved in obtaining a career you want, the answer is a definite yes.

"Can't I just leave everything to chance like most people and hope I get what I want?" you ask.

You can, but if your ultimate goal is to succeed in some aspect of the computer industry, the idea is to do everything possible to give yourself the best opportunity for success.

Planning for a successful career does take some work. As your own career manager, you are going to be responsible for your career every step of the way. In the end, however, it will be worth it. You will be rewarded with the wonderful career that you want and deserve.

4

GET READY, GET SET, GO: PREPARATION

Opportunity Is Knocking: Are You Ready?

Whether I'm giving seminars about getting the career of your choice, a workshop on obtaining success in some other facet of life, or coaching someone on the phone, I always ask the same question.

"If opportunity knocks, are you ready to open the door and let it in?"

While there are those who quickly say, "Yes," others say, "What do you mean? If opportunity knocks, I'll get prepared."

Unfortunately, that's not the way it always works. Sometimes you don't have a chance to prepare. Sometimes you need to be prepared at that very moment or you could lose out on an awesome opportunity.

Let's look at a couple of scenarios. First, imagine you are walking along the beach thinking about your career. "I wish I had a job as an information technology security manager," you say out loud, even though no one is there to hear you. "I wish I could find a really great job opening in a really large, prestigious company," you continue, planning how success might come your way. As you're walking, the surf washes up and you see something shiny. You reach down

to see what it is and pick up what appears to be a small brass lamp. All this time, you're still planning your career as you're walking. "I wish I had an interview for that job right now," you say as you absentmindedly rub the side of the lamp.

You see a puff of smoke and a genie appears. "Thank you for releasing me," he says. "In return for that, I will grant you your three wishes."

Before you have a chance to ask, "What wishes?" you find yourself in an office sitting in front of a table where the human resources director, the chief technology officer, and a number of other people are asking you questions and interviewing you for the job of your dreams. Evidently, the genie had been listening to you talking to yourself and picked up on your three wishes.

Here's the opportunity you've been wishing for! You're sitting at the interview you wished for, and are being interviewed by the powers that be at one of the large, prestigious companies you wanted to work for. Are you ready? Or is this big break going to pass you by because you're not prepared?

Let's look at another scenario. In this scenario imagine you have a fairy godmother who comes to you one day and says, "I can get you a one-on-one meeting with the head of the search committee looking for the next CIO of one of the most prestigious corporations in the country." The only catch is you have to be ready to walk in his office door in half an hour. Would you be ready or would you miss your big break because you weren't prepared? If your answer is, "Hmm, I might be ready—well, not really," then read on.

Want to think about another one? Let's imagine you are on your way to a weekend vacation in Las Vegas. You sit down in your seat on the plane and a man sits down next to you. You've seen him before, but where?

"I don't know why you look so familiar," you say to him.

All of a sudden you remember. The gentleman sitting next to you is the editor in chief of one of the most prestigious technology magazines in the country. "I just saw you on CNN talking about changes in technology," you say to him, "you were great."

"Thank you," he says. "What do you do?"

"Actually I don't have a job yet," you tell him. "I'm graduating from State College with a double major in computer sciences and journalism in June. I don't suppose you're looking for a new reporter."

"Are you on your school newspaper?" he asks.

"I review new software and have done a couple of reviews on hardware and peripherals," you tell him. "I also write a column for the local weekly on technology."

You chat back and forth about technology for a bit and he says, "We have an internship program, but the deadline for applying is today. You don't by any chance have a resume in that bag, do you?"

Can you take advantage of the opportunity sitting right next to you? Or would you let the opportunity pass you by because the only thing you were prepared to do was go on vacation?

Here's the deal on opportunity. It may knock. As a matter of fact it probably will knock, but if you don't open the door, opportunity won't stand there forever. If you don't answer the door, opportunity, even if it's your opportunity, will go visit someone else's door.

While you might not believe in genies, fairy godmothers, or even the concept that you might be in the right place at the right time, you should believe this. In life, and your career, you will run into situations where you need to be ready "now" or miss your chance. When opportunity knocks, you need to be ready to open the door and let it in.

How can you do that? Make a commitment to get ready now. It's time to prepare. Ready, set, let's go!

Look Out for Opportunities

Being aware of available opportunities is essential to taking advantage of them. While it's always nice when unexpected opportunities present themselves, you sometimes have to go out looking for them as well.

How many times have you turned on the television or radio and learned about an opportunity you wished you had known about so you could have taken advantage of it? How many times have you opened the newspaper and read about an opportunity someone else experienced?

Would you rather open the newspaper and read a feature story profiling a couple of friends who started a social networking site that they sold for millions of dollars or be one of those friends? Would you rather see a press release congratulat-

The Inside Scoop

For some reason that we never understood, my grandmother always kept a suitcase packed. "Why?" we always asked her.

"You can never tell when you have an opportunity to do something or go someplace," she replied. "If you're ready, you can go. If you're not prepared you might miss an opportunity."

Evidently she was right. Here's her story.

My grandfather was a physician. After he died, my grandmother worked at a number of different jobs both to keep herself busy and to earn a living. At one point she worked as a sales associate in a women's clothing store in a well-known resort hotel. The hotel always had the top stars of the day in theater, music, film, and television performing in nightclub shows on holiday weekends. One weekend, Judy Garland was doing a show at the hotel. According to the story we were told as children, Judy Garland wanted a few things from the clothing store and called the store to see if someone could bring up a few pieces for her to choose from.

The store was busy and the manager assigned my grandmother the job. She quickly chose some items and brought them up to the star's room. Judy was pleased with my grandmother's choices and after talking to her for a short time, evidently was impressed with her demeanor and attitude.

While signing for the purchases, she said to my grandmother, "I need a nanny for my children. I think you would be the right one for the job. I'm leaving tomorrow morning. If you're interested, I need to know now." Without missing a beat, my grandmother took the job and by the next afternoon was on the road with Judy Garland, serving as nanny to her children.

While clearly she didn't give two weeks notice to her sales job, being at the right place at the right time certainly landed her an interesting job she seemed to love. I don't really remember how long she kept the position. What I do know, however, is that when an interesting opportunity presented itself, my grandmother was ready. Had she not been ready or hesitated, no doubt, someone else would have gotten the job.

The moral of the story is that when opportunity knocks, you have to be ready to open the door.

ing the new director of marketing of a big software firm or be the director of marketing?

Would you rather have a chance meeting with the head of a search committee for a job as the CIO of a large corporation or hear from your friend that she ran into the individual?

No matter what your aspirations are in the computer industry or what segment of the industry you want to pursue, you want to be the one taking advantage of every available opportunity.

Here's the deal: If you don't know about opportunities, you might miss them. It's important to take some time to look for opportunities that might be of value to you.

Where can you find opportunities? You can find them all over the place. Read through the papers, listen to the radio, look through the trade journals, and watch television. Check out newsletters, companies, corporations, trade associations, organizations, Web sites, and college campuses.

Even if you're not a student, schools, universities, and colleges often offer seminars or have programs that might be of interest and are open to the public for a small fee. Contact associations and ask about opportunities. Network, network, network, and network some more, continually looking for further opportunities.

What kind of opportunities do you have? What types of opportunities are facing you? Is an eBay powerseller giving a seminar? Is the CIO of a large corporation going to speak at a business conference? Is your local college giving a seminar on careers in IT? Have you heard that the newspaper is looking for ideas for a new weekly column on some aspect of personal computing?

Is the author of a book on designing Web sites doing a book signing at the local bookstore?

Have you heard of an opening as a department head in the IT department in the company in which you are working? Did you hear about a contest where the prize is a one-on-one meeting with Bill Gates? Is your college or university hosting an IT career fair?

These are all potential opportunities. Be on the lookout for them. They can be your keys to success.

Keep track of the opportunities you find and hear about in a notebook or, if you prefer, use the Opportunities Worksheet provided.

Opportunities Worksheet

Self-Assessment and Taking Inventory

Let's now make sure you're ready for every opportunity. One of the best ways to prepare for something is by first determining what you want and then seeing what you need to get it. Remembering that you are your own career manager, this might be the time to do a self-assessment.

What's that? Basically your self-assessment involves taking an inventory of what you have and what you have to offer and then seeing how you can relate it to what you want to do. Self-assessment involves thinking about you and your career goals.

Self-assessment helps you define your strengths and your weaknesses. It helps you define your skills, interests, goals, and passions, giving you the ability to see them at a glance. Your self-assessment can help you develop and write your resume and make it easier to prepare for interviews.

Do you know what you want? Do you know what your strengths and weaknesses are? Can you identify the areas in which you are interested? Can you identify what's important to you in your career?

"But I already know what I want to do," you say. "This is a waste of my time. Do I have to do this?"

No one is going to make you do this. However, many people find that answering these questions now can help your career dreams come to fruition quicker. It may give you insight into something you hadn't yet thought of. It might help you fine-tune an idea for a career. It often helps give you the edge others might not have.

Doing a self-assessment is a good idea no matter what segment of the computer industry you are interested in pursuing. Before someone takes a chance on you they are going to want to know about you. If you have this done, you'll be prepared.

Strengths and Weaknesses

We all have certain strengths and weaknesses. Strengths are things you do well. They are advantages that others may not have. You can exploit them to help your career. Weaknesses are things that you can improve. They are things you don't do as well as you could.

What are your strengths and weaknesses? Can you identify them? Why are these questions important? Because once you know the answers, you will know what you need to work on and improve.

For example, if one of your weaknesses is you're shy and you don't like speaking in front of groups of people, you might take some public speaking classes or you might force yourself to network and go into situations that could help make you more comfortable around people. If you need better written communication skills,

⭐ Tip from the Top

If there is something that you need to do or that you determine can help you in your career, do it—now! Don't procrastinate. In other words, don't put off until tomorrow what could have been done today (or at least this week). If you need more education, certification, additional skills, or anything else, don't put it off until you "have time." Get it now! If you need to work on your resume or your portfolio do it now and get it done. Procrastinating can seriously affect your career because it means you didn't get something done that needed to be accomplished. Just the sheer thought of having to get something done takes time and energy. Instead of thinking about it, do it!

Tip from the Coach

If a human resource director, head-hunter, recruiter, interviewer, or college admissions officer asks what your weaknesses are, try to indicate a weakness that might also be thought of as a strength. For example, you might say something like, "I'm a perfectionist. I like things to be done right." Try not to give anyone in those positions information on any of your real weaknesses. Remember that as friendly as these people might seem during interviews, their job is screening out candidates. You don't want to give an interviewer or anyone else a reason not to hire you.

Tip from the Top

Accept the fact that at almost every interview you go on you will be asked about your strengths and weaknesses. Preparing a script ahead of time, so you know what you are going to say and are comfortable saying it, gives you the edge.

you might take a couple of writing classes to make you a better writer.

Are you a good salesperson who could be great? Think about taking some classes or workshops in selling. Are you a good presenter who could be spectacular? Think about taking a workshop or seminar in presenting. Do your programming skills need updating? Consider taking a class or workshop. Is your lack of certification holding you back? Get certified.

The Inside Scoop

A good way to deal with an interviewer asking you how you will deal with a specific weakness that they identify is by telling them that you are actively trying to change it into a strength. For example, if one of your weaknesses is you don't like speaking in public, you might say you are working on turning that into a strength by taking a public speaking class. Telling an interviewer you are working on your shortcomings helps him or her form a much better picture of you.

Do your interpersonal skills need some help? A class or seminar might be what you need. Do you need to learn how to organize your time better? Look for a time management seminar. Are you always stressed? Take a course in stress management. Do your negotiation skills need fine-tuning? You know what you need to do. Take a class.

Take some time now to define your strengths and weaknesses. Then jot them down in a notebook or use the blank Strengths and Weaknesses Worksheet provided on page 73. Be honest and realistic. On the following pages are a couple of sample worksheets to help you get started. The first is for someone who wants a career as a computer technician. The next is for someone interested in a career as a brand manager for a computer company.

Now that you know some of your strengths and weaknesses, it's time to focus on your personal inventory. Your combination of skills, talents, and personality traits are what helps determine your marketability.

What Are Your Skills?

Skills are acquired things that you have learned to do and you can do well. They are tools that you can use to help sell yourself. Keep in mind that there are a variety of relevant skills. There

Strengths and Weaknesses Worksheet:
Career as a Computer Technician

My Strengths

I have a lot of energy.
I can get along with almost everyone.
I can follow instructions.
I'm a team player, yet can work on my own.
I have strong technical troubleshooting skills.
I have strong analytical skills
I am good at teaching others things in a simple-to-understand manner.
I'm creative.
I have a good memory.
I have leadership skills.
I am great at motivating and inspiring others to do their best.
I have Microsoft certified systems engineer credentials.

My Weaknesses

I'm late a lot of the time.
I'm not good with numbers.
I don't test well.
I'm not organized.

What's important in my career?

I want a career as a computer technician. I want to do system setups and networking. I also want to do repair and troubleshooting. I want to work for a company handling large projects for different clients. That way I'll always have a challenge. I also want to be a mentor to young people seeking a career in the field. I eventually want to have my own computer business.

are job-related skills that you use at your present job. Transferable skills are those that you used on one job and that you can transfer to another. Life skills are skills you use in everyday living, such as problem solving, time management, decision making, and interpersonal skills. Hobby or leisure time skills are skills related to activities you do during your spare time for enjoyment. These might or might not be pertinent to your career. There are also technical skills connected to the use of machinery. Many of these types of skills overlap.

Most people don't realize just how many skills they have. They aren't aware of the specialized knowledge they possess. Are you one of them?

While it's sometimes difficult to put your skills down on paper, it's essential so you can see what they are and where you can use them

---

Strengths and Weaknesses Worksheet: Career As a Brand Manager for a Computer Company

My Strengths

I am organized.
I get along with others.
I have strong interpersonal skills.
I have great communications skills.
I'm creative.

I have great sales skills.
I'm a team player.
I have a bachelor's degree with a major in computer sciences and business.
I have a master's degree in marketing.

My Weaknesses

I'm a perfectionist.
I am an overachiever.
I have a difficult time being on time for things.
I don't like speaking in front of groups of people.
I get stressed easily.

What's important in my career?

I want to work as a brand manager and learn all there is about the branding of computers. I then want to move my career more into the marketing field and hope to find a job as the director of marketing for a large computer company

---

in your career. Your skills, along with your talents and personality traits, make you unique. They can set you apart from others and help you not only land the career of your dreams, but succeed in it as well.

Once you've given some thought to your skills, it's time to start putting them down on paper. You can either use the blank Skills Worksheet provided on page 74 or a page in a notebook.

Begin with the skills you know you have. What are you good at? What can you do? What have you done? Include everything you can think of, from basic skills on up, and then think of the things people have told you you're good at.

Don't get caught up thinking that "everyone can do that," so a particular skill of yours is not special. All your skills are special. Include them all in your list.

Review these skill examples to help get you started. Remember, this is just a beginning.

◎ Computer proficiency
◎ Programming capabilities
◎ Public speaking
◎ Time management
◎ Analytical skills
◎ Problem-solving skills
◎ Organizational skills
◎ Presentation skills
◎ Counseling skills
◎ Writing skills

Strengths and Weaknesses Worksheet

My strengths:

_____

_____

_____

My weaknesses:

_____

_____

_____

What's important in my career?

_____

_____

_____

_____

_____

◎ Listening skills
◎ Verbal communications
◎ Management
◎ Selling
◎ Language skills
◎ Leadership skills
◎ Math skills
◎ Decision-making skills
◎ Negotiating skills
◎ Art skills
◎ Money management
◎ Word processing skills
◎ Computer repair
◎ Teaching skills

◎ Customer service
◎ Cooking
◎ Web design

★ Tip from the Top

Keep in mind that some skills also need talent. For example, writing is a skill. It can be learned. To be a great writer, however, you generally need talent. Cooking is a skill. To be a great chef, you need talent. Teaching is a skill. The best teachers, however, are also talented.

◎ Singing

◎ Songwriting

◎ Acting

◎ Playing an instrument

◎ Interior decorating

◎ Playing a sport

Your Talents

You are born with your talents. They aren't acquired like skills, but they may be refined and perfected. Many people are reluctant to admit what their talents are, but if you don't identify and use them, you'll be wasting them. What are your talents? You probably already know what some of them are. What are you not only good

---

Skills Worksheet

_____

_____

_____

_____

_____

_____

_____

_____

_____

at, but better at than most other people? What can you do with ease? What has been your passion for as long as you can remember? These will be your talents.

Are you a talented teacher, inspiring students to want to learn? Does your talent lie in being able to make even complicated things easy to learn?

Are you a talented computer graphic artist? What about a talented Web designer? Can you make a Web site look better than almost anyone else you know?

Are you a talented negotiator? Can you bring two sides to an agreement when no one else can? Are you a prolific writer? A great fund-raiser?

Can you tell stories in such a manner that people listening want to hear more? Do you tell jokes in such a manner that those listening just can't stop themselves from laughing? Can you make people feel comfortable with a simple look?

Does your talent fall in science? How about math? What about art? Do you have that "eye" to be able to see just the right employee for a specific job? Can you look at someone and just know that with a little training and work, he or she can be great?

Think about it for a bit and then jot your talents in your notebook or in the blank Talents Worksheet on page 76. Here are a couple of examples to get you started.

Talents Worksheet – Sample 1

I have good interpersonal skills. I get along with most people.

People feel comfortable telling me things.

I am multilingual and can speak English, Spanish, and French.

People feel they can relate to me.

I am funny and can break the ice with a joke to make people feel comfortable.

I have the ability to make people around me feel good about themselves.

Talents Worksheet – Sample 2

I am a talented writer and can bring stories to life with my words.

I am very creative.

I have a great sense of humor. I can make almost everyone I'm around feel better by making them laugh.

I have the ability to inspire people.

I have the ability to motivate people.

I am a great public speaker.

I am very persuasive.

Talents Worksheet

_____

_____

_____

_____

_____

_____

_____

Your Personality Traits

We all have different personality traits. The combination of these traits is what sets us apart from others. There are certain personality traits that can help you move ahead no matter what aspect of the industry you want to pursue. Let's look at what some of them are.

- ◎ Ability to get along well with others
- ◎ Adaptable
- ◎ Ambitious
- ◎ Analytical
- ◎ Assertive
- ◎ Caring
- ◎ Charismatic
- ◎ Clever
- ◎ Compassionate
- ◎ Competitive

- ◎ Conscientious
- ◎ Creative
- ◎ Dependable
- ◎ Efficient
- ◎ Energetic
- ◎ Enterprising
- ◎ Enthusiastic
- ◎ Flexible
- ◎ Friendly
- ◎ Good listener
- ◎ Hard worker
- ◎ Helpful
- ◎ Honest
- ◎ Imaginative
- ◎ Innovative
- ◎ Inquisitive
- ◎ Insightful

◎ Life-long learner
◎ Observant
◎ Optimistic
◎ Outgoing
◎ Patient
◎ Passionate
◎ Personable
◎ Persuasive
◎ Positive
◎ Practical
◎ Problem solver
◎ Reliable
◎ Resourceful

◎ Sense of humor
◎ Self-starter
◎ Self-confident
◎ Sociable
◎ Successful
◎ Supportive
◎ Team player
◎ Understanding

What are your special personality traits? What helps make you unique? Think about it, and then jot them down in your notebook or in the Personality Traits Worksheet below.

Personality Traits Worksheet

_____

_____

_____

_____

_____

_____

_____

_____

_____

Special Accomplishments

Special accomplishments make you unique and often will give you the edge over others. What are your special accomplishments?

Have you won any awards? Were you awarded a scholarship? Were you asked to deliver a paper at a national conference? Have you won a writing competition? Did you do especially well in school? Did you win salesperson of the year?

Were you the president of your class? Were you the chairperson of a special event? Have you won a community service award? Were you nominated for an award even if you didn't win?

Has an article about you appeared in a regional or national magazine or newspaper? Have you been a special guest on a radio or television show? Are you sought out as an expert in some area of technology? Are you sought out as an authority in E-commerce? Being an expert on anything will set you apart from others.

All these things are examples of some of the special accomplishments you may have experienced. Think about it for a while and you'll be able to come up with your own list of accomplishments. Once you identify your accomplishments, jot them down in your notebook or on the Special Accomplishments Worksheet below.

Special Accomplishments Worksheet

_____

_____

_____

_____

_____

_____

_____

_____

_____

_____

Education and Training

Education and training are important to the success of your career, no matter what you want to do. Depending on what area of the computer industry you are pursuing, a college education may or may not be mandatory. One way or another, a college background will generally be preferred or at least helpful in your career. In some cases, a post-secondary education may also be helpful.

In addition to your formal education, there may be other opportunities that will prove useful in your career. These may encompass classes, courses, seminars, workshops, programs, on-the-job training, and learning from your peers. Every opportunity you have to learn anything can be a valuable resource in your career, and your life.

What type of education and training do you already possess? What type of education and training do you need to get to the career of your dreams? What type of education and training will help you get where you want to go?

Would some extra classes help you reach your career goal? Is there a special seminar that will help give you the edge? How about a course in a different computer language? What about a workshop in public speaking? What about a class in time management? How about a stress management seminar? What about a seminar in facilitating? How about an immersion class in a second language?

Do you need some classes to get certified in your field or to help move your career forward? Sometimes, even if certification isn't necessary, it will give you the edge over other applicants.

Do you need to get your master's degree? What about your Ph.D.? How about taking some workshops or seminars or attending some conferences? The options are yours.

Now is the time to determine what education or training you have and what you need so you can go after it.

Fill in the Education and Training Worksheet on page 80 with your information so you know what you need to further your career and meet your goals.

Location, Location, Location: Where Do You Want to Be?

Location can be an important factor in your career. Where do you need to live to if you want a great career in the computer industry? Is one location better than another? Here's the good news! Depending on what you want to do, careers in the computer industry are available throughout the country.

There are a ton of options. Depending on what you want to do, you might work in a rural setting, the suburbs, or a large city. You might work on the East Coast, the West Coast, or the middle of the country. Sometimes you get to choose. Other times you have to go where the jobs are.

Education and Training Worksheet

What education and training do I have?

_____

_____

What education or training do I need to reach my goals?

_____

_____

What classes, seminars, and workshops have I taken that are useful to my career aspirations?

_____

_____

_____

What classes, seminars, workshops, and courses can I take to help advance my career?

_____

_____

_____

Where is the right location for you? While you need to be in the location where there are openings, remember this: You want to be in an area where you will be comfortable. If you love the hustle and bustle of a city, you might not be comfortable setting up your life in a small, rural town. On the other hand, if you grew up in a small rural area and love that type of life, you might not want to live in a city. Some people are more flexible than others. Only you can decide where you want to be.

Use the Location Worksheet on the next page to help you decide where you want to look for a job.

Location Worksheet

Type of area I reside in now:

_____

Location of job or career choice I want:

_____

Other possible locations:

_____

Reviewing Your Past

Let's now look at your past. What have you done that can help you succeed in your career in the segment of the computer industry in which you want to work?

Make a list of all the jobs you have had and the general functions you were responsible for when you held them. Then, make a list of the volunteer activities in which you have participated. Look at this information and see what functions or skills you can transfer to your career in the computer industry.

Remember that many skills are transferable. It doesn't necessarily matter if all your skills are directly related to the computer industry.

"Give me some examples," you say.

Were you a counselor at a camp? Were you a tutor? Did you lead a study group in college? Have you taught Sunday school? Did you work as a high school teacher? The skills utilized in these activities may help you in your career as a trainer.

Have you worked as an administrative assistant? Were you a key holder in a retail store?

Have you held jobs in corporate America? The skills used in these situations might help in a career in the administration or management segment of the computer industry.

Have you held a job as a reporter for a local newspaper? Did you work on your school newspaper? That shows that you know how to develop and write an article or news story and can do it in a timely fashion. These skills can easily be transferred if you are interested in a career as a reporter or journalist in technology. They might also be transferred if you are interested in writing textbooks or for a career as a technical writer.

Have you volunteered handling the publicity for a not-for-profit group? Have you worked as a marketing director in a different industry? All these skills can be transferred to work in marketing or publicity in the computer industry.

Have you volunteered to do the newsletter for a local not-for-profit organization? You can transfer your skills to a career in desktop publishing.

Have you worked in retail sales? Have you sold advertising for a newspaper? How about selling commercials for television or radio stations? Have you worked as a real estate salesperson? Do you love selling? Are you good at it? You could use your sales skills in a career in retail or wholesale sales of computers, peripherals, or software.

Have you been developing Web sites and MySpace pages for your friends? Transfer your skills to a career developing Web sites for a company or organization.

Remember, the idea is to use your existing education, training, talents, skills, and accomplishments to get your foot in the door. Once in you can find ways to move up the ladder so you can achieve the career of your dreams. When going over your list of past positions include both part-time jobs you have had as well as full-time positions. Don't forget to include your volunteer and civic activities. Look at the entire picture, including not only your jobs but also your accomplishments and see what they might reveal about you.

"Like what?" you ask.

Did you graduate from high school in three years instead of four? That illustrates that you're driven and can accomplish your goals. Were you the chairperson for a not-for-profit charity event? That illustrates that you take initiative, work well with people, can delegate, and organize well. Do you sing in your church choir? Have you volunteered to handle the choir's music? This shows you can sing and that you have the dedication to attend rehearsals. Handling the music illustrates your organizational skills.

Now that you have some ideas, think about what you've done and see how you can relate it to your dream career. Everything you have done in your life, including your past jobs, volunteer and civic activities, and other endeavors can help create your future dream career in the computer industry.

Using Your Past to Create Your Future

When reviewing past jobs and volunteer activities, see how they can be used to help you get closer to the career you are seeking in the computer industry. Answer the following questions:

◎ What parts of each job accomplishment or volunteer activity did you enjoy?
◎ What parts made you happy?
◎ What parts gave you joy?
◎ What parts of your previous jobs excited you?
◎ What skills did you learn while on those jobs?
◎ What skills can be transferred to your career in the segment of the computer industry in which you are interested in pursuing?
◎ What accomplishments can help your career in the computer industry?

Jot down your answers in your notebook or use the "Using Your Past to Create Your Future" worksheet provided.

The more ways you can find to use past accomplishments and experiences to move closer to success in your career in computers, the better off you will be. Look outside the box to find ways to transfer your skills and use jobs and

---

★ Tip from the Top

If you're just out of school, your accomplishments will probably be more focused on what you did while in school. As you get more established in your career, your accomplishments will be more focused on what you've done during your career.

activities as stepping-stones to get where you're going.

Passions and Goals

Once you know what you have, it's easier to determine what you need to get what you want. You've made a lot of progress by working on your self-assessment, but you have a few more things to do. At this point, you need to focus on exactly what you want to do.

In what area of the computer industry do you want to be involved? What are you interested in? Do you love working on the Web? Do you want to work in programming? Do you want to develop software? Do you want to design computers? Is it your dream to own a computer repair shop?

Do you want to work directly in the computer industry or do you want to work with computers in another industry?

Do you want to work hands-on or is it your dream to work in management?

Do you want to work in systems analysis? What about in some aspect of programming? Do you want to work in operations? How about database administration? Is it your dream to work in support? What about a career in

Using Your Past to Create Your Future		
Past Job/ Volunteer Activity/ Accomplishment	**Parts of Job/ Volunteer Activity/ Accomplishment that I Enjoyed**	**Skills I Learned and Can Transfer to Career in the Computer Industry**

communication or networks? Do you want a career as a data security specialist?

Do you want to be a college or university instructor or professor teaching others about computer sciences?

Are you dreaming of a career as the marketing director of a large computer company? Do you want to be a brand manager? Do you want to be the person representing a computer or peripheral on a television shopping channel?

There are so many opportunities. It's all up to you. You just need to follow your dreams.

You began working on determining exactly what you wanted to do earlier in the book. Continue to refine your list of things that you enjoy and want to do. Previously you defined your career goals. Now that you've assessed the situation, are your goals still the same?

What are your passions? What are your dreams? Think about these things when making your career choices. You owe it to yourself to have a career that you love, that you're passionate about, and that you deserve. Now, with a bit of effort, you're on your way!

5

JOB SEARCH STRATEGIES

If you've decided that your dream career is in some aspect of the computer industry, you're in luck. Computers have literally changed the way we do everything and as a result, impact all of our lives. The range of job opportunities computers and related technology have created is tremendous. There are thousands of jobs in the various segments of the industry as well as the peripherals. One of them can be yours!

We've covered some of the various opportunities in previous chapters. Some jobs are easier to obtain. Others may be more difficult. This section will cover some traditional and not so traditional job search strategies.

It's important to recognize that getting the job is just the beginning. What you want is a career.

Using a Job to Create a Career

Unfortunately, you can't just go to the store and get a great career. Generally, it's something you have to work at and create. How do you create your dream career? Developing the ultimate career takes a lot of things, including sweat, stamina, and creativity. It takes luck and being in the right place at the right time. It takes talent, education, and training. It takes persever-

ance and passion. And it takes faith in yourself and knowing that if you work hard for what you want and don't give up, you will get it.

You have to take each job you get along the way and make it work for you. Think of every job as a rung on the career ladder, every assignment within that job as a stepping-stone. To complete the puzzle takes a lot of pieces and a lot of work, but it will be worth it in the end.

Every job you get along the way helps to sharpen your skills and adds another line to your resume. Every situation is an opportunity to network, learn, and most of all to get noticed.

If you know what your ultimate goal is, it is much easier to see how each job you do can get you a little closer. Every situation, no matter how small or insignificant you think it may be, gives you another experience, hones your skills, helps you to gain confidence, and gives you the opportunity to be seen and discovered.

> ## Tip from the Coach
> It may take some time to get where you want to in your career. Try to make your journey as exciting as your destination.

85

Tip from the Coach

Don't get so caught up in getting to your goal that you don't enjoy your journey.

Every job can lead you to the career you've been dreaming about.

One of the things you should know is that while almost anyone can get a job, not everyone ends up with a career. As was discussed in a previous section of the book, the difference between a job and a career is that a job is a means to an end. It's something you do to get things done and to earn a living. Your career, on the other hand, is a series of related jobs you build using your skills, talents, and passions. It's a progressive path of achievement.

When you were a child, perhaps your parents dangled the proverbial carrot on a stick in front of you, tempting you to eat your dinner so that you could have chocolate ice cream and cake for dessert. Whether dinner was food you liked, didn't particularly care for, or a combination, you probably ate it most of the time to get to what you wanted—dessert. In this case, your dessert will be ultimate success in some segment of the computer industry.

Use every experience, every job, and every opportunity for the ultimate goal of filling your life with excitement and passion while getting paid. Will there be things you don't enjoy doing and jobs you wish you didn't have along the way? Perhaps, but there will also be things you love doing and jobs you look back on and remember with joy.

The Inside Scoop

We all have said, "Why didn't I think of that?" at one time or another in our lives. We have all said, "Why isn't there a way to do this or that?" We all have wished we could use our passion and imagination to create a great career. Just so you know, you can!

One night in 2005 three friends in their 20s who met while working at PayPal went to a party. Like many of us do, they took some videos during the evening. And like many of us like to do, they wanted to share the video with some other friends. Frustrated with trying to e-mail the videos, the three friends, Chad Hurley, Steve Chen, and Jawed Karim, decided that if they were finding it difficult, so might others who wanted to share their videos.

They saw a need, an opportunity, and within a short time, a possible solution. On February 14, 2005, the three young men registered the domain name, YouTube. The rest is history. Through creativity, passion, a bit of networking, and a lot of hard work, the three young men built YouTube into the social networking site we know today. Less than two years later, on October 9, 2006, Google paid $1.65 billion in stock for the purchase of YouTube.

Think this type of thing only happens to the other people? Think it can't happen to you? Well, as I keep telling you, it can, but it helps to be proactive. This is just one of many stories that illustrate how great things can happen when you have an idea, some passion, and are willing to work at it. There are hundreds more.

Whatever your goal, go after your passion and create a career you can love. You just might be someone else's inspiration.

Your Career: Where Are You Now?

Where are you in your career now? Are you still in school? Are you just starting out? Are you in another field and want to move into a career in the computer industry? Do you know what you want to do with the rest of your life?

If you already know what you want to do, great! You're in good shape. You need only to prepare by getting the education, training, and experience and you're ready to find the job or jobs which will lead you to your dream career. If not, read on.

Moving into the Computer Industry: Career Changing

Are you currently working in another industry but really want to be in some segment of the computer industry? If so, you're not alone. Many people dream about having a certain career from the time they were very young, and for a variety of reasons, end up in other careers in other industries. Is this you? If so, read on.

Perhaps at the time you needed a job, any job. Possibly it looked too difficult to obtain a career doing what you wanted. Maybe you couldn't afford the time or money to finish your education. Maybe you just didn't know how to go about it. Maybe you weren't ready. Maybe people around you told you that you were pipe dreaming. Maybe they told you that a career in the segment of the computer industry in which you were interested was not what you wanted to do. Maybe you were scared. Or maybe someone offered you a job in a different industry and you took it for security. There might be hundreds of reasons why you wanted a career in the computer industry, but you didn't pursue it at the time. The question is, do you want to be there now?

"Well," you say, "I do, but . . . ."

Before you go through your list of "buts," ask yourself these questions. Do you want to give up your dream? Do you want to live your life saying, "I wish I had," and never trying?

Wouldn't you rather find a way to do what you wanted than never really be happy with what you're doing? Wouldn't it be great to look at others who are doing what they want and know that you are one of them? You can! You just have to make the decision to do it!

First of all, it's important to realize that if you have proven yourself in your career, even if it is in another industry, it's an indicator to a potential employer that you can do the same for them. Past accomplishments and skills in one career will be helpful in your new career so make sure you use them to your advantage.

How can you move into a career in the computer industry from a different industry? How can you change your career path? It depends on the segment of the industry in which you aspire to work, but it's not as hard as you think.

What you need to do is take stock of what you have and what you don't have. Then see

---

⭐ Tip from the Coach

Are you living someone else's dream? You can't change your past, but you can change your future. If your dream is to work in an aspect of the computer or technology industry, go for it. Things might not change overnight, but the first step you take toward your new career will get you closer to your dream. Every day you put it off, is one more day you're wasting doing something you don't love. You deserve more. You deserve the best.

how and where you can transfer your skills and accomplishments to find ways you can use them in the career of your choice.

"What if I want to be something like a game developer? What if I want to be a software engineer? What if I want to be a CIO? Don't I need to do more than just transfer skills?" you ask.

Yes, as a rule you will. You still can transfer any applicable skills, but if your dream is to work in some segments of the computer industry and you are either just starting your career or want to move into one of those areas, you probably are going to have to get some additional education, training, or certification before going on your job search. But that doesn't mean you can't do it.

Let's take a moment to look at some ways you can transfer skills. Do you have teaching skills? What about using your skills to become a corporate hardware or software trainer? What about teaching people how to use their home computers or software programs? Maybe you want to teach computer technology in a high school. How about teaching programming in college? What about teaching Web design? There are a ton of other opportunities. You just have to think about it for a bit.

Do you have strong writing skills? Consider seeking a position with a software company, computer company, or peripheral vendor in the public relations or marketing department. Think about a career as a Web content editor. What about a job as a technology reporter for a newspaper or periodical? How about a career as a technical writer, producing documentation for hardware, software, and peripherals?

Are your skills in marketing? Consider a position in the marketing department of a hardware or software company. What about being the marketing director of a Web site? Again,

there are a ton of opportunities. You just have to look for them.

Are your skills in promotion? How about transferring your skills to a career promoting Web sites? Maybe you want to develop Web-based contests and promotions to help promote companies or draw traffic.

Are your skills in the number crunching area? What about seeking out a position in the accounting or bookkeeping department of an ISP, hardware, or software company?

Do you have office skills? Are you a good manager? Do you have good organizational skills? Consider a job as an administrative assistant in a technology company. Think about working as a customer service supervisor in an ISP.

Can you explain things easily? Do you understand how computers work from the inside out? What about a career in technical support? Have you been fixing everyone's computer as a hobby? What about using your skills for a career in computer repair?

Are your skills in sales? Lucky you! The possibilities are endless. Every industry needs sales people, and the computer industry is no different. Whether you're selling advertising or equipment, you can always find a great job. Maybe you want to sell advertising for Web sites. Perhaps you want to sell Internet services. Maybe you want to sell computers? Perhaps you want to sell hosting services? Maybe you want to sell the services of programmers. The sky is the limit.

Do you have skills in retailing? E-commerce is growing on the Web by leaps and bounds. What are your skills? Can you find a way to transfer them to this growing way of shopping? If so, you're on your way. Whether you look for a job working for a large online shopping site like QVC.com or a smaller, more regional e-commerce site, there are a ton of opportunities available.

"Wait a minute," you say, "what if I don't want to work in the area where my skills are? What if I want to do something totally different? What then?"

Here's the deal. Use your skills and your talents to get your foot in the door. Once in, you have a better opportunity to move into the area you want.

Can you do it? Yes! Thousands of people are successful in the computer industry. You can be too!

Should you quit your present job to go after your dream? And if so, when should you do it? Good questions. Generally, you are much more employable if you are employed. You don't have that desperate "I need a job" look. You don't have the worries about financially supporting yourself and your family if you have one. You don't have to take the wrong job because you've been out of work so long that anything looks good.

It's best to work on starting your dream career while you have a job to support yourself. Ideally you'll be able to leave one job directly for another much more to your liking.

Words from the Wise

If you are working at another job until you get the one you want, it's not a good idea to keep harping on the fact that you're only there until you get your big break or the job of your dreams. If your supervisor thinks you are planning on leaving, not only will you probably not get the choice assignments, but also co-workers who may be stuck in the job you are using as a stepping-stone often feel jealous.

The Inside Scoop

In your journey to obtaining your perfect career, you might take some jobs that you consider stepping-stones and are not where you ultimately want to end up in your career. No matter what type of career you aspire to, it is essential that you remember your ultimate goal. Don't get so wrapped up in the job you have that you forget where you're going.

Over the years I've often seen people take a job because the money was there even though it wasn't exactly what they wanted. Then, as time goes on, they are offered more money or promotions and find it difficult to give it up, even to pursue their goals. Don't get so busy that you forget where you're going and what you want. If you have a dream, don't forget your goals.

Of course, in some situations, you might want to (or need to) devote most of your time to your career. Only you can make the decision on how to go about your starting your career. Take some time to decide what would be best for you.

You must focus in on exactly what you want to do, set your goals, prepare your action plan, and start taking actions now. You're going to have to begin moving toward your goals every day—a job which can lead to the career of your dreams.

We've already discussed that you are usually more marketable if you are currently employed. This doesn't mean you shouldn't work toward your goals. Continue searching out ways to get where you're going.

"Working takes all my energy," you say, "I don't have time to do everything. If I'm working, I just don't have enough time to put into creating my dream career."

You're going to have to make time. It's amazing how you can expand your time when you need to. Remember your action plan? It's imperative that you carve time out of your day to perform some of your actions.

If you think you don't have the time, look at your day a little closer. What can you eliminate doing? Will getting up a half an hour earlier give you more time to work on your career? How about cutting out an hour of television during the day or not surfing the Internet for an hour? Even if you can only afford to take time in 15-minute increments, you usually can find an hour to put into your career.

Moving from One Segment of the Computer Industry to Another

Are you working in one segment of the computer industry and want to work in another? Are you, for example working at an ISP in technical customer support and want to work in programming? Are you a Web administrator who wants a career as the corporate director of security? Are you a systems programmer who wants to work in application programming? Are you a professor teaching computer science who wants to write textbooks? Are you a Web content editor who wants to move into a position as a Web site marketing director? Are you working in corporate software development, but dream about developing games? Are you in a similar situation?

What do you want to do? Check out the requirements for the job you want. Look into what education or training you need to reach your goals. Find a mentor. Ask questions. Find what you need to do to get the career of your dreams and then do it!

What should you not do? To begin with, don't give up before you get started. Don't get so caught up in how difficult something will be that you don't look for a way to do it. Most of all, don't discount your dreams.

Let's say you are a technical customer support person at an ISP and want to become a software engineer. What do you do? You already have an associate's degree in computer science and are working toward your bachelor's. After some research you find that most companies prefer to hire individuals who hold a minimum of a bachelor's degree in either computer science, software engineering, or computer systems. What classes have you already taken that are applicable? What other types of classes do you need to take? What kind of program can help you move into the job of your dreams? If you research what you need to do and take it step by step, you will be on your way to getting the job of your dreams.

Finding the Job You Want

Perseverance is essential to your success, no matter what you want to do, what area of the computer industry you want to enter, and what career level you want to achieve. Do you want to know why most people don't find their perfect job? It's because they gave up looking before they found it.

Difficult as it might be to realize at this point, remember that your great career is out there waiting for you. You just have to locate it. How do you find that elusive position you want? You look for it!

Basically, jobs are located in two areas: the open job market and the hidden job market. What's the difference? The open job market includes those jobs that are advertised and announced to the public. The hidden job market is composed of jobs that are not advertised or announced to the public.

Where can you find the largest number of jobs? Are they in the hidden job market or the open job market? A lot depends on exactly what you want to do in the industry. While many jobs are advertised in the open market, you need to be aware that there are a great many jobs that aren't advertised. Why?

There are a few reasons. Some employers don't want to put an ad in the classified section of the newspaper because it might result in hundreds of responses or more.

"But isn't that what employers want?" you ask. "Someone to fill job openings?"

Of course they want their job openings filled, but they don't want to have to go through hundreds of resumes and cover letters to get to that point. It is much easier to try to find qualified applicants in other ways, and that is where the hidden job market comes in.

This doesn't mean, however, that you shouldn't look into the open market. The newspaper is full of positions. However, the smart thing to do to boost your job hunt is utilize every avenue to find your perfect job. With that being said, let's discuss the open job market before discussing the hidden job market in more detail.

The Open Job Market

When you think of looking for a job where do you start? If you're like most people, you head straight for the classifieds section of the newspaper. While, as we just noted, this strategy may not always be the best bet, it's at least worth checking out depending on what type of position you are seeking. Let's go over some ways to increase your chances of success in locating job openings this way.

The Sunday newspapers usually have the largest collection of help wanted ads. Start by focusing on those. You can never tell when an employer will advertise job openings, though, so you might also want to browse through the classified section on a daily basis if possible.

Will you find a job you want advertised in your local hometown newspaper? That depends on what type of job you're seeking and where you live. If you live in a small town that has no technology companies and you're looking for a position in technology, probably not. If you're looking for a position in computer repair or working with an ISP, your chances may be better.

What do you do if you don't live in the area where you want to look for a job? How can you get the newspapers? Larger bookstores and libraries often carry Sunday newspapers from metropolitan cities in the country. If you're interested in getting newspapers from specific areas, you can also usually order short-term subscriptions. One of the easiest ways to view the classified sections of newspapers from around the country is by going online to each newspaper's Web site. The home page will direct you to the classified or employment section. Start your search there.

What do you look for once you get the papers? That depends on the specific job you're after, but generally look for key words. If you want a job in programming, for example, you would look for key words such as "Lead Systems Programmer," "Senior Systems Programmer," "Manager of Operating Systems Programming," "Project Manager, Programming," "Applications Programmer," "Senior Applications Programmer," and so on. If you are looking for a job as a marketing director for a technology company, you might look for key words such as "Marketing Director," "Marketing,"

"Computers," "Technology," "Software Company-Marketing," or "Hardware Company-Marketing," for example.

Don't forget to look for specific company names as well. "Dot.net ISP," "ABC Software," "Best Computer Company," and so on.

In some cases, all the jobs in technology are in a specific section of the classifieds. In others, the jobs are scattered throughout the section.

In many situations, large companies also use boxed or display classified ads. These are large ads that may advertise more than one job and usually have a company name and/or logo. There may also be ads for employment agencies specializing in jobs in a specific area of computers or technology.

The Trades, Industry Publications, Newsletters, and Web Resources

Where else are jobs advertised? The trades are often a good source. Trades are periodicals geared toward a specific industry. Every industry has trade magazines and newspapers and the computer industry is no exception.

Where do you find them? Contact the trade association geared toward the specific area of the industry in which you are interested. (Trade associations are listed in Appendix I in the back of this book.)

How can you use the trades to your advantage? Read them faithfully. If you don't want to invest in a subscription, go to your local or college library to see if they subscribe. See if your local bookstore has them available. Many of the trades also have online versions of their publication. Browse through the "Help Wanted" ads in the classified section of each issue to see if your dream job is there.

Newsletters related to various areas of the computer and technology industry might offer other possibilities for job openings. What about Internet Web sites such as Monster.com, Hotjobs.com, and other employment sites? What about career sites geared specifically toward computer and technology jobs? What about job posting sites?

Don't forget company Web sites. Many of these sites have specific sections listing career opportunities at their organization. It's worth checking out. Remember that companies don't necessarily have to be specifically computer or technology oriented to have opportunities. Companies in all industries need the services of people in all aspects of the computer and technology industry.

Are you already working in the industry and seeking to move up the career ladder? Many companies post their employment listings in the human resources department or in employee newsletters. What if you don't have a job there already and are interested in finding out about internal postings? This is where networking comes into play. A contact at the company can keep you informed.

If you're still in college or you graduated from a school that offered programs in the area in which you are interested, don't forget to check with the college career services office. In many cases, companies searching to fill specific positions may go to colleges and universities where they know there are specific programs.

Employment Agencies, Recruiters, and Headhunters

Let's take a few minutes to discuss employment agencies, recruiters, and headhunters. What are they? What's the difference?

Employment agencies may fall into a number of different categories. They may be temp agencies, personnel agencies, or a combination of the two. Temp agencies work with companies to provide employees for short term or fill-in work. These agencies generally specialize in a number of career areas. Some agencies even provide workers for longer-term projects. Some agencies may also provide contract workers or freelancers to handle specific projects.

How do they work? Basically, a company tells an agency what types of positions they are looking to fill and the temp agency recruits workers they feel are qualified for those positions. The business then pays the agency and the agency pays the employee.

When you work in this capacity, you are not working for the company. You are an employee of the temp agency. Generally, in this type of situation, you do not pay a fee to be placed.

Personnel agencies, on the other hand, work in a different manner. These agencies try to match people who are looking for a job with companies that have openings. When you go to a personnel agency they will interview you, talk about your qualifications, and if the interviewer feels you are suitable, will send you to speak to companies that have openings for which you are qualified. You may then meet with someone in the human resources department of the company with the opening. You may or may not get the job. There are no guarantees using a personnel agency.

Words from the Wise

If you are going to use an employment agency to help you find a job, remember to check before you sign any contracts to see who pays the fee, you or the company. There is nothing wrong with paying a fee. You simply want to be aware ahead of time of what the fee will be.

Tip from the Coach

Employment agencies in most states are required to be licensed and registered with the Department of Labor. Check out employment agencies before you get involved.

If you do get hired, you will generally have to pay a portion of your first year's salary to the personnel company that helped you get the job. In some cases, the employer will split the fee with you. Check ahead of time so you will have no surprises.

You should not be required to pay anything up front. You may be asked to sign a contract. Before you sign anything, read it thoroughly and understand everything. If you don't understand what something means, ask.

Recruiters, headhunters, and executive search firms are all similar. These firms generally have contracts with employers who are looking for employees with specific skills, talents, and experience. It is their job to find people to fill those positions.

The difference between recruiters, headhunters, and executive search firms, and the employment or personnel agencies we discussed previously is that you (as the job seeker) are not responsible for paying a fee. Rather, the fee will be paid by the employer.

How do these companies find you? There are a number of ways. Sometimes they read a story in the paper about you or see a press release about an award you received. Sometimes someone they know recommends you.

In some cases, companies just cold call people who have jobs similar to those they are trying to fill and ask if these people know anyone who might be looking for a similar job who you might recommend. You might recommend someone or you might even say you are interested yourself.

What if no one calls you? Are you out of luck? Not at all. It's perfectly acceptable to call recruiters and headhunters yourself.

What you need to do is find firms that specialize in the area of the computer industry you aspire to work. So, for example, if you are a software engineer looking for a job in that field, you would look for executive recruiters that specialize in placing people in software engineering, software development, or technology.

How do you find these recruiters? There are over 5,000 executive recruiting agencies in the United States. You can search out firms on the Internet or look in the Yellow Pages of phone books from large, metropolitan areas.

You might check out trade magazines and periodicals. Many have advertisements for recruiters in their specific career area. You also can also call the human resources department of companies you are interested in working with directly and ask them which recruiting agency (if any) they use.

Why do companies look to recruiters to find their employees? Generally, it's easier. They have someone screening potential employees, looking for just the right one. Because recruiters don't generally get paid unless they find the right employee, they have the perfect incentive.

Should you get involved with a recruiter? As recruiters bring job possibilities to you, there really isn't a downside. As a matter o fact, even if you have a job that you love, it's a good idea to keep a relationship with headhunters and recruiters. You can never tell when your next great job is around the corner.

Here's a few thing which can help when you are working with a recruiter.

◎ Tailor your resume or CV to the specific sector of the industry in which the recruiter works. You want your qualifications to jump off of the page.
◎ Make sure you tell your recruiter about any companies to which you do not want your resume sent. For example, you don't want your resume sent to your current employer. You might not want your resume sent to a company where you just interviewed, etc.
◎ Call and check in with the recruiter on a regular basis.

The Hidden Job Market

While a good number of jobs are advertised, let's talk a bit about the hidden job market. Many people think that their job search begins and ends with the classified ads. If they get the Sunday paper and their dream job isn't in there, they give up and wait until the next Sunday. I am betting that once you have made the decision to have a career in some aspect of the computer industry, you're not going to let something small like not finding a job opening in the classifieds stop you. So what are you going to do?

While there may be job openings in which you are interested advertised in the classifieds, it's essential to realize that many jobs are not advertised at all. Why? In addition to not wanting to be inundated with hundreds of resumes and phone calls, some employers may not want someone in another company to know that they are looking for a new marketing director, publicity director, or chief information officer until they hire one. As a matter of fact, they may not want the person who currently holds the job to know that he or she is about to be let go. Whatever the reason, once you're aware that all jobs aren't advertised you can go about finding them in a different manner.

Why do you want to find jobs in the hidden job market? The main reason is because you will have a better shot at getting the job. Why? To begin with, there is a lot less competition. Because the positions aren't being actively advertised, there aren't hundreds of people sending in resumes trying to get the jobs. Not everyone knows how to find the hidden job market, nor do they want to take the extra time to find it, so you also have an edge over other potential job applicants. Many applicants in the hidden job market also often come recommended by someone who knows about the opening. This means that you are starting off with one foot in the door.

How does the hidden job market work? Basically, when a company needs to fill a position, instead of placing an ad, they quietly look for the perfect candidate. How do they find the candidates without advertising? Let's look at some ways this is accomplished and how you can take advantage of each situation.

◎ Employees may be promoted from within the company.
  ▫ That is why it is so important, once you get your foot in the door and get a job, to keep yourself visible in a positive manner. You want supervisors to think about you when an opening occurs. For example, if you're working as a programming analyst and you want to become a project manager, during a conversation with your supervisor you might say something like, "After I finish my work, I would be glad to help with any other parts of the project where you might need some assistance. I'm really interested in learning all I can about projects like this. I find it fascinating how all the pieces come together.

In the same vein, if you are working in the publicity department a software vendor and your goal is a career in marketing, drop subtle hints during conversations with the supervisors in both your department and the marketing department. You might, for example, say something like, "I love working in publicity. Learning how to properly publicize the products and the company was one of my goals when I decided to work at this company. I also always wanted to learn more about marketing." You're not saying you don't like your job. You're not saying you want to leave your job. What you're doing is planting a seed. If you have been doing an amazing job in your current position and anything opens up in marketing, you just might be suggested for the job.

◎ An employee working in the company may recommend a candidate for the position.
  ▫ This is another time that networking helps. Don't keep your dreams to yourself. Tell others what type of job you're looking for and what your qualifications are. You can never tell when a position may become available. Employers often ask their staff if they know anyone who would be good for this job. If you shared your qualifications and dreams, someone just might recommend you.

◎ Someone who knows about an opening may tell their friends, relatives, or coworkers, who then apply for the job.

  ▫ In some cases, it's not another employee who knows about an opening, but it might be someone who has contact with the company. For example, a project manager at one company might be at a conference and hear that another company is looking for a new director of information. He or she might tell his brother's neighbor to call up and apply for the job. He or she might also mention it to a colleague who mentions it to someone else.

◎ Sometimes it may be someone outside the company who hears about the job. The UPS delivery person, for example, may be delivering packages to a company when he or she overhears a conversation about the Webmaster leaving. If you had networked with the UPS delivery person and mentioned you were looking for a job like that, he or she might stop by and tell you about the opportunity. Then, all you would have to do is contact the company.

◎ People may have filled in applications or sent resumes and cover letters to the company asking that they be kept on file. When an opening exists, the human resources department might review the resumes and call one of those applicants.

  ▫ Even if you there are no jobs advertised, it is often worth your while to send a cover letter and your resume to the human resources department asking about openings. Be sure to ask that your resume be kept on file.

◎ Suitable candidates may place cold calls at just the right time.

  ▫ Difficult as it can be to place cold calls, it might pay off. Consider committing yourself to making a couple of cold calls every day. Do some research. Then, depending on the area of the industry in which you are interested in working, finds some potential companies and call the director of human resources in an attempt to set up an interview. Who can you call? Depending on what type of job you are looking for, you might call almost any company that might be able to use your services. The beauty of a cold call is that it can be made to anyone.

◎ People may have networked and caught the eye of those who need to fill the jobs.

  ▫ Finding positions in the hidden job market is a skill in itself. One of the best ways to do this is by networking. Through networking you can make contacts and your contacts are the people who will know about the jobs in the hidden market.

⭐ The Inside Scoop

When making a cold call, try to get the name of the person you're trying to reach ahead of time so you can ask for someone by name. How? Just call the company and ask the receptionist.

Using New Technology to Find Jobs

Somewhere in between the open job market and the hidden job market there are an array of other channels to find your perfect job. New technology has changed the way many employers look for potential employees and has changed the way many people look for jobs, especially in the computer industry.

Using an integrated job search encompassing as many methods as possible will help you have the best chance at success. What does that mean?

In addition to traditional job search methods, you might want to utilize one or more other options. Let's look at a few of them.

- ◎ Online job boards
    - ▫ These can offer a plethora of possibilities to job seekers. Surf the Internet looking for job boards specific to your area of career interest. Once you find them, browse through them on a regular basis. You might want to check them out, even if you have the job of your dreams. You never can tell when an even better opportunity will present itself. If you don't know about it, you can't take action.
- ◎ Online resume posting sites
    - ▫ Sites like monster.com, careerbuilder.com and a host of others, including many geared specifically to the IT industry, allow you to post your resume so potential employers can view it. There are pros and cons to doing this.
        - ◇ On the pro side, you can get your resume in front of thousands of potential employers who might be looking for someone with your skills, talents, and passion. Today, many employers regularly review these sites in an effort to find the best employee. Many have found this saves hundreds of thousands of dollars annually in recruiting employees.
        - ◇ On the con side, you never really know who is seeing your resume. In some cases, you are inundated by phone calls and/or e-mails from people that have absolutely nothing to do with your career.

Some are trying to sell you something. Others are scams.

- What do you need to know?
  - ◇ The resume you post online needs to be formatted differently than the resume that you print out and mail or deliver in person to someone. The resume that you post online will need to be a plain text or text-only version. It might also be referred to as text only. What that means is that you won't be able to use a lot of formatting or highlighted text. Your plain text version either will be used to copy and paste into online forms provided by online resume sites or will be posted directly into online resume databases. Depending on the situation, you might also need an e-mail version of your resume, which is also a text-only document. Some people also use HTML versions of their resume.
- What else do you need to know?
  - ◇ Don't haphazardly post your resume all over the Internet. Choose two or three of the main resume posting sites and a couple of the more popular sites targeted to your specific industry.
  - ◇ Some insiders suggest omitting the dates you worked at a specific company as well as the actual names of companies where you held jobs. Instead they recommend writing an accurate generic description of the type of company for which you worked.

  - ◇ Be careful of posting your personal information. You should be aware that you can often control the posting of your personal information with your resume. Some sites offer the option of blocking your personal information to all but potential employers. Some have other options. You may, for example, want to omit your address and phone number and use your e-mail as your contact information. Be sure to check your e-mail frequently so you don't miss a message about a potential job possibility.
  - ◇ You should also be sure to check the site's privacy policy. Some sites sell your information, some don't. Check before you post your info.
- ◎ Blogging
  - Many people are now using blogging as a tool to find jobs. What exactly is a blog? Short for Web log, basically it's a Web page (or Web site) on which you can share your comments, thoughts, opinions, ideas, stories, etc., on a regular basis. Many people use blogs as a sort of personal diary or journal discussing what they are thinking, what they are doing, or what is going on in their life. Blogs may have text, images, videos, and links to other Web sites. In many cases, people reading your blog leave comments, almost creating your own online community. How can you use a blog to help your career? There are a number of ways.

◇ Blogging helps you expand your network. As we have discussed throughout the book, the more people in your network, the better chances you have of finding your perfect job. Your blog can help introduce you to people online. It can tell them what you do, what you have done, and what your aspirations are. Done correctly, you can weave in your accomplishments and your resume.

◇ Additionally, you can link your resume to your blog. In this manner, potential employers can learn more about you.

◇ When people begin to read your blog, they begin to feel that they know you. You begin to build credibility. This can be extremely helpful in your career.

◇ People tend to believe what they read. Later in the book, we're going to discuss how becoming an expert in one or more areas can help your career. Using your blog effectively, you can let people know about your expertise.

◇ Potential employers and recruiters often Google your name to see what they can find out about you. Will you be a good match? Will you fit in? What does your blog say about you?

◇ In some cases, potential employers, especially those seeking individuals with specialized skills, will Google blogs with the specific purpose of seeing who is out there with those skills.

◇ If you are interested in freelancing or consulting, your blog can help get your name out there and give you credibility.

▫ What do you need to know?

◇ If you are using your blog for professional purposes, keep your blog professional. Don't talk about how your kids had the stomach flu, you had a fight with your husband, or you broke up with your girlfriend.

◇ Update your blog on a regular basis so people start to look forward to new content.

◎ Social networking sites

▫ Social networking sites are another option for finding jobs that can turn into wonderful careers. How do they work? Essentially, you register with the site and put up your profile.

◎ Where do you find social networking sites?
- ⊡ You can surf the net. Some of the more familiar sites include Facebook, MySpace, Ryze, and LinkedIn.
- ⊡ What do you need to know?
  - ◇ Don't give up other types of networking just because you are involved in online networking. You want to use online networking in conjunction with your other networking opportunities, not instead of it. Use it in conjunction with face-to-face networking, not instead of it.
  - ◇ Be very careful about posting personal, unprofessional information on the Internet. In addition to Googling your name, potential employers and recruiters may visit your MySpace or Facebook page to see what you've said. Writing something like "My hobby is drinking until I pass out" or having racy photos online will not sit well with most employers.

Networking in the Computer Industry

Often, it's not just what you know, but who you know. Contacts are key in every industry and the computer and technology industries are no exception. Networking is, therefore, going to be an important part of succeeding. It is so important that in some situations it can often make you or break you.

"How?" you ask.

If you don't have a chance to showcase your skills and your talents to the right people, it's difficult to get the jobs you want, the promotions you want, and the career of your dreams.

Networking is important in every area of the computer and technology industry, no matter what segment you aspire to work. The fact of the matter is that without the power of networking it is often difficult to get your foot in the door. That doesn't mean you can't get your foot in the door, it just means it is harder.

Earlier chapters have touched on networking. Because of its importance to your career success we will continue discussing it throughout the book. What is essential to understand is that networking isn't just something you do at the beginning of your career. It's something you're going to have to continue doing for as long as you work.

How do you network? Basically, you put yourself into situations where you can meet people and introduce yourself. Later in the book we will discuss more about networking basics and offer some networking exercises that will be useful; however, what you should be doing at this point is learning to get comfortable walking up to people, extending your hand, and introducing yourself.

"Hi, I'm Tina Keating. Isn't this an interesting event? What a great opportunity this was to learn more about Web design," you might say at a seminar.

Voice of Experience

You never want to be in the position where someone remembers that they met you and thinks that you would be perfect for a job, yet they have no idea how to contact you. Don't be stingy with your business cards. Give them out freely.

The person you meet will then tell you his or her name and perhaps something about him or herself. You can then keep talking or say, "It was nice meeting you. Do you have a business card?"

Make sure you have your business cards handy and when you are given a card, give yours as well.

Every situation can ultimately be an opportunity to network, but some are more effective than others. Look for seminars, workshops, and classes that professionals in the area of the computer industry in which you are interested potentially might attend.

Why would an industry professional be at a workshop or seminar? There are many reasons. They might want to network just like you do, they might want to learn something new, or they might be teaching or facilitating the workshop.

Where else can you meet and network with professionals in the computer or technology industry? What about trade association meetings? What about conferences? What about at their place of work?

"But I can't just walk into someone's office who I don't know and introduce myself," you say.

You're right. That probably won't work. So what can you do?

If you don't know someone in the type of company you want to work, you're going to have to get creative in your networking. How can you network with employees of those companies? Here's a strategy you might want to try.

Find one or two organizations or companies in which you might be interested in working and locate the physical address.

Choose a day when you have some time to spare. Generally, it needs to be on a weekday because those are the days most business takes

---

> ### ★ Tip from the Top
> When networking at an event, don't just zero in on the people you think are important industry insiders and ignore the rest. Try to meet as many people as you can. Always be pleasant and polite to everyone. You never can tell who knows who and who might be a great contact later.

---

place. Get dressed in appropriate clothing, and go to the location of the company you've chosen. Now stand outside the building and look around. Are there restaurants, coffee shops, diners, or bars nearby? There probably are. Does the company have a cafeteria or lunchroom? Is it open to the public? Why does all this matter?

Because people working in these offices have to eat lunch somewhere, they have to get their coffee somewhere. After work on Friday night they might want to stop at the bar on the corner for happy hour.

What does that mean to you? If you can determine where the company employees hang out, you can put yourself in situations in which to network with them.

Can you find out which restaurants, diners, and coffee shops the employees frequent? You often can, if you stand outside around lunchtime and watch to see who goes where.

Some office buildings have thousands of employees in different businesses. How do you know which are the employees from the company you have targeted? You might have to eavesdrop a little and listen for clues in things people say as they walk out the door. You might stop in the building and ask someone. Get on the elevator and ask the elevator operator. Ask the security guard standing in the lobby. You might even stop into a couple of the coffee shops, diners, or restaurants and ask the host or hostess: "Hi, I was supposed to have a lunch meeting with someone from ABC Software and I'm embarrassed to say, I'm not sure which coffee shop the meeting was set for," you might say. "Do a lot of the employees from there come in here or is it the coffee shop down the street?"

At this point, the hostess will either give you a blank look that means you probably are in the wrong place (or she really doesn't know) or tell you that you are indeed in the right location. She might even say, "Yes, we just did a take-out order for them a few minutes ago," or something to that effect.

Once you've found the correct location, wait until it's nice and busy and there is a slight line. People will usually talk to other people, even if they don't know them, when they are standing in lines. Start up conversations and hope that you're standing near the people from the organization you're looking for. What about sitting at the counter if there is one? If you get lucky, you might end up sitting next to someone from the very organization you are targeting.

This whole process is often a lot easier if you are trying to network with people who work at a company where there is a cafeteria or coffee shop in the building. If there is, the odds are you will be running into people who work there.

The tricky part in this entire procedure is being able to network in this type of situation. Some people are really good at it and some people find it very difficult. What you're dealing with when doing this is first finding the correct people and then starting a conversation with them that may let you turn them into networking contacts. Done right, it can pay off big time.

You might meet someone, for example, who works in one of the administrative offices and strike up a conversation. You never can tell what may happen from there. You might mention you were thinking about filling in an application because you were looking for a job in the company's IT department. Your new contact might say, "I don't think there are any positions in that department, but the Webmaster just put in her letter of resignation." You might get a referral, set up an interview, or even end up with a job.

Does this technique always work? Sometime it does and sometimes it doesn't. The important thing to know is that it might help you get your foot in the door when you otherwise might not have.

If you find networking in this manner difficult, it might be easier for you to do at a bar during a "happy hour" because people tend to talk more in these situations. Remember, though, that while it's okay to drink socially, your main goal is to network and make contacts. You won't do yourself any favors becoming intoxicated and then acting outrageously or saying something inappropriate.

★ The Inside Scoop

It's great to network with those at the top, but a good and often more practical strategy is to try networking with the assistants and support team. The people at the top might not always remember you; those a step or two down the line usually will. Additionally, a recommendation from these people about you to their boss can do wonders for your career.

Where else might people helpful to your career congregate? What about joining trade associations specific to the area of the computer or technology industry in which you're interested in working?

Are they having any conferences? Do they have regular meetings? Are they holding any type of networking events? In addition to attending, you might want to find out if they need any volunteers to help with the event.

Why? To begin with, it's a good way to be visible. It is also more beneficial to your career to meet the executive director of a trade association or the president or the HR director of a company when you're being introduced as a volunteer who helped pull an event together than knocking on his or her door and saying, "Hi, do you have a minute?"

Where else? What about joining the local chamber of commerce and volunteering to work on some events? What about volunteering to help with one of their fund-raisers?

What about attending a job fair? These events are wonderful opportunities to meet with people involved in the industry. Even if you don't score an interview or find a job, you might make some amazing contacts. Who might be there? You might meet HR directors or other company representatives, you might meet recruiters, or you might just meet other job seekers. All these people can be tremendous networking contacts.

While there are general job fairs where you may find potential opportunities in the computer industry, many organizations also hold job fairs that specialize in jobs involving computers or the technology industry. Where do you find them? They may be advertised in the newspaper, trade journals, or online.

Be sure when you attend these events that you dress appropriately and bring copies of your resume. Stop at each booth that interests you and talk to the individual manning the booth. Make sure you pick up business cards and any other pertinent information.

Instead of just attending the job fair, consider volunteering to help out. Why? Because the HR directors, company representatives, recruiters, and other key people who are there may just see you in the different light. You will be illustrating that you are willing to do that little extra, that you have a good work ethic, and that you can be a commodity. It will also be easier to network with the vendors participating in the event.

How else can you get to the right people? Sometimes all it takes is making a phone call. Consider calling an industry trade association, for example, ask to speak to the communications or public relations director and tell him or her about your career aspirations. Ask if he or she would be willing to give you the names of a couple of industry people that you might call.

For example, you might contact the public relations director of a video gaming company and ask whom you might talk to if you were interested in a career in that field. You might contact a technology reporter and ask if he or she can give you insight into career opportunities. You just might be surprised by the response.

"Why would anyone want to help me?" you ask.

Most people like to help others. It makes them feel good. Don't expect everyone to be courteous or to go out of the way for you, but if you find one or two helpful people, you may wind up with some useful contacts.

To get you started thinking, here's a sample script of how such a conversation might go.

Jackie Conner, Game Development Association Public Relations Director: Hello, Jackie Conner.

You: Hi, this is Kevin James. I'm not sure if you're the right person to speak to about this, but would it be okay if I tell you what I'm looking for so you can point me in the right direction?

Jackie Conner: Sure, go ahead

You: Thanks. First, I'm not selling anything. I'm getting my bachelor's degree in computer science and programming in May. My goal is to have a career in some aspect of the gaming industry. I want to create games that everyone is talking about—you know, innovative games that no one can stop playing. I don't really know any of the right people to bounce this off of. I was wondering if you might have some ideas about whom I could talk to or how I can meet with some people within the industry. I'm not sure what to do after I graduate or even what direction to go. I know there are opportunities. I just don't really know where they are. I was hoping you would be able to give me some suggestions.

Jackie Conner: I wish I could help, but I'm not sure who I could suggest right now. Sorry.

You: Well, at this point, I'm just trying to get my foot in the door. Don't you have any suggestions at all of people who might be able to give me a couple of names?

Jackie Conner: You probably could contact anyone in membership. I'm not sure who, specifically, could help you though.

You: I would appreciate any help. Would it be a big imposition for me to come in one day when you're not too busy to just meet with you for a couple of minutes, just to get a couple of ideas? I would appreciate any help. I promise I won't take a lot of your time.

Jackie Conner: I'm pretty busy for the next few weeks and I'm not sure how I could really help. We have our annual conference at the end of the month. I'm sorry. I'm really swamped. My assistant is on maternity leave and our conference coordinator was just in an accident so things are really piling up.

You: I know how that is. I've helped put on a few conferences here at the university. I'm on the student activities board. Anyway, I don't want to keep you. Thanks for your time. Can I leave my number?

Jackie Conner: Not a problem. I don't know if you would be interested, but I could get you a pass to our conference. In addition to the seminars, we have a number of networking sessions. You're on your own for transportation and accommodations, but it might be worth it to you. The conference is in Some City. Are you interested?

You: Wow, thanks, that would be great. I would love that.

Jackie Conner: Why don't you fax your information over and I'll make sure you get a conference pack. The number is 111-222-3333. Be sure to stop by at the conference and introduce yourself.

You: Thank you. Let me run something by you. I would love to repay your generosity by giving you some help with the conference. I have classes in the morning, but I can make phone calls in the afternoon or input information into the computer or something if that would help. I'm familiar with the registration software. I could also call the speakers to verify their time slots. It would be great experience for me and you need the help.

Jackie Conner: That might work. Why don't you come in and we can talk. If it works out, I have some money in the budget for temps. If you're working for the conference we can even pay for your transportation and accommodations.

You: Wow. That would be great. I'm going to e-mail my resume as soon as we hang up. I can come in tomorrow afternoon if that is good for you.

Jackie Conner: I look forward to meeting you.

See how easy it is? You just have to ask.

"But what if someone says no?" you ask. "What if they won't help?"

That might happen. The conversation may not go in the direction you want it to. Some people will say no. So what? If you don't ask, you'll never know.

"But what do I say if someone says no?"

Simply thank them nicely for their time and hang up. Don't belabor the point. Just say, "Thanks anyway. I appreciate your time."

It will be difficult the first couple of times you make a call like that, but as you begin to reach out to others it will get easier. Pretty soon, you won't even think about it.

Where else can you network? A lot of that depends on what segment of the computer industry you are targeting. Look for opportunities.

"But how do I get through to the industry professionals?" you ask.

You have to be creative. For example, let's say you read a story in the paper about an upcoming event to benefit a not-for-profit organization. The organization is honoring the CIO of a large, prestigious company in your area. What do you do? First of all, make sure you go.

"I can't afford to go to a big fund-raiser," you say.

Get creative. Volunteer to be a host or hostess. Offer to help check people in. See if you can cover the event for the newspaper. Think outside of the box.

Events don't always have to be oriented to the career area you are pursuing to be good networking opportunities. You might want to join organizations like Kiwanis or Rotary and go to their meetings. You might want to join the chamber of commerce and go to their events. Why? Industry professionals attend these events. It's a good place to meet people on a more even playing field.

Remember that these are business functions. Behave professionally and make sure to watch for any opportunities to network—the main reason that you're there. Here are some tips on what to do and what not to do:

◎ Do not bring anyone with you. Go alone. It will give you more opportunities to meet people.
◎ Do not smoke, even if other people are. You can never tell what makes someone

> ### ⭐ Tip from the Coach
>
> Remember that networking is a two way street. If you want people to help you it's important to reciprocate. When you see something you can do for someone else's career, don't wait for them to ask for help. Step in, do it, and do it graciously.

remember you. You don't want it to be that you smell of tobacco.

◎ Don't wear strong perfume, cologne, or aftershave. Aside from the possibility of some people being allergic to it, you don't want this to be the reason people remember you.

Here are some things you should do.

◎ Do bring business cards to give out to everyone.
◎ Do bring a pen and small pad of paper to take down names and phone numbers of people who don't have cards.
◎ Do meet as many people as possible. If given the opportunity, briefly tell them what your goal is and ask if they have any suggestion about who you can contact.

Follow up on the contacts and information you gather at these meetings. Don't neglect this step or you will have wasted the opportunity. Call, write, or e-mail contacts you have made in a timely fashion. You want them to remember meeting you.

The Right Place at the Right Time

Have you ever looked down while you were walking and seen some money lying on the ground? It could have been there for a while, but no one else happened to look down at that time. You just happened to be in the right place at the right time.

It can happen anytime. Sometimes you hear about an interesting job opening from an unlikely source. You might, for example, be standing in a long line at the bakery. The woman in back of you asks if you would mind if she went ahead of you because she is rushing out of town to visit her son. It seems she needs to pick up the bakery's famous chocolate cake because it is her son's favorite and he misses it since moving away to take a new job two hours away.

You of course agree to let her get ahead of you. While standing in line chatting she mentions how proud she is of her son. It seems he has become the director of development for a well-known e-commerce shopping site.

"I love that site," you say. She asks what you do. "I just graduated from college in May with a double major in journalism," you tell her.

"I don't suppose your son needs someone to write a column on fashion?" you ask, half kidding. "I've been sending out resumes, but haven't found a job yet. It's my dream to write about fashion. I did a bi-weekly column when I interned at the Some City Times."

"Was that you?" the woman asked. "I really enjoyed that. I remember reading the column you wrote on updating your wardrobe. It made shopping a lot easier."

"Thanks," you say. "You're next. Have a great trip. Here, take my card. I enjoyed chatting with you."

Tuesday morning your phone rings. It's the woman's son. It seems that during her visit, his mom told him about meeting you and your columns. He thought a regular column on fashion would be great for the site. He checked out your old columns online and like them, especially the way you added humor to your stories. He also thought you might be able to moderate a fashion blog on the site. He wants to know when you can come for an interview.

You go and guess what? You got the job!

Think it can't happen? It can and it does. It's just a matter of being in the right place at the right time and taking advantage of a potential opportunity.

There is no question that being in the right place at the right time can help. The question is however, what is the right place and the right time and how do you recognize it?

The simple answer is; it's almost impossible to know what the right place and right time are. You can, however, stack the deck in your favor. How? You can put yourself in situations where you can network. Networking with people outside of the industry can be just as effective and important as networking with industry professionals.

The larger your network, the more opportunities you will have to find the job you want. The more people who know what you have to offer and what you want to do, the better. Who do you deal with every day? Who do these people know and deal with? Do any of these people in your network and your extended network know about your dream career working in the computer industry?

★ Words from the Wise

If you are currently employed, never use your company e-mail when contacting another company for a job.

If you aren't employed, and don't have to worry about a current boss or supervisor hearing about your aspirations, then spread the news about your job search. Don't keep it a secret. The more people who know what you're looking for in a career, the more people there are who potentially can let you know when and where there is a job possibility.

If I haven't stressed it enough, if at all possible do not keep your career aspirations to yourself. Share them with the world.

Cold Calls

What exactly is a cold call? In relation to your career, a cold call is an unsolicited contact in person, by phone, letter, or e-mail with someone you don't know in hopes of obtaining some information, an interview, or a job. It is a proactive strategy.

Let's focus on the cold calls you make by phone. They are much like the call we just discussed with the gaming development trade association public relations director.

Many find this form of contact too intimidating to try. Why? Because not only are you calling and trying to sell yourself to someone who may be busy and doesn't want to be bothered, but you are also afraid of rejection. None of us like rejection. We fear that we will get on the phone, try to talk to someone, and they will not take our call, hang up on us, or say no to our requests.

The majority of telemarketing calls made to homes every day are cold calls. In those cases the people on the other end of the phone aren't trying to get a job or an interview. Instead, they are attempting to sell something such as a product or a service. When you get those calls, the first thing on your mind is usually how to get off the phone. The last thing you want to do is buy anything from someone on the other end. But the fact of the matter is that people do buy things from telemarketers if they want what they're selling.

With that in mind, your job in making cold calls is to make your call compelling enough that the person on the other end responds positively. Why would you even bother making a cold call to someone? It's simply another job search strategy and it's one that not everyone attempts, which gives you an edge over others.

How do you make a cold call? It's really quite simple. If you want to make a cold call to a potential employer, you just identify who you want to call, then put together a script to make it easier for you, and then make your call. Keep track of the calls you make. You may think you'll remember who said what and whom you didn't reach, but after a couple of calls it gets confusing. Check out the Cold Call Tracking Worksheet sample below for the type of information you should record. Then use the blank Cold Call Tracking Worksheet provided on the opposite page to track cold calls you make.

Who do you call? That depends on who you're trying to reach. You might call technology companies, corporations, schools, ISPs, consulting firms, headhunters, trade associations, Web design companies, and so on. Every call you make is a potential opportunity that can pan out for you.

Here's an example.

You: Hi, Ms. Rosen. This is Fred Johnston. I'm not sure you're the right person to speak to, but I was hoping I could tell you what I am looking for and perhaps you could point me in the right direction.

Cold Call Tracking Worksheet

Company	Phone Number	Name of Contact	Date Called	Follow-up Activities	Results
BRG Web Design	111-222-2222	Nicki Johnston	5/6	Send resume.	Asked for resume, will get back to me after reviewing my qualifications
Best Internet Service	111-111-1111	Dave Toner	5/9	Send resume.	Will keep resume on file, no current opening. Call back in a few months.
Hills Department Store	111-222-3333	Glen Morris, Director of E-Commerce	5/9	E-mailed resume.	Will review resume and get back to me.
Campo Corporation	111-999-0000	Taylor Thomas	5/11		Call back in two weeks.

Cold Call Tracking Worksheet

Company	Phone Number	Name of Contact	Date Called	Follow-up Activities	Results

Are you in the middle of something now or would it be better if I call back later?

Ms. Rosen: What can I do for you?

You: I was wondering if you know of any opportunities blogging for your company?

★ Voice of Experience

You will find it easier to make cold calls if you not only create a script, but practice it as well. In order to be successful in cold calling you need to sound professional, friendly, and confident.

Ms. Rosen: What exactly do you want to do?

You: I'm interested in doing corporate blogging. You know, to help a company increase their presence on the Web. It's being used more and more for marketing purposes.

Ms. Rosen: We don't have any positions like that here.

You: I understand. I'm trying to get some leads on where to call. Do you have any suggestions? I have my bachelor's degree in communications and

I'm working on getting my master's. I interned at WIWO in the news department for a short time until they moved me into the WIWO-online. I started a blog for the *Janet James Show* and it really took off. Then I started the blog for the entire station.

Ms. Rosen: You worked at with Janet James? I loved that show. It's too bad they cancelled it.

You: I wish they hadn't cancelled it too. It was a really fun job.

Ms. Rosen: You know, you might want to speak to our marketing director. In addition to working here at Great Foods, she is also the president of one of the industry trade associations. She might be able to give you some leads on names.

You: That would be great.

Ms. Rosen: Her name is Lucy Burns. You can reach her at extension 3050. Tell her I suggested you call her. Let me transfer you right now.

You: Thanks for your help. I appreciate it.

As you can see, it's not all that difficult, once you get someone on the phone.

"But what if they say no?" you ask.

So they say no. Don't take it personally. Just go on to your next call and use your previous call as practice.

Where do you find people to call? Browse company Web sites for names. Read trade journals. Read the newspaper. Look for magazine articles and feature stories. Watch television and listen to the radio. Go through the Yellow Pages. You can get names from almost anyplace. Call up. Take a chance. It may pay off.

Depending on where you're calling and the size of the company, in many cases when you

> ⭐ **Tip from the Coach**
> Expect rejection when making cold calls. Some people may not want to talk to you. Rejection is a lot easier to deal with when you decide ahead of time it isn't personally directed toward you.

start your conversation during a cold call, the person you're speaking to will direct you to the human resources (HR) department. If this is the case, ask who you should speak to in HR. Try to get a name. Then, thank the person who gave you the information and call the HR department, asking for the person whose name you were given. Being referred by someone else in the company will often get you through. Try something like this:

You: Good afternoon, would Lucy Burns be in?

Secretary: Who's calling?

You: Fred Johnston. Ms. Rosen suggested I call.

Believe it or not, the more calls you make, the more you will increase your chances of success in getting potential interviews and the job of your dreams.

If you're really uncomfortable making the calls, or you can't get through to the people you're trying to reach by phone, consider writing letters. It takes more time than a phone call, but it is another proactive method for you to potentially get through to someone.

Creating Your Own Career

Do you want one more really good reason to find the hidden job market? If you're creative and savvy enough, you might even be able to create a position for yourself. What does that mean? Here an example.

Let's go back to Fred Johnston. The company he called didn't have a position for a blogger. If he sells the idea, he might just be able to create a position for himself doing what he wants to do.

Can you create your own position? If you are creative, have some initiative, and are aggressive enough to push your idea you can.

What you have to do is come up with something that you could do for a company that isn't being done now or you could do better.

Do you have any ideas? Put fear aside and think outside the box. Get creative. Come up with an idea, develop it fully, put it on paper so you can see any problems, and then fine-tune them. Then call up the company that you want to work with, lay out the idea, and sell them on it. You've just created your own job!

6

TOOLS FOR SUCCESS

The right tools can make it easier to do almost any job. Imagine, for example, trying to paint your house without the right brushes, quality paint, and a good ladder. It could happen, but it would probably be more difficult to do a really good job. Imagine trying to bake a cake without measuring spoons, measuring cups, pans, and a good working oven. You might be able to do it, but your chances of success are diminished.

Obtaining jobs and creating a wonderful career is a project in itself. Tools can make it easier. Every trade has its own set of tools that help the tradesman (or woman) achieve success—tools which, if unavailable, would make their job more difficult, if not impossible, to accomplish.

Whatever area of the computer industry you are pursuing there are certain tools that can help you achieve success faster as well. These may include things like your resume, CV, business and networking cards, brochures, career portfolio, and professional reference sheets, among others. This chapter will help get you started putting together these tools.

Your Resume as a Selling Tool

Whether utilizing publicity, ads in newspapers or magazines, television or radio commercials, billboards, banners on the Web, or a variety of additional marketing vehicles there is virtually no successful company that does not advertise or market their products or services in some manner.

Why do they do this? The main reason is to make sure others are aware of their product or service so they can then find ways to entice potential customers to buy or use that product or service.

What does this have to do with you and your career? When trying to succeed in any career, it is a good idea to look at yourself as a product.

What this means in a broad sense is that you will be marketing yourself so people know you exist, so they begin to differentiate you from others, and so they see you in a better light.

How can you entice potential employers to hire you? How can you help people in the industry to know you exist?

The answer is simple. Start by making your resume a selling tool! Make it your own personal printed marketing piece. Everyone sends out resumes. The trick is making yours so powerful that it will grab the attention of potential employers.

Resumes are important no matter what area of the computer field you are pursuing. Does your resume do a great job selling your creden-

Tip from the Coach

Your resume will be useful at every level of your career. It is not a "do it once, get a job, and never need it again" document.

Words from the Wise

If you're using different versions of resumes, make sure you know which one you send to which company. Keep a copy of the resume you use for a specific job with a copy of the cover letter you send. Do it every time. Otherwise when sending out numerous resumes and letters it's very easy to get confused.

tials? Does it showcase your skills, personality traits, and special talents? Is your resume the one that is going to impress the employers or human resources directors who can call you in for that all important interview and ultimately land you the job you are after? Is it going to land you the job you've been dreaming about?

If an employer doesn't know you, their first impression of you might very well be from your resume. This makes your resume a crucial part of getting an interview that might ultimately lead to your dream job.

A strong resume illustrates that you have the experience and qualifications to fill a potential employer's needs. How can you do this? To begin with, learn to tailor your resume to the job you're pursuing. One of the biggest mistakes people make in job hunting is to create just one resume and then use it every single time they apply for a position, no matter what the job.

If this is what you've been doing, it's time to break the habit. Begin by crafting your main resume. Then edit it to fit the needs of each specific job opening or opportunity for which you are applying.

"But," you say, "Let's say I want to work in technical customer support. Can't I use the same resume for every technical customer support job I apply for?"

Here's the answer in a nutshell. You can use the same resume only if you are going for the exact same type of job. For example, you might use the same resume if you are applying for two

jobs as technical customer support technician in two similar types of ISPs.

However, if you are applying for one job as technical customer support technician in an ISP dealing with residential customers and another as a technical customer support technician for business customers, you might want to tailor your resume to each job, highlighting any skills and experiences relevant to each position.

Before computers became commonplace, preparing a different resume for every job was far more difficult. In many cases, people would prepare one resume and then have it professionally printed by a resume service or printer. That was it. If you wanted to change your resume, you had to go back to the printer and have it done again, incurring a major expense.

Today, however, most of us have access to computers, making it far easier to change

Tip from the Top

When replying to a job advertisement, use words from the advertisement in both your resume and your cover letter. It makes you look like more of a fit with the company's expectations.

resumes at will. Do you want to change your career objective? What about the order of the components on your resume? Do you want to add something? Do you want to delete something? You are in control. You can create the perfect resume every time with the click of a mouse.

Always keep a copy of each resume on your computer and make sure you note the date it was done and its main focus. For example, you might save your resumes as "Director of Web site Marketing_Retail resume Nov 9"; "Director of Web site Marketing_University resume Nov 9"; and so on.

How can you make your resume a better marketing tool? Present the information in a clear, concise manner, highlighting your best assets. Organize things in an order that makes it easy for someone just glancing at your resume to see the points that sell you best and will make the person want to take a second look.

⭐ Tip from the Top

Always keep updated copies of your resume on a CD or a flash drive. You can never tell when your computer hard drive will die just at the time someone tells you about a great opportunity or you see an advertisement for the perfect job. If your resume is on a CD or other media, you simply need to just put it in another computer, tailor your resume for that particular job, and send it off. You can also toss a CD or a USB flash drive in your briefcase or bag to keep with you if you are away from home and want to add something to your resume quickly. Adding a handwritten line when you change your phone number or address or even whiting-out the wrong information just is not acceptable.

The decision about the sequence of items in your resume should be based on what is most impressive in relation to the position you are pursuing. Do you have a lot of work experience? Put that information first. Are your accomplishments extraordinary? If so, highlight those first. Do you have little experience, but you just graduated cum laude with a degree in computer science? Then perhaps your education should be where your resume should start.

Sometimes it helps when creating your own resume to imagine that you just received it in the mail yourself. What would make you glance at it and say, "Wow"? Would you continue reading or would you glance at it and hope that there was a more interesting resume coming in?

One of the most important things to remember is that there really is no right or wrong type of resume. The right one for you will end up being the one that ultimately gets you the position you want. There are so many ways to prepare your resume that it is often difficult to choose one. My advice is to craft a couple different ones, put them away overnight, and then look at them the next day. Which one looks better to you? That probably will be the style you want to use.

Here are some tips that might help:

◎ Tailor each resume for every position.
◎ Make sure you check for incorrect word usage. No matter what position you're pursuing, most employers prefer to have someone who has a command of the English language. Check to make sure you haven't inadvertently used the word "their" for "there," "to" for "too" or "two," "effect" for "affect," "you're" for "your," "it's" for "its," and so on.

◎ Don't rely solely on your computer's spell and grammar checker. Carefully go over your work yourself as well.

◎ Every time you edit your resume or make a change, check carefully for errors.

◎ It is very easy to miss a double word, a misspelled word, or a wrong tense. Have a friend or family member look over your resume. It is often difficult to see mistakes in your own work.

◎ As tempting as it is to use different colored inks when preparing your resume, don't. Use only black ink.

◎ Use a good quality paper—at least 40-pound weight—for printing your resumes. Paper with texture often feels different, so it stands out. While you can use white, beige, or cream colored papers, soft light colors such as light blue, salmon pink, gray, or light green will help your resume stand out from the hundreds of white and beige ones.

◎ Make sure your resume layout looks attractive. You can have the greatest content in the world, but if your resume just doesn't look right, people may not actually read it.

◎ You know the saying, "You can't judge a book by its cover"? Well, you really can't, but if you don't know anything about the book or its contents you just might not pick it up unless the cover looks interesting.

◎ When sending your resume and cover letter, instead of using a standard, number-10 business envelope and folding your resume to fit in it, use a large manila envelope. That way you won't have to fold your resume, and your information gets there looking clean, crisp, and flat. This is especially important if you are sending a scannable resume.

◎ Don't use odd fonts or typefaces. Why? In many large companies, resumes are scanned. Certain fonts don't scan well. What should you use? Helvetica, Times, Arial, and Courier work well.

◎ Many fonts don't translate well when e-mailing. What looks great on the resume on your computer may end up looking like gibberish at the recipient's end—and you probably will never know. Use Helvetica, Times, Arial, or Courier.

◎ If you are e-mailing your resume, you also want to make sure it looks as pleasing to the recipient as does is when you look at it. E-mail your resume to yourself to see how it looks.

◎ When preparing your resume, make your name larger and bolder than the rest of the text. For example, if your resume is done in 12-point type, use 14-, 16-, or 18-point type for your name. Your name will stand out from those on other resumes.

◎ Remember to utilize white space effectively. Margins should be at least one inch on each side as well as on the top and bottom of each page. White space also helps draw the reader's attention to information.

★ Words from the Wise

No matter what color paper you use for your resume and cover letters, make sure they photocopy well. Some colored papers photocopy dark or look messy. Even if you aren't photocopying your resume, a potential employer might.

Resume Formats

You should be aware that there are a number of different formats for preparing your resume, depending on how you are using it. These include:

◎ *Printed resume:* Your printed resume is the traditional resume you would prepare when you are going to print it out and send it or bring it to a potential employer or recruiter or bring it with you to an interview. It is generally attractively formatted and may contain bulleted lists and highlighted words. No matter what other type of resume you use, you always need to have a printed resume ready.

◎ *Scannable resume:* A scannable resume is one that can be scanned into a company's computer as an image and stored electronically. With the help of OCR (optical character recognition) software, the text of the resume can then be read and searched by keywords. These keywords are helpful when employers are looking for employees with certain skill sets. Your scannable resume will not be as graphically attractive as your traditional, printed resume because visuals like bold and italicized fonts, increased font sizes, borders, and bullets may confuse the OCR software reading your resume. In a scannable resume, you will be using spacing to separate categories and sections. Instead of bullets, you generally can use asterisks.

▫ Keywords, like categories such as education, experience, and so on, in your scannable resume will be in a separate section. Keywords are the words that can help get your resume pulled for review. These words illustrate that you have the relevant skills for the specific job the employer is looking to fill. The more keywords you have that match those the reviewer is looking for, the better the likelihood your resume will be one that is chosen to be reviewed by a human being.

▫ In the keyword summary section, place your skills, traits, and areas in which you are knowledgeable. These might include:

◇ General transferable skills such as leadership, communications skills, writing skills, negotiating skills, organization skills, decision making, and so on.

◇ Industry-specific skills such as customer support, marketing, computer repair, database management, Web design, programming skills, systems analysis, market research, new product launch, application prototyping, help desk support, and so on.

◇ Business or organization buzz words such as consensus building, corporate administration, profit improvement, profit and loss responsibility, strategic planning, profit improvement, and so on.

◇ Specific software applications and programming languages in which you are competent such as C ++, Flash, Java, XHTML, TCP/IP, IntranetWare, Windows NT Server 4.0, Microsoft Excel, CAAT, so on.

◇ Traits that employers might be looking for such as strong ethics, team player, motivated, achievement oriented, etc.

◇ Education, certification, or credentials employers might be looking for such as B.S. in computer science, certified network administrator, Microsoft certified systems engineer, Novell certified engineer, and so on.

▫ Specific job titles such as software engineer, systems analyst, database manager, marketing manager, etc.

▫ Use nouns and phrases in your keyword summary instead of action verbs when you can. Instead of "designed Web sites" for example, say "Web site designer." Use action verbs throughout the rest of your resume.

▫ Some people list their keywords in the keyword summary separating each word with a comma or a period. Others integrate their keywords into a career summary statement. The choice is yours.

▫ Just because you use your keywords in a summary at the beginning of your resume doesn't mean you can't elaborate and use the words (with action verbs) in the body of your resume as well.

▫ Print your scannable resume on white paper. Use a laser printer if possible. If your resume is more than one page, print each page on a separate sheet. Make sure your name is the first thing on top of each page.

▫ If you are including more than one phone number, such as your home phone and cell, put each on a separate line.

The Inside Scoop
In order to increase the chances of your scannable resume having keywords necessary for a specific job, check out keywords that appear in similar job descriptions and use those keywords to describe your qualifications.

◎ *E-mail resume:* If you choose to e-mail your resume you may send it as an attachment or paste it into the body of your e-mail. The difference is that when you e-mail it as an attachment, your recipient will receive it with all the formatting intact, meaning you can still have a graphically pleasing resume. When you paste your resume into the body of the text, you will generally lose all the formatting, because you will be using plain text.

◎ *Electronic resumes:* Electronic resumes are used in a number of different situations. They are done in plain text, which is often referred to as text only or ASCII text. Using plain text means that you won't have the ability to highlight text or do any attractive formatting. The plain text version of your resume can be used in a number of ways.

▫ You may use it by copying and pasting it into the body of an e-mail.

▫ You might use it to copy and paste into online forms provided by online resume posting sites or when applying to specific jobs online.

▫ You may use it to post directly into online resume databases.

▫ Depending on the situation, you might also need an e-mail version of your resume that is also a text-only document.

- ▢ You can easily prepare your resume in text only format by making a copy of your resume in a word processing program such as Microsoft Word and then saving it as plain text or text only. Be aware that you will lose the formatting, which is what your goal is at this point.
- ▢ Be sure to go over your resume and make all lines flush left. Take out any extra spaces.
- ▢ You will probably notice that bullets you have may have changed to asterisks or dashes. That is okay too.
- ▢ Send your plain text resume to yourself to make sure it looks good before sending it to a potential employer or posting it online.

◎ *Web-based resume:* A Web-based resume is an HTML version of your resume. It is done as a Web page. It can be simple or elaborate. Why would you need a Web-based resume? There are a number of reasons. Basically, it is easy to access. If you are speaking to a potential employer, you need to merely point him or her to your Web resume. A potential employer might also happen to find your resume when surfing the Internet. One

---

The Inside Scoop

In order to have a Web-based resume, you need to have access to Web space. If you surf the Internet you can often find sites which will let you post your resume free of charge. Many colleges and ISPs also offer free Web space for hosting a personal page.

Tip from the Top

Always bring a copy of your printed resume when you are going on an interview.

---

of the really good reasons to have a Web based resume is because it gives you the ability to link to samples of your work. While this is helpful in any industry, it can be extremely helpful in the computer industry.

Redefining Your Resume

You probably already have a resume in some form. How has it been working? Is it getting you the interviews you want? If it is, great. If not, you might want to consider redefining it.

You want your resume to stand out. You want it to illustrate that you are successful in your past accomplishments. You want potential employers to look at your resume and say to themselves, "That's who I want working here!"

How do you do that? Make your resume compelling. Demonstrate through your resume that you believe in yourself, because if you don't believe in you, no one else will, either. Show that you have the ability to solve problems and bring fresh ideas to the table.

First, decide how you want to present yourself. What type of resume is best for you? There are a couple of basic types of resumes. The chronological resume lists your jobs and accomplishments, beginning with the most current and going backward. Functional resumes, which may also be referred to as skills-based resumes, emphasize your accomplishments and abilities. One of the good things about this type of resume is that it allows you to lay it out in a manner that spotlight your key areas, whether they be your qualifications, skills, or employment history.

What's the best type of resume for you? That depends on a number of factors, including where and what level you are in your career. If you are just entering the job market and you haven't held down a lot of jobs, but you have relevant experience through internships and/or volunteer activities, you might use the functional type. If, on the other hand, you have held a number of jobs in the field and climbed the ladder with each new job, you might want to use the chronological variety. You can also sometimes combine elements from both types. This is called a combination resume. As I noted earlier, there is no one right way. You have to look at the whole picture and make a decision.

Use common sense. Make sure your best assets are prominent on your resume. Do you have a lot of experience? Are your accomplishments above the bar? Did you graduate cum laude? Do you have a master's degree? Do you have a Ph.D.? Have you won awards in the industry? Determine what would grab your eye and find a way to focus first on that.

What Should Your Resume Contain?

What should you include in your resume? Some components are required and some are optional. Let's look at some of them.

What do you definitely need? You absolutely need your name, address, phone number, and e-mail address. You also should have your education, and any training, as well as your professional or work experience. You want to include your work accomplishments and responsibilities so potential employers know what you have done and what you can bring to the table. What else? You should include certifications, licenses, professional affiliations and memberships, honors, awards, and any additional professional accomplishments.

What else might you want to put in your resume? Your career objective, a summary of skills, and a career summary.

What should you not put in your resume? Your age, marital status, any health problems, current or past salaries, and whether or not you have children. What else should you not include? Any weakness you have or think you have.

Career Summary

Let's take a moment to discuss your career summary. While a career summary isn't a required component, it often is helpful when an employer gets huge numbers of resumes and gives each a short glance. A career summary is a short professional biography no longer than 12 lines that tells your professional story. You can do it in a number of ways. Here's an example:

Seasoned, creative Web designer with over 10 years of experience in creating award-winning Web sites. Have designed high impact, innovative Web sites for a variety of clients in both the corporate world and the entertainment industry, including pharmaceutical companies, financial institutions, film studios, entertainment television shows, and record labels. Ability to effectively work with project managers, programmers, and information architects creating attention grabbing, innovative Web sites. Track record of completing projects on time and under budget. Certification in Web Design/Computer Graphics. Competent in Adobe Illustrator, PhotoShop, QuarkXPress, and Microsoft Front Page. Excellent communication and problem-solving skills. 2008 president of Some State Web Designers Association.

A potential employer looking at this might think, "This Jean Nester is certified in Web design and computer graphics. She is competent in various programs. She has won awards for her Web sites. She seems to have the ability to get along with others and has good communications skills. She looks fairly motivated. Why don't I give her a chance to tell me more and bring her in for an interview?"

"What if I just got out of school and don't have a lot of experience? What would my career summary look like?" you ask.

In situations like this you have to look toward experience and jobs you held prior to graduating. How about this:

Recent graduate of State University with major in computer science. (4.0 GPA.) Member of State University, IT-Club. Taught noncredit courses to seniors on Creating Personal Web sites and Blogging For Fun. Created database program for University Bookstore to help track sales. Customer support tech for ICS Internet Service.

If you prefer, you can use a bulleted list to do your career summary.

◎ Motivated network administrator with eight years of experience
◎ Proficient in design, integration, and management of multi-tiered databases
◎ Expert in WAN and LAN networks and network protocols
◎ Excellent problem-solving and troubleshooting skills
◎ Detail oriented
◎ Proven project manager
◎ Ability to bring projects in on time and under budget

Career Objective

Do you need a career objective in your resume? It isn't always necessary, but in certain cases it helps. For example, if you are just starting out in your career, having a career objective or a specific goal illustrates that you have some direction. It illustrates that you know where you want to go in your career.

When replying to an advertisement for a job opening, make sure your career objective on your resume is as close to the job you are applying for as possible. For example, if you are applying for a job as a Web content developer for a health information site for women, you might make your career objective, "To work in a situation combining my passion for providing helpful health information to women with my love of researching, writing, and graphic arts."

If, on the other hand, you are sending your resume to a company "cold," or not for a specific job opening, don't limit yourself unnecessarily by stating a specific career objective. If you use a career objective in this type of situation, make sure it is general.

In many instances, you might send copies of your resume with a cover letter to companies you want to work for that aren't actively looking to fill a job. Your hope is to garner an interview. If your resume indicates one specific career goal, you might be overlooked for another position. In cases such as this, try to make your career objective (if you use one) more general. Remember, you want the person reviewing your resume to think of all the possible places you might fit in the organization.

Education

Where should you put education on your resume? That depends. If you recently graduated from college, put it toward the top. If you graduated a number of years ago, put your education toward the end of your resume. Do you need to put the year you graduated? Recent graduates might want to. Otherwise, just indicate the college or university you graduated from, your major, and degree.

"What if I went to college, but didn't graduate? What should I put on my resume?" you might ask.

If you went to college but didn't graduate, simply write that you attended or took coursework toward a degree. Will anyone question you on it? That's hard to say. Someone might. If questioned, simply say something like, "I attended college and then, unfortunately, found it necessary to go to work full time. I plan on getting my degree as soon as possible. I only have nine credits left to go, so it will be an easy goal to complete."

Similarly, if a job requires a graduate degree and you are working toward one but haven't completed the educational requirements, simply put down that you are taking the coursework toward your degree.

In addition to your college education, you also want to include any certification courses or seminars you have taken. Don't forget to include any relevant noncredit courses, seminars, and workshops you have attended as well. While you probably wouldn't want to include classes like flower arranging (unless this has to do with your job in some way), you might include educational courses that are not industry oriented, but might help you in your career, such as public speaking, writing, grant writing, communications, or team work.

Professional and Work Experience

List your work experience in this section of your resume. What jobs have you had? Where did you work? What did you do? What were your accomplishments?

How far back do you go? That once again depends on where you are in your career. Don't go back to your job as a babysitter when you were 15, but you need to show your work history.

In addition to your full-time jobs in or out of the area of the industry in which you are seeking employment, include any part-time work that relates to the segment of the industry you are pursuing as well as any jobs that illustrate skills, accomplishments, or achievements.

Skills and Personality Traits

There's an old advertising adage that says something to the effect of, "Don't sell the steak, sell the sizzle." When selling yourself through your resume, do the same. Do not only state your skills and personality traits—make them sizzle! Do this by using descriptive language and key phrases.

Need some help? Here are a few words and phrases to get you started.

◎ Creative
◎ Dedicated

◎ Hardworking
◎ Highly motivated
◎ Energetic
◎ Self-starter
◎ Fully knowledgeable
◎ Strong work ethic
◎ Team player
◎ Problem solver

Tip from the Coach
When writing about your accomplishments, use action words to illustrate your experience—words like *achieved*, *accomplished*, *demonstrated*, *inspired*, *motivated*, and *supervised*.

Accomplishments and Achievements

What have you accomplished in your career in or out of technology or the computer industry? Have you been recognized as a team leader? Have you increased Web traffic to a company site? Have you developed a new innovative method of social networking?

Have you increased software sales? Have you garnered nationwide publicity for your company? Have you written a weekly technology column? Have you won an industry award? Have you written an acclaimed article on some aspect technology or computers? Have you developed a software program that can guard against identity theft?

Have you implemented an innovative program? Have you successfully supervised other team members? Did you develop a program that resulted in a patent? Have you been asked to present a paper at a conference?

Have you started a blog that has taken off? Have you volunteered to teach senior citizens basic computer skills? Have you increased E-commerce sales? Have you developed a new application? Have you developed a game that was purchased by one of the leading gaming manufacturers?

Your achievements inform potential employers not only about what you have done, but also about what you might do for them.

Sit down and think about it for a while. What are you most proud of in your career?

What have you done that has made a difference or had a positive impact on the company for which you worked? If you are new to the work force, what did you do in school? What about in a volunteer capacity?

Just as you made your skills and personality traits sizzle with words, you want to do the same thing with your accomplishments and achievements. Put yourself in the position of a human resources director or the owner of a company for a moment. You get two resumes. Under the accomplishments section one says, "Created e-commerce Web site." The other says, "Developed a new, innovative e-commerce Web site for women's clothing retail outlet. Increased bottom line sales by 78 percent within one year. Within two years site was voted one of the top 10 retail sites by online customers."

Which resume would catch your eye?

You can help your accomplishments and achievements sizzle by using action verbs to describe them. Use words like *achieved*, *administered*, *applied*, *accomplished*, *assisted*, *strengthened*, *managed*, and others.

Honors and Achievements

When drafting your resume, include any honors you have received, whether or not they have anything to do with the area of the computer industry you are pursuing. Honors help set you apart from other candidates. Did one of your newspaper articles win a journalism award? Did you run for your local library board of directors and win the seat? Were you honored with the "Volunteer of the Year" award at a local hospital? How about the community service award from your local civic group. While these accomplishments might have nothing to do with the computer industry, they do show that you are a hard worker and good at what you do.

Community Service and Volunteer Activities

If you perform community service or volunteer activities on a regular basis, include it on your resume. Community service and volunteer activities you perform illustrate to potential employers that you "do a little extra." Additionally, you can never predict when the person reviewing your resume might be a member of the organization with which you volunteer. An unexpected connection like that can help you stand out in a positive way. Additionally, illustrating that you are involved in the not-for-profit world may be a plus to potential employers.

Hobbies and Interests

What are your hobbies and interests? Do you collect old baseball cards? Do you have a collection of vintage baseball bats? Do you collect cookbooks? Do you collect NASCAR memorabilia? Are you a hiker? Do you volunteer with a literacy program? Are you a CASA volunteer? Are you involved in pet rescue? While many career counselors feel that hobbies or personal interests have no place on a professional resume, I disagree.

Why? Here's a secret. You can never tell what will cause the person or persons reviewing the resumes to make a connection. Perhaps he or she has the same hobby as you. Perhaps he or she is a volunteer with a literacy program

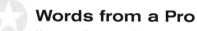

Words from a Pro

If you are instructed to send references with your resume, attach them on a separate sheet of paper with your cover letter.

in which you participate. Anything that causes you to stand out in a positive manner or that causes a connection with your potential interviewer will help your resume garner attention, helping you to land an interview.

You should be aware that there are some exceptions to including hobbies and interests on your resume. You don't want to include these things on resumes you are sending to recruiters or headhunters. You probably also don't want to include them on resumes you post online or on Web based resumes.

References

The goal for your resume is to have it help you obtain an interview. If you list your references on your resume, be aware that someone may check them to help them decide if they should interview you. You don't really want people giving their opinions about you until you have the chance to sell yourself. With this in mind, it usually isn't a good idea to list your references on your resume.

If you are uncomfortable with this, include a line on your resume stating, "references are available upon request."

Your Resume Writing Style

How important is writing style in your resume? Very important. Aside from conveying your message, your writing style helps to illustrate that you have written communication skills.

When preparing your resume, write clearly and concisely and do not use the pronoun "I"

> ### ★ Tip from the Coach
>
> Don't stress if you can't fit your resume on one or two pages. While most career specialists insist a resume should only be one or two pages at most, I strongly disagree. You don't want to overwhelm a potential employer with a 10-page book, but if your resume needs to be three or four pages to get your pertinent information in, that's okay. Keep in mind, though, that lengthy resumes or CVs (curriculum vitae) are generally used by high-level professionals with many years of experience and work history to fill the additional pages. If your resume is longer than normal, you should use a brief career summary at the beginning so a hiring manager can quickly see what your major accomplishments are. If they then want to take their time to look through the rest of the resume, your information will be there.

to describe your accomplishments. Instead of writing, "I conducted an IT department budget assessment. I found a way to save $300,000," try, "Conducted an IT department budget assessment saving the company $300,000 over a two year period." Note the inclusion of a time period. It's good to be specific about your achievements.

Instead of, "I implemented an online merchandising effort that increased sales," try, "Implemented an online merchandising effort that increased sales over 30 percent within one year."

Creating Industry-Specific Resumes

How can you create resumes specific to the area of the industry you are pursuing? Once you've created your basic resume, tailor each for the specific position or area you are pursuing, and find ways to relate your existing skills to that resume.

Use all your experiences, talents, and skills to help you obtain the career you want. Transfer skills and experience when you can.

One thing you should never do is lie on your resume. Don't lie about your education. Don't lie about your work experience. Don't lie about places you've worked. Don't lie about what you've done. If you haven't picked up on it yet, *do not lie*. Once someone knows you have lied, that is what they will remember about you and they may pass on that information to others.

"Oh, no one is going to find out," you might say.

Don't bet on it. Someone might find out by chance, deduce the truth based on knowledge within the industry, or hear the facts from a co-worker or industry colleague. Someone, just by chance, may be surfing the Internet and see your name. When the truth comes out, it can blow up in your face.

"By that time, I'll be doing such a good job, no one will fire me," you say.

That's the best-case scenario and there's a chance that could happen, but think about this. Once someone lies to you, do you ever trust that person again? Probably not, and no one will trust you or anything you say, either. That will hurt your chances of climbing the career ladder. The worst-case scenario is that you will be fired, left without references, lose some of your contacts, and make it much more difficult to find your next job.

If you don't have the experience you wish you had, try to impress the human resources director, hiring manager, or recruiter with other parts of your resume and your cover letter. If you have the experience and you are trying to advance your career, this is the time to redefine your resume. Add action verbs. Add your accomplishments. Make your new resume shine. Create a marketing piece that will make someone say, "We need to interview this person. Look at everything he has done."

When creating your resume, you want it to reflect your knowledge of the industry. Be sure your resume shows evidence of skills, experience, productivity, and your personal commitment to the area of the industry you are pursuing.

Your CV—Curriculum Vitae

What exactly is a CV or curriculum vitae? What's the difference between a CV and a resume? That depends who you ask. Some people use the words interchangeably. Some say a resume is a one- or two-page summary of your employment history, experience, and education and a CV is a longer, more comprehensive, detailed synopsis of your qualifications, education, and experience. So what's the answer?

Generally, it's somewhere in between. Your resume is a summary of your employment history and education that highlights your skills, talents, and education. Your CV would be a longer, detailed synopsis of these things plus teaching and research experience you might have, articles or papers you have published, research projects you have done, presentations

---

Tip from the Coach

One of the mistakes that many people make when preparing their resume is that they keep adding accomplishments without deleting any of the earlier or less important ones. While it's very tempting to do this, it's not always the best idea.

---

you have made, and so on. The CV gives you the opportunity to list every paper, project, presentation, etc.

How do you know which type of document to use? Generally, it depends on the type of job for which you are applying. You will often use your CV instead of a resume if you are applying for a job in corporate administration or research, among other things.

What About References?

References are another of your selling tools. Basically, references are the individuals who will vouch for your skills, ethics, and work history when a potential employer calls. A good reference can set you apart from the crowd and give you the edge over other applicants. A bad one can seriously hinder your career goals.

It's always a good idea to bring the names, addresses, and phone numbers of the people you are using for references with you when you apply for a job or when you are going on an

---

Words from the Wise

As people often use the words CV and resume interchangeably, don't assume that just because someone asks you for your CV, that they actually want that particular document. They might really want your resume.

The Inside Scoop

Instead of just making your resume an outline of your accomplishments, make it a powerful marketing tool.

interview. If you're asked to list them on an employment application, you'll be prepared.

Who should you use for references? To begin with, you'll need professional references. These are people you've worked with or who know you on a professional level. They might be current or former supervisors, bosses or project managers, the director of a not-for-profit organization you've worked with, internship program coordinators, former professors, satisfied clients, and so on.

Do your references have to be from the computer industry? If you have references within the industry, it can't hurt. What you are looking for, however, are people you can count on to help sell you to potential employers. Those will be your best references.

Always ask people if they are willing to be a reference before you use them. Only use people you are absolutely certain will say good things about you. Additionally, when searching out your references, try to find people who are articulate and professional.

Who would be a bad reference? A boss who fired you, a supervisor you didn't get along with, or anyone who you had any kind of problem with, whatsoever. Do not use these people for references, even if they tell you that they'll give

---

The Inside Scoop

If you give your references an idea of exactly what type of job you're pursuing, what skills are important in that position, or even what you want them to say, you stand a better chance of them leading the conversation in the direction you want it to go. You might tell a reference, for example, that you're applying for a position as an online content editor for a large Web site that sells toys. The job description calls for someone who has excellent written communication skills, is highly creative, organized, and has the ability to multitask. In most cases, when your reference gets a call, he or she will remember what you said and stress your important selling points, including not forgetting that you have a degree in early childhood education.

---

you a good one. They might keep their word, but they might not, and you won't know until it's too late.

"What if I didn't get along with my supervisor?" you ask. "Isn't a potential employer going to call her anyway?"

You are right. Your potential employer probably will call your former supervisor. The trick is getting a list of three to five good references. That way, no matter what anyone else says, you still look good.

You might be asked to list references on an employment application, but it's a good idea to prepare a printed sheet of your professional references that you can leave with the interviewer. Basically, this sheet will contain your list of three to five references, including their names, positions, and contact information. As with your resume, make sure it is printed on good-quality paper.

Here's an example to get you started.

Tip from the Coach

In some cases, employers might ask for personal references as well as professional references. These are people such as family, friends, or neighbors who know you well. Be sure to have a list of three to five personal references as well as their contact information readily available in case you need it.

PROFESSIONAL REFERENCE SHEET FOR LAURA SEGAL

Mr. James Evans
CIO
Tri-County Bank Corporation
131 Broadway
Anytown, NY 11111
(111) 555-5555
evansj@tri-countybans.com

Mr. George Malick
Intern Supervisor
SPA Software
251 Route 9W
Anytown, NY 11111
(111) 222-3222
malickg@spasoftware.com

Professor Clifford Brown
Department Head,
    Computer Science & Technolgy
Some City University
Some City, NY 12222
(222) 444-5555
cliffbrown@somecityu.edu

Ms. Claire James
Sunset Computer Graphics, Inc.
132 Sunset Road
Anytown, NY 11111
(111) 333-3333
clairj@sunsetcg.net

Personal References

In addition to professional references, you might also be asked to provide personal references. These are friends, family members, or others who know you. You probably won't need to print out a reference sheet for your personal references, but make sure you have all their contact information in case you need it quickly.

As with professional references, make sure the people you are using know you are listing them as references. Give them a call when you're going on an interview to let them know someone might be contacting them. Ask them to let you know if they get a call.

Letters of Recommendation

As you go through your career, it's a good idea to get letters of recommendation from people who have been impressed with your work. Along with references, these help give potential employers a better sense of your worth. How do you get a letter of recommendation? You usually simply have to ask. For example, let's say you are close to completing an internship.

Say to your supervisor, "I've enjoyed my time here. Would it be possible to get a letter of recommendation from you for my files?"

Most people will be glad to provide this. In some cases, people might even ask you to write it yourself for them to sign. Don't forego these opportunities, even if you feel embarrassed about blowing your own horn. The easiest way to do it is by trying to imagine you aren't writing about yourself. In that way you can be honest and write a great letter. Give it to the person and say, "Here's the letter we discussed. Let me know if you want anything changed or you aren't comfortable with any piece of it." Nine times out of ten, the person will just sign the letter as is.

Who should you ask for letters of recommendation? In many cases, people will be the same ones you ask to be your reference. If you are still in school or close to graduating, you might ask professors with whom you have developed a good relationship. Don't forget internship coordinators or supervisors, former and current employers, executive directors of not-for-profit, civic, or charity organizations you have volunteered with, and so on.

In some situations the people you ask may just write generic letters of recommendation stating that you were a pleasure to work with, or were good at your job. If the person writing the letter knows the type of position you're pursuing, he or she might gear the letter to specific skills, traits, and talents needed.

Your letters of recommendation will become another powerful marketing tool in your quest to career success in the computer industry. What do you do with them? Begin by photocopying each letter you receive on high-quality, white paper, making sure you get clean copies. Once that's done you can make them part of your career portfolio, send them with your resume when applying for position, or bring them with you to interviews.

Creating Captivating Cover Letters

Unless instructed otherwise by a potential employer or in an advertisement, always send your resume with a cover letter. Why? Mainly because if your resume grabs the eye of someone in the position to interview you, he or she often looks at the cover letter to evaluate your written communications skills as well as to get a sense of your personal side. If your letter is a good one, it might just get you the phone call you've been waiting for. On the other hand, a poorly written letter might just keep you from getting that call.

What can make your letter stand out? Try to make sure your letter is directed to the name of the person to whom you are sending it instead of "Hiring Manager," "Director of Human Resources," "To Whom It May Concern," or "Sir or Madam."

"But, the name of the person isn't in the ad," you say, "how do I know what it is?"

You might not always be able to get the correct name, but at least do some research. You might, for example, call the company advertising the opening and ask the name of the person to which responses should be directed.

If you are sending your resume to a company cold, it's even more important to send it to a specific person. It gives you a better shot at someone not only reviewing it, but taking action on it.

It's okay to call the company and say to the receptionist or secretary, "Hi, I was wondering if you could give me some information? I'm trying to send my resume to someone at your company and I'm not sure who to send it to. Could you please give me the name of the human resources director (or whoever you are trying to target)?"

If he or she won't give the name to you for some reason, say thank you and hang up. While organizations generally will freely give out this type of information, there may be some companies that, for various reasons, will not give out names easily.

How do you get around this? Wait until lunchtime or around 5:15 p.m. when the person you spoke to might be at lunch or done with their workday, call back and say something to the effect of, "Hi, I was wondering if you could please give me the spelling of your HR director's name?"

If the person on the other end of the phone asks you to be more specific about the name simply say, "Let's see I think it was Brownson or something like that. It sounded like Brown something."

Don't worry about sounding stupid on the phone. The person at the other end doesn't know you. This system usually works. Believe it not, most companies have someone working there whose name sounds like Brown or Smith.

The person on the phone may say to you, "No, we don't have a Brownson. What department are you looking for? It was HR wasn't it?"

When you say yes, he or she will probably say, "Oh, that's not Brownson, it's John Campbell. Is that who you're looking for?"

Then all you have to say is, "You know what, you're right, sorry, I was looking at the wrong notes. So that's C-A-M-P-B-E-L-L?"

Voila! You have the name. Is it a lot of effort? Well, it's a little effort, but if it gets you the name of someone you need and ultimately helps get you an interview, isn't it worth it?

By the way, this technique not only works for getting names you need, but other information as well. You might have to be persistent and it might take you a few tries, but it generally always gets you the information you need.

You also can sometimes get names from the Internet. Perhaps the company Web site lists the names of their key people. Key names for large companies may also often be located on Hoovers.com, an online database of information about businesses. While the site is a paid service, many of the key names you may need are available free of charge.

Do what you can to get the names you need. It can make a big difference when you direct your letters to someone specific within the company.

No matter which segment of the computer industry in which you are trying to locate a job, those who are in the position to hire you may be receiving a large number of resumes, letters,

and phone calls. What can help your cover letters stand out? Make them grab the attention of the reader. How? Make sure your cover letters are creative.

Take some time and think about it. What would make you keep reading? Of course, there will be situations where you might be better off sending the traditional "In response to your ad letter." But what about trying out a couple of other ideas?

Take a look at the first sample cover letter. Would this letter grab your attention? Would it make you keep reading? Chances are it would. After grabbing the reader's attention, it quickly offers some of the applicant's skills, talents, and achievements. Would you bring in Charles Summers for an interview? I think most employers would.

CHARLES SUMMERS
111 North Street
Different Town, NY 22222
Phone: 111-999-9999
charless@moreinernet.com

Ms. Clara Toomey
Human Resources Manager
Compton University
Some City, NY 11111

Dear Ms. Toney:
Congratulations!
I'm pleased to inform you that you have just received the resume that can end your search for Best Department Store's new corporate online-marketing director. In order to claim your "prize," please review my resume and call as soon as possible to arrange an interview. I can guarantee you'll be pleased you did!

As the assistant director of marketing at JG Fashions, I helped coordinate the marketing activities for a year before being promoted to the position of full-fledged marketing director. During my two-year tenure in this position, I developed and implemented a variety of new local and regional advertising campaigns as well as a number of innovative promotional programs designed to enhance awareness our new Web site. With the help of these programs our sales increased 43 percent in Web sales alone!

In this position I additionally developed a number of strategic partnerships, generating large amounts of media attention for all entities involved in the news and online.

While I love what I do now, my dream and passion has been a career marketing the Web site of a large, prestigious department store.

I welcome the challenge and opportunity to work with Best Department Stores and believe my experience, skills, talents, and passion would be an asset to your company.

I look forward to hearing from you.

Sincerely yours,
Mark Hilton

While a creative cover letter may grab the attention of the reader, sometimes when applying for certain positions, creativity just isn't appropriate. Here's an example of a simple letter for someone applying for a job as an Internet support representative. Notice that it uses a story of sorts, to grab the attention of the reader.

DEREK HUFF
381 South Street
Different Town, NY 33333
Phone: (222) 999-9999
derkehuffl@moreinternet.com

Allen Wallace, Hiring Manager
GHL Internet Services
102 Third Avenue
Anytown, NY 22222

Dear Mr. Wallace:

I am submitting my resume for the position of Internet support representative in response to your advertisement in the September 15 edition of the *Anytown Times*.

I'm sure you are receiving many resumes from potential applicants with the technical skills to handle this position. As you will note from my resume, I possess all the skills you require, but I have many more I believe will be helpful in this position.

I have people skills. I have customer service skills, and I have good judgment. I have the ability to listen when a customer is speaking, calm him or her down if necessary, and help solve the problem quickly and efficiently.

I have the knack of explaining how to do technical things in an easy-to-understand manner. I know what it is like for a customer to be frustrated and need a solution. I have compassion. I have understanding. And I have the ability to make everyone of your customers that I deal with happy that they are your customers.

Last semester, I started a volunteer program at my college helping people in the area solve computer problems and Internet issues via a hotline. While our free service was available to anyone who called, the majority of our callers were older people new to computers and the Internet.

Some problems were simple while others were more complicated. At the end of the night, however, I knew that whoever called in with a problem had their problem solved. And when that happens, you know you have made a difference in someone's day.

While I know this type of job might be filled with challenges, I am sure it is also filled with the joy of helping people find solutions. I would welcome the opportunity to work with GHI Internet Services in this capacity.

I would very much appreciate the opportunity to meet with you to further discuss this opportunity. I look forward to hearing from you.

Sincerely,
Derek Huff

If you are applying for a technical job such as a programmer, software engineer, game developer, project manager, security specialist, and so on, be sure your cover letter highlights your technical knowledge and skills. For example:

◎ Microsoft certified systems administrator (MCSA) credentialed.
◎ Technical expertise in Windows, Linux, Java, Oracle, Visual Basic, and HTTP.

- Comprehensive experience in a range of operating systems including DOS, Windows XP, and Vista.
- Technical proficiency in various platforms and network protocols.

More Selling Tools—Business and Networking Cards

The best way to succeed at almost anything is to do everything possible to stack the deck in your favor. Most people use a resume to sell themselves. As we just discussed, done right, your resume can be a great selling tool. It can get you in the door for an interview. But putting all your eggs in one basket is never a good idea. What else can you do to help sell yourself? What other tools can you use?

Business cards are small but powerful tools that can positively impact your career if used correctly. We've discussed the importance of business cards throughout the book. Let's look at them more closely.

Whatever level you're at in your career, whatever area of the computer industry you're interested in pursuing, business cards can help you get further. If you don't have a job yet, business cards are essential. At this point, they may also be known as networking cards because that is what they are going to help you do. If you already have a job, business cards can help you climb the ladder to success. Get your business cards made up, and get them made up now! They will be very useful in your career.

The Inside Scoop

Don't try to save money by making business cards on your computer. They never really end up looking professional and you don't really end up saving any money.

Tip from the Coach

Business cards are networking cards. You give them to people you meet so they not only remember you and what you do, but how to contact you if necessary. These are important no matter what aspect of the computer industry you aspire to succeed.

Why are cards so important? For a lot of reasons, but mainly because they help people not only remember you, but find you. Networking is so essential to your success in the computer industry that once you go through all the trouble of doing it, if someone doesn't remember who you are or how they can contact you, it's almost useless.

How many times have you met someone during the day or at a party and then gone your separate ways? A couple days later, something will come up where you wish you could remember the person's name or you remember their name, but have no idea how to get a hold of them.

How badly would you feel if you found out that you met someone, told him or her that you were looking for a job, they ran into someone else who was looking for someone with just your skills and talents, and they didn't know how to get a hold of you? Business cards could have helped solve that problem.

Tip from the Top

If you are currently employed, your employer will often provide you with business cards. If you are employed and looking for a job, make a second set of business cards to give out with your personal (not business) information.

Samples of Business and Networking Cards

Nancy Green

Career Goal: Position in Database Administratioin
Master's Degree in Computer Science—State University

P.O. Box 1800   Phone: 111-000-1111
Anytown, NY 11111   Cell: 111-999-0000
nancygreen@someinternet.com

Anthony Charles

Software and Hardware Trainer

P.O. Box 222   Phone: 111-444-6666
Anytown, NY 11111   Cell: 111-111-1111
anthonycharles@someinternet.com

---

630 Deer Run Avenue
Anytown, NY 11111
rogerlawson@internet.com

Rodger Ballister

Web Designer
ballisterWeb@ballister.com

Phone: 111-999-0000
Cell: 111-112-2222

When was the last time you ran into someone successful who didn't have business cards? They boost your prestige and make you feel more successful. If you feel more successful, you'll be more successful.

So, what's your next step? Start by determining what you want your business cards to look like. There are a variety of styles to choose from. You might want to go to a print shop or an office supply store such as Staples or Office Max to look at samples or you can create your own style.

Order at least 1,000 cards. What are you going to do with that many cards? You're going to give them to everyone. While everyone might not keep your resume, most people in all aspects of business keep business cards.

What should your cards say? At the minimum include your name, address (or P.O. box), and phone number (both home and cell if you have one). It's a good idea to add in your job or your career goal or objective. You might even briefly describe your talents, skills, or traits. Your business card is your selling piece so think about what you want to sell. Check out some of the samples to get ideas.

Remember that cards are small, and that limits the number of words that can fit so the card looks attractive and can be read easily. If you want more room, you might use a double-sided card (front and back) or a double-sized card that is folded over, in effect giving you four times as much space. I've seen both used successfully. The double-sized card can be very effective for a mini-resume.

You have a lot of decisions on how you want your business cards to look. What kind of card stock do you want? Do you want your card smooth or textured, flat or shiny? What about color? Do you want white, beige, or a colored card? Do you want flat print or raised print? What fonts or typefaces do you want to use? Do you want graphics? How do you want the information laid out? Do you want it straight or on an angle? The decisions are yours. It just depends on what you like and what you think will sell you the best.

Brochures Can Tell Your Story

While you're always going to need a resume, consider developing your own brochure, too. A brochure can tell your story and help you sell yourself. Sometimes, something out of the ordinary can help grab the attention of someone important.

What's a brochure? Basically, it is a selling piece that gives information about a product, place, event, or person, among other things. In this situation, the brochure is going to be about you. While your resume tells your full story, your brochure is going to illustrate your key points.

Why do you need one? A brochure can make you stand out from other job seekers.

What should a brochure contain? While it depends to a great extent on what segment of the computer industry you are pursuing, there are some basic things you should include.

Of course, you need your name and contact information. Then add in your selling points. Maybe those are your skills. Perhaps they are your talents or accomplishments. What about something unique or special that you do? Definitely try to illustrate what you can do for a company and what benefits they will obtain by hiring you. A brief personal biography is often helpful to illustrate your credentials and credibility. What about including three or four quotes from some of your letters of recommendation? For example:

◎ "One of the best interns we ever had participate in our internship program." Glen Jones, DHA Computers.
◎ "A real team player who motivates the team." Janice Crystal, Marcent Engineering.
◎ "One of our most requested software trainers." Joan Windmere, Windmere & Associates.

Keep your wording simple. Make it clear, concise, and interesting.

What should your brochure look like? The possibilities are endless. Brochures can be simple or elaborate. Your brochure can be designed in different sizes, papers, folds, inks, and colors. You can use photographs, drawings, illustrations, or other graphics.

If you have graphic design ability and talent, lay out your brochure yourself. If you don't, ask a friend or family member who is talented in that area. There are also software programs that help you design brochures. With these programs you simply type in your information and then print it out. Some people with access to a laser color copier and/or printer create their own professional looking pieces.

The beauty of doing it yourself is that after you've sent out a number of brochures you can improve and redesign them if they aren't doing anything for you and send out another batch. Be very sure, however, that your brochure looks professional or it will defeat the purpose.

If you want to design your brochure, but want it printed professionally, consider bringing your camera-ready brochure to a professional print shop. Camera-ready means your document is ready to be printed, and any consumer print shop should be able to help guide you through the steps needed to prepare your work for them.

⭐ Tip from the Coach

You don't need 1,000 brochures. Start off with 100 or so and see how they work for you. If you're not seeing results, you may need to rework your brochure to make it a valuable marketing tool. Remember that for brochures to be effective you have to send them out, so be sure you start working on a list of companies or people you want to target.

In addition to print shops, you might also consider office supply stores like Staples and Office Max that do printing.

If you don't feel comfortable designing your own brochure, you can ask a printer in your area if there is an artist on staff. Professional design and printing of a brochure can get expensive. Is it worth it? Only you can decide, but if it helps get your career started or makes the one you have more successful, probably the answer is yes.

Can brochures be effective? I certainly think so. Not only do I know a great number of people who have used them successfully in a variety of industries, I personally used one when I was breaking into the music business and have continued using them ever since. Here's my story.

At the time, I was sending out a lot of resumes and making a lot of calls in an attempt to obtain interviews. I had learned a great deal about marketing and noticed that many companies used brochures. My father, who was a marketing professional, suggested that a brochure might just be what I needed. By that time I had realized that if I wanted to sell myself, I might need to market myself a little more aggressively than I was doing, so I decided to try the brochure idea.

We designed a brochure that was printed on an 11-by-17-inch paper folded in half, giving me four pages to tell my story. We artistically placed a head shot on the front page and printed it in hot pink ink. The inside was crafted with carefully selected words indicating my accomplishments, skills, talents, and the areas in which I could help a company that hired me. The brochures were professionally printed and I sent them to various record labels, music instrument manufacturers, music publishers, music industry publicity companies, artist managers, and so on. I started getting calls from some of the people who received the brochure, obtained a number of interviews, and a even landed a couple of job offers. None of them, however, interested me.

Five years after I sent out my first brochure, I received a call from a major record company that told me that at the time they first received my brochure they didn't need anyone with my skills or talents, but they thought the brochure was so unique that they kept it on file. Voila! Five years passed, they needed an individual with my skills and someone remembered my brochure, pulled it out, and called me. By that time I was already on the road with another group and couldn't take the job, but it was nice to be called.

What was really interesting, however, is that companies and people to which I originally sent that first brochure years ago still remember it. They can describe it to a T, and many of them still have it in their files.

When creating your brochure, make sure it represents the image you want to portray. Try to make it as unique and eye catching as possible.

You can never tell how long someone is going to keep it before they call you.

Your Career Portfolio: Have Experience, Will Travel

People in creative careers have always used portfolios to illustrate what they have done and can accomplish. You can do the same.

What exactly is a career portfolio? Basically, it's a portfolio, binder, or book that contains your career information and illustrates your best work. In addition to the traditional printed components of your portfolio, many people in the computer industry are also using multimedia components, including video, PowerPoint, and Web pages. Your portfolio is a visual representation of what you have done and often illustrates what your potential might be.

Why do you need one? Because your career portfolio can help you get the positions you want and that is what this is all about. Consider this question. What would you believe more? Something someone told you or something you saw with your own eyes? If you're like most people, you would believe something you saw. And that's what a good career portfolio can do for you. It can provide actual illustrations of what you've done and what you can do.

For example, you might tell a potential employer that you can write press releases. Can you really? If you have samples in your portfolio, you can pull out a couple and show your work.

What would be more impressive to you? Reading over someone's resume and reading that he or she won the Software Developer of the Year Award or actually seeing a copy of the award certificate?

Have you written press releases about your accomplishments that led to articles in the paper? Have others done articles or feature stories about you that appeared in the media?

Copies of all these documents can be part of your career portfolio. Often, if you have buzz around you, potential employers feel you will be an asset to the company, giving you an edge over another applicant.

Don't think that your portfolio will only be useful when you are first trying to land a job. If you continue adding new accomplishments, skills, and samples of projects you've worked on, your portfolio will be useful in advancement throughout your career. Of course, as time goes on, omit some of your earlier documents and replace them with more current ones.

Having an organized system to present your achievements and successes is also helpful when going through employment reviews, or asking for a promotion or a raise. It also is very effective in illustrating what you've done if you're trying to move up the ladder at a different company.

Over the years, I consistently get calls from people who have been to our seminars or called for advice who continue to use their career portfolios successfully in their careers in every

---

⭐ Tip from the Top

When compiling your portfolio be careful not to use any confidential work or documents from a company, even if you were the one who wrote the report or the letter. A potential employer might be concerned about how you will deal with their confidential issues if you aren't keeping others' confidences.

industry. Work on developing your career portfolio and this simple tool can help you achieve success as well.

Your portfolio is portable. You can bring it with you when you go on interviews so you can show it to potential employers. You can make copies of things in your portfolio to give to potential employers or have everything at hand when you want to answer an ad or send out cold letters.

How do you build a detailed portfolio illustrating your skills, talents, experiences, and accomplishments? What goes into it? You want your portfolio to document your work-related talents and accomplishments. These are the assets that you will be selling to potential employers. Let's look at some of the things you might want to include.

- ◎ Your profile
- ◎ Resume
- ◎ Bio
- ◎ Reference sheets
- ◎ Skill and abilities
- ◎ Degrees, licenses, and certifications
- ◎ Experience sheet
- ◎ Summary of accomplishments
- ◎ Professional associations
- ◎ Professional development activities (conferences, seminars, and workshops attended as well as any other professional development activities)
- ◎ Awards and honors
- ◎ Volunteer activities and community service
- ◎ Supporting documents
- ◎ Samples of work
- ◎ Newspaper, magazine, and other articles and/or feature stories about you
- ◎ Articles you have written and published
- ◎ Reports you've done
- ◎ Web sites you've designed
- ◎ Applications you've developed
- ◎ Letters of recommendation
- ◎ Letters or notes people have written to tell you that you've done a good job
- ◎ Photos of you accepting an award or at an event you worked on
- ◎ Photos of events you were involved in
- ◎ News stories or feature articles generated by your execution or supervision of a project

Remember that this list is just to get you started. Some of the components may relate to you and some may not. You can use anything in your portfolio that will help illustrate your skills, talents, and accomplishments.

In order to make it easier to locate information in your portfolio, you might want to develop a table of contents and then utilize dividers.

Tip from the Top

Make good-quality copies of key items in your portfolio to leave with interviewers or potential employers, agents, etc. Visit an office supply store to find some professional-looking presentation folders to hold all the support documents you bring to an interview.

Words from a Pro

If you're dealing with an unknown printer or company, ask to see samples of their work ahead of time. Then be sure to get a "proof" that you can check for errors and approve before your folders are printed.

Here's a sample of a profile that a programmer might use in his portfolio. Use it to give you an idea on getting started on yours.

Whatever segment of the computer industry you are pursuing, use every tool you can to make sure you get the edge over others who want the same success as you do.

Sample of Profile for Career Portfolio

PROFILE
Lonnie Masters

Education:
- ◎ State University–Master of Science
  - ▫ Computer Information Systems
- ◎ State University–Bachelor's Degree
  - ▫ Major: Information Technology

Additional Training:
- ◎ Seminar: Software Development and Documentation
- ◎ Seminar: Administering ENS for NetWare
- ◎ Workshop: Flash
- ◎ Workshop: Web Development and Design Certification
- ◎ Workshop: Systems Administration
- ◎ Seminar: Web Page Design

Qualifications:
- ◎ Hardworking, dedicated, focused, motivated, and energetic
- ◎ Creative thinker
- ◎ Competent in a variety of computer languages
- ◎ Strategic planning
- ◎ Repair and maintenance
- ◎ Verbal and written communication skills
- ◎ Trilingual (English, Spanish, French)

7

GETTING YOUR FOOT IN THE DOOR

Whether I'm giving a career seminar or doing a career consultation, people looking for advice on getting that perfect job consistently tell me that if they only could get their foot in the door they would be on their way. In a way they're right.

One of the keys to a great career in any industry is getting your foot in the proverbial door. The computer industry is no exception. If you can just get that door open—even if it's just a crack—you can slip your foot in, and then you're on the road to success. Why? Because once you get your foot in, you have a chance to sell yourself, sell your talent, and sell your products or services.

Seems easy, but the problem is sometimes the hardest part is getting your foot in the door. Whether you simply walk in off the street to see someone or call to make an appointment, you often are faced with the same situation. You need to get past the receptionist, the secretary, or whoever the "gatekeeper" happens to be between you and the person with whom you want to speak.

Here's what you need to know. Whenever there is a job opening, someone will get the job and, unfortunately, someone will not. Rejection is often part of the process in getting a job. However, to feel rejected when you didn't even get the chance to really be rejected because you can't get through to someone is quite another thing.

It's not personal, but the secretary, receptionist, assistant, and even the person you're trying to reach, often think of you and most other unsolicited callers as unwanted intruders who waste their time. It doesn't really matter whether you're trying to sell something or get a job: Unless they can see what you can do for them, it's going to be hard to get through.

In reality you are trying to sell something. You're trying to sell you, your skills and your talents. You're trying to get a job. What you need to do, however, is try not to let the gatekeepers know exactly what you want.

I am in no way telling you to lie or even stretch the truth. What I'm telling you to do is find a way to change their perception of you and what you want. Get creative.

Some areas of the computer industry are easier to enter while other segments are more competitive. And while there generally always is a gatekeeper, sometimes it's easier to get past him or her.

You might not think you have to worry about getting past a gatekeeper if you are pursuing a career in one of the segments of the computer industry that is in great demand, but you can never tell. You might, for example, want to interview in a company in which it may be more difficult to get a job. You might want to go after a project manager position that others want too. You might want to work as a chief information officer at a large corporation where there are a hundred other people who want the same job as you. You might want to get a coveted internship in gaming development at one of the major gaming companies. You might even want to create your own position. There are so many possibilities where there could be a gatekeeper in your way that it is always good to be prepared.

In many situations you might be answering an advertisement or visiting the human resources offices of a company to fill in an application. If, for example, you are applying for an advertised job, you might not have to worry about getting past the gatekeeper, but that doesn't mean he or she isn't there.

No matter which segment of the industry you are pursuing, there will be times when you need to get past a gatekeeper so you can get your foot in the door. Before you rush in and find the door locked, let's look at some possible keys to help you get in.

Will you need every key all the time? Probably not, but once you learn what some of the keys are, you'll have them if you need them.

Getting Through to People on the Phone

Let's start with the phone. If your goal is to talk to a specific person or make an appointment, it's important to know that many high-level business people don't answer their own phone. Instead, they rely on secretaries, receptionists, or assistants to handle this task. And that's not even counting the dreaded voice mail.

You can always try the straightforward approach. Just call and ask to speak to the person you are looking for. If you get through, you have your foot in the door. If not, it's time to get creative.

Let's look at a couple of scenarios and how they might play out. In the first scenario David Fox is trying to land an interview in an attempt to create a position as an technology reporter.

Scenario 1

Receptionist: Good afternoon, WIOU.

You: Hello, this is David Fox. May I please speak to Tracy Spencer?

Receptionist: Does he know what this is in reference to?

You: No, I'm looking for a job as a technology reporter and would like to see if I could arrange an interview.

Receptionist: I'm sorry, Mr. Spencer isn't looking to fill any positions at this time. Thank you for calling.

You: Okay. Thanks. Good-bye.

With that said, you're done. Is there something you could have said differently that might lead to a better ending? Sometimes mentioning a job to the gatekeeper is not a good idea. Let's say you are trying to create your own position or you are going after a position that is so coveted that those already working in the company may not be that open to helping those on the outside. What can you do? Creativity is the name of the game.

Let's look at another scenario.

Scenario 2

Secretary: Good afternoon, WIOU.

You: Is Mr. Spencer in please?

Secretary: Who's calling?

You: David Fox.

Secretary: May I ask what this is in reference to?

You: Yes, I was trying to set up an informational interview. Would Mr. Spencer be the person who handles this or would it be someone else?

[Asking the question in this manner means that you stand a chance at the gatekeeper giving you a specific name that you can call if Mr. Spencer is the wrong person.]

Secretary: Informational interview for what purpose?

You: I was interested in exploring the interest radio listeners have in technology issues, I thought that, as the program director, Mr. Spencer might be someone who might have some knowledge in that area. Would he be the right person?

[Make sure you are pleasant. This helps the person answering the phone want to help you.]

Secretary: You probably would be better off speaking to our station owner, James Ernst. Would you like me to switch you?

[What you are really doing is helping her get you off the phone even if it means she is dumping you on someone else.]

You: Yes, that would be great. What was your name?

[Try to make sure you get the name. In this manner, when you get transferred, the person answering at the other end will be more apt to help you.]

Secretary: Nancy Black.

You: Thanks for your help. I really appreciate it.

Secretary: I'll switch you now.

Shari Jones: James Ernst's office. This is Shari Jones, may I help you?

You: Hi, Ms. Jones, Nancy Black suggested that Mr. Ernst might be the right person for me to speak to. I'm working on a project and interested in exploring the interest people who listen to radio have in technology-oriented issues. Ms. Black said Mr. Ernst might be able to give me some information on that demographic.

Ms. Jones: What type of project are you working on? Is this a school project or something else?

You: No, I'm out of school. As a matter of fact I just graduated from State University in May. I have my bachelor's in computer science. I'm teaching a class on creating personal Web sites at the local community college.

[Notice that you are not really answering her question. And while you are really just teaching a two-day class, you also mentioned you were teaching something. If Ms. Jones is multitasking or really isn't paying attention, she might take that to mean you already have a full-time job. At this point, Ms. Jones probably will either say, "Sorry, Mr. Ernst is very busy," or keep pumping you for information.]

Ms. Jones: Mr. Ernst is out of the office this week. He should be back next Monday, but he is very busy next week.

You: I understand he is busy and I really don't want to impose on his time. Do you think he would have 10 minutes for me if I stop in sometime next week or would it be better to call him? Technology is so important to all of us today. I'm really interested in hearing his thoughts on this.

Ms. Jones: I know Mr. Ernst is very interested in technology himself. As a matter of fact, the reason he is out of town is he went to a seminar on using the Internet to increase station revenue.

You: I bet that is interesting.

Ms. Jones: Did you say you were teaching at the local community college? Mr. Ernst is on the board of directors at the college. He was on the committee to start a new program in computer science there. Actually, he might really enjoy speaking to you. He is pretty busy next week, but he might be able to spare a few minutes on Wednesday. Would that work for you?

[Do not say, "Let me check my calendar." If at all possible, take the time you are given for the meeting, no matter what else you have to juggle around.]

Ms. Jones: I'm going to double check with Mr. Ernst when he calls in. If you don't hear from me, why don't you come over around 9:30 a.m. Wednesday? Do you have our address?

You: It is 101 First Street, isn't it?

Ms. Jones: You're right. That's where our offices are located. You also might want to speak to Hilary Simpson from the *Daily Times*. She is on the college board with Mr. Ernst. She worked with him trying to get the computer science program into the college. She might be able to give you some information on technology and the print media. I know she thinks it's important, because I hear she's looking for a technology reporter for a new column.

You: I bet that would be an interesting job.

Ms. Jones: Give her a call. Her number is 444-9999. Her secretary's name is Mary. Tell her I told you to call.

You: Thanks so much for your help. I'm going to call as soon as I hang up. You've been really helpful. I'll see you next week.

Once you get into the meeting with Mr. Ernst you might or might not be able to talk him into the idea of creating a position for a technology reporter. You might even be able to talk him into a new technology talk show for the radio station. It all depends how convincing you are.

No matter what, however, by calling him you have networked your way into another meeting at the newspaper. And you have heard about a position as a technology reporter or columnist for the paper, a position you have not seen advertised.

I can hear you saying, "That kind of thing doesn't really happen."

To that I reply, it can and it does. I've seen it happen numerous times. It can happen to you too. In order for it to happen, however, you have to find ways to get past the gatekeeper.

Here's another scenario.

Scenario 3

Receptionist: Good afternoon, DRE Entertainment.

You: Hi, I'm working on a project involving careers and career opportunities in computer technology in the entertainment industry. Do you know who in your company I might speak to that might know something about that area?

[Here is where it can get a little tricky. If you are very lucky, the receptionist will just put you through to someone in publicity, public relations, or human resources. If you're not so lucky, he or she will ask you questions.]

Receptionist: What type of project?

You need to be ready with a plausible answer. What you say will, of course, depend on your situation. If you are in college, you can always say you are working on a project for school. If not, you can say you are doing research on the various career opportunities in computer technology in entertainment. If you have writing skills, you might contact a local newspaper or magazine to see if they are interested in an article on computer-oriented careers in the entertainment industry (or whatever segment of the industry you are targeting). If you can't find someone to write for, you can always write a story on "spec." This means that if you write a story, you can send it to an editor on speculation. They might take it and they might not. Don't think about money at this point. Your goal here is to get the "right people" to speak to you and get an appointment.

This method of getting to know people is supposed to give you credibility, not make you seem untrustworthy. The idea will only be effective if you really are planning on writing an article or a story and then carry through.

One of the interesting things about writing an article (whether on spec or on assignment) is that you can ask people questions and they will usually talk to you. They won't be looking at you as they might be if you were looking for a job.

Voice of Experience

Make sure you get the correct spelling of the name of everyone who helps you. Send a short note, thanking them for their help, immediately. This is not only good manners, it helps people remember who you are in a positive way.

What you've done in these situations is changed people's perception about why you are talking to them. One of the most important bonuses of interviewing people about their careers is that you are making invaluable contacts.

While it might be tempting, remember to use this opportunity to ask questions and network; do not try to sell yourself. After you write the article, you might call up one of the people you interviewed, perhaps the human resources director, and say something like, "You made a career in Web development for an entertainment site so interesting, I'd like to explore a career like that. Would it be possible to come in for an interview or to fill in an application?" Or, "Until I spoke to you, I didn't realize I could use my degree in computer science to work at a company like yours. Would it be possible to come in and speak to you again about possible opportunities?"

What can you do if none of these scenarios work? The receptionist may not be very eager to help. He or she may have instructions to "not let anyone through." It may be his or her job to block unsolicited callers and visitors from the boss. What can you do?

Here are a few ideas that might help. See if you can come up with some others yourself.

◎ Try placing your call before regular business hours. Many executives and others you might want to talk to come in early, before the secretary or receptionist is scheduled to work.

◎ Try placing your calls after traditional business hours when the secretary probably has gone for the day. The executives and others you want to reach generally don't punch a time clock and often work late. More importantly, even if people utilize voice mail, they may pick up the phone themselves after hours in case their family is calling.

◎ Lunch hours are also a good time to attempt to get through to people. This can be a little tricky, however. The executive may use voice mail during the lunch hour period or he or she may go out to lunch. On the other hand, you might get lucky.

◎ Sometimes, others in the office fill in for a receptionist or secretary and aren't sure what the procedure is or who everyone is. While you might not get through on the first try, you might use this type of opportunity to get information. For example, you might ask for the person you want to speak to and when the substitute tells you he or she isn't in and asks if you want to leave a message, say something like, "I'm moving around a lot today. I'll try to call later. Is Mr. Brown ever in the office after 6:00 p.m.?" If the answer is yes, ask

if you can have his direct extension in case the switchboard is closed.

Remember the three "Ps" to help you get through on the phone. You want to be:

◎ Pleasant
◎ Persistent
◎ Positive

Always be pleasant. Aside from it being general good manners to be nice to others, being pleasant to gatekeepers is essential. Gatekeepers talk to their bosses and can let them know if you were annoying or obnoxious. When someone tells you their boss "never takes unsolicited calls or accepts unsolicited resumes," tell them that you understand. Then ask what they suggest. Acknowledge objections, but try to come up with a solution.

Be persistent. Just because you don't get through on the first try doesn't mean you shouldn't try again. Don't be annoying, don't be pushy, but don't give up. People like to help positive people. Don't moan and groan about how difficult your life is to the secretary. He or she will only want to get you off the phone.

Persistence and the Guilt Factor

Don't forget the guilt factor. If you consistently place calls to "Mr. Jenkins" and each time his secretary tells you he is busy, unavailable, or will call you back and he doesn't, what should you do? Should you give up? Well, that's up to you. Be aware that persistence often pays off. In many cases, after a number of calls, you and the secretary will have built up a "relationship" of sorts. As long as you have always been pleasant, he or she may feel guilty that you are such a nice person and his or her boss isn't calling you back. In these cases, the secretary may give you a tip on how to get through, tell you to send

---

⭐ **Words from the Wise**

Friday afternoon is the worst time to call someone when you want something. The second worst time is early Monday morning.

> ⭐ **Voice of Experience**
>
> While persistence can work, don't be annoying. Calling more than once a day or in most cases, even more than once a week (unless you are given specific instructions to do so by the secretary, receptionist, or the assistant to the person you are trying to contact) will put you on the annoying list.

something in writing, or ask the boss to speak to you.

Voice mail is another obstacle you might have to deal with. This automated system is often more difficult to bypass than a human gatekeeper. Many people don't even bother answering their phone, instead letting their voice mail pick up the calls and then checking their messages when convenient.

Decide ahead of time what you're going to do if you get someone's voice mail. Try calling once to see what the person's message is. It might, for example, let you know that the person you're calling is out of town until Monday. What this will tell you is that if you are calling someone on a cold call, you should probably not call until Wednesday, because they probably will be busy when they get back in town.

If the message says something to the effect of, "I'm out of town. If you need to speak to me today please call my cell phone," and then provides a phone number, don't call. You don't need to speak to him or her; you want to. There is a big difference between needs and wants. You are cold calling a person who doesn't know you to ask for something. It is not generally a good idea to bother people outside of the office.

However, if you call a few times and keep getting the voice mail, you're going to have to make your move. Leave a message something like this.

You: Hi, this is Jerry Strong. My phone number is (111) 444-4444. I'd appreciate it if you could give me a call at your convenience. I look forward to hearing from you. Have a great day.

If you don't hear back within a few days, try again.

You: Hi, Mr. Green. This is Jerry Strong. (111) 444-4444. I called a few days ago. I know you're busy and was just trying to reach you again. I look forward to hearing from you. Thanks. Have a great day.

You might not hear from Mr. Green himself, but one of his assistants might call you. What do you do if you don't get a call back? Call again. How many times should you call? That's hard to say. Persistence may pay off. Remember, the person on the other end may start feeling guilty that he or she is not calling you back and place that call.

Be prepared. When you get a call back, have your ducks in a row and be ready and able to sell yourself. Practice ahead of time if need be and leave notes near your phone.

I suggest when making any of these calls that you block your phone number so that no one knows who is calling. To permanently block your

> ⭐ **Words from the Wise**
>
> Be aware that even if you block your number, certain companies pay to "see" your number anyway. Generally, these are companies utilizing toll free numbers such as 800 or 877 phone numbers, but in certain cases companies utilizing toll numbers may also unblock your number.

phone number from showing on the receiver's caller ID, call your local phone company. Most don't charge for this service. You can also block your phone number on a temporary basis by dialing *67 before making your call. Remember that as soon as you hang up, this service will be disabled, so you will need to do this for each call.

Getting Them to Call You

While persistence and patience in calling and trying to get past the receptionist is usually necessary, you may need something else, too. You want something to set you apart, so busy executives not only want to see you, but remember you. You want them to give you a chance to sell yourself.

What can you do? Creativity to the rescue! The amount of creativity will depend, to a great extent, on the specific company or organization to which you are trying to get through.

Your goal is to get the attention of the important person who can give you a chance to sell yourself. Once you have his or her attention, it's up to you to convince them that they should work with you.

Let's look at some ideas that I have either personally used or that others have told me worked in their quest to get an individual's attention so they could get a foot in the door. Use these ideas as a beginning. Then try to develop some others of your own. You are limited only by your own creativity and ability to think outside of the box.

My Personal Number-One Technique for Getting Someone to Call You

I am going to share my number one technique for getting someone to call you. I have used this technique successfully over the years to get people to call me in a variety of situations and

industries at various levels in my career. I first came up with this technique after I graduated from college when I was entering the workforce and wanted to get a job in the music industry.

At the time, there was no book to give me ideas. There was no career coach. There was no one who really wanted to help, and I desperately needed help to get a job.

I had tried all the traditional methods. I tried calling people, but most of the time I couldn't get past the gatekeeper. When I did, no one called me back. I had tried sending out resumes. As I had just graduated from college, I had no "real" experience. I didn't know anyone and didn't even know anyone who knew anyone. I needed a break. Here's what I did.

When I was younger my parents used to take raw eggs, blow out the contents, and then decorate the shells. Every one always commented on how nice they were and how different they were. One day, for some reason, the eggs popped into my mind, and I came up with my method to get people to call me back. Here's how it works.

Get a box of eggs. Extra-large or jumbo work well. While either white or brown eggs can be used, start with white ones because of the coloration differences in brown eggs. Wash the raw eggs carefully with warm water. Then dry the shells well.

There are two ways to do the next step, depending on what you have at hand. In the first method, you don't need any special equipment other than a needle or pin and a straw. The other method is easier, but you will need to purchase a small egg blower.

Let's start with the first method. Hold one egg in your hand, and using a large needle or pin, punch a small hole in the top of the egg. The top is the narrower end. Then, carefully punch a slightly larger hole in the other end of the egg.

You might need to take the needle or pin and move it around in the hole a bit to make it larger. Keep any pieces of shell that break off.

Now, take a straw and place it on the top hole of the egg. Holding the egg over a bowl, blow into the straw, blowing out the contents of the egg. This may take a couple of tries. Because of concerns with salmonella, do not put your mouth directly on the egg.

Keep in mind that the bigger you have made the hole, the easier it will be to blow the contents out of the egg. However, you want the egg to look as "whole" as possible when you're done. The bigger the hole, the harder this is to accomplish.

After blowing the contents out of the egg, carefully rinse out the shell, letting warm water run through it. Get the egg as clean as possible. Shake the excess water out of the egg and leave it to dry thoroughly. Depending on the temperature and humidity when you are preparing the eggs, it might take a couple of days.

After getting the raw egg out of the shell this way for years, I found there was an easier method. Believe it or not, there actually is a small tool called an egg blower you can buy for under $10 to do this project. These egg blowers simplify the process of emptying and cleaning the inside of the eggs. You can find egg blowers like the Blas-Fix Egg Blower, Aunt Marge's Egg Blower, or similar tools in craft stores or online. They will speed up the process of preparing the eggs.

Do at least three eggs at one time in case one breaks or cracks during the next step. You might want to do more. After you get the hang of this, you're going to want to keep a few extra prepared eggs on hand for when you want to get someone's attention fast and don't have time to prepare new ones.

Next, go to your computer and type the words, "Getting the attention of a busy person

is not easy. Now that I have yours, could you please take a moment to review my resume?" You can customize the message to suit your purposes by including the name of the recipient if you have it or specifying your background sheet or whatever you want the recipient to look at and consider. Then type your name and phone number.

Use a small font to keep the message to one or two lines. Neatly cut out the strip of paper with your message. Roll the strip around a toothpick. Carefully insert the toothpick with the strip of paper into the larger of the hole in the egg. Wiggle the toothpick around and slowly take the toothpick out of the egg. The strip of paper should now be in the shell.

Visit your local craft store and pick up a package of those small moveable eyes, some miniature plastic or felt shaped feet, and white glue or a glue gun. Glue the miniature feet to the bottom of the egg, covering the hole. Make sure you use the glue sparingly so none goes on your message. Now, glue on two of the moving eyes making the egg look like a face.

Go back to your computer and type the following words. "CRACK OPEN THIS EGG FOR AN IMPORTANT MESSAGE." Print out the line and neatly cut it into a strip. You might want to use bright-colored paper. Glue the strip to the bottom of the feet of the egg.

Now you're ready. Take the egg and place it in a small box that you have padded with cotton, bubble wrap, or foam. These eggs are very fragile, and you don't want the egg to break in transit!

Wrap the egg filled box in attractive wrapping paper and then bubble wrap to assure it won't move around. Put your resume (background sheet or other information) and a short cover letter into an envelope. Put it on the bottom of a sturdy mailing box. Place the egg box over it.

Make sure you use attractive clean boxes and pack the egg as carefully as possible. Address the box. Make sure you include your name and return address. Then either mail, UPS, FedEx, DHL, or messenger it to the office of the person you are trying to reach. (Do not bring it yourself or you will be defeating the purpose.) Even if that person has a secretary opening his or her mail, the chances are good that the "gift" will be opened personally. In the event that a secretary opens the package, he or she will probably bring the egg into the boss to crack.

So now the recipient has the egg in front of him or her. He or she will probably break it open, see the message, and glance at your resume. Here's the good news. By the time the person breaks open the egg, he or she won't even notice the hole on the bottom and usually has no idea how you got the message in there. Generally, most people who have seen this think it is so neat that they want to know how you did it, so they call you to ask. (Believe it or not, everyone has someone they wish would call them back.)

Once you have the person you wanted to contact on the phone, your job is to get an interview. You want to get into their office and meet with them. When you get that call, tell the recipient of the egg that you would be glad to show him or her how you did it; but it's kind of complicated to explain over the phone. Offer to show them how it is done and ask when they would like you to come in.

Voila! You have an appointment. Now all you have to do is sell yourself.

Is your resume sitting in a pile of countless others? Do you want your resume to stand out from among the hundreds that come in? Do you want an interview but can't get one? Are you having difficulties getting people to call you back? Need some help? Then read on!

While I love the egg idea and have used it to obtain appointments, call backs, and to get noticed throughout my career, there are other ideas that work, too. You might want to try a couple of these.

Have you ever considered using these simple items to help you succeed? If you haven't, perhaps now is the time.

- ◎ Fortune cookies
- ◎ Chocolate chip cookies
- ◎ Candy bars
- ◎ Mugs
- ◎ Pizzas
- ◎ Roses

Fortune Cookies

Almost no one can resist cracking open a fortune cookie to see what the "message" says. This can be good news for your career.

Some fortune cookie companies make cookies similar to the ones you get in Chinese restaurants, but with personalized messages inside. What could you say? That depends on what you are looking for. How about something like, "Human Resources Director who interviews Michael Cashman will have good luck for the rest of the day. Michael's lucky number: 111-222-3333."

Whatever message you choose, remember that you generally need to make all the messages the same or it gets very expensive to have the cookies made. You also need to either print cards on your computer or have cards printed professionally that read something to the effect of, "Getting the attention of a busy person is not easy. Now that I have yours, could you please take a moment to review my resume?" Or, "Getting the attention of a busy person is not easy.

Now that I have yours, I was hoping you could take a few moments to give me a call." (Or set up an appointment or anything else you want to say.) Make sure your name and phone number are on the card.

Put a couple of cookies with the card and your resume or other material in a clean, attractive mailing box and address it neatly. Make sure you address the box to someone specific. For example, don't address it to Director of IT Department, Community General Hospital. Instead address it to Mr. James Knowles, Director of IT, Community General Hospital. Don't send it to Personnel Services, CBE Computers. Instead send it to Andrew Brooks, Personnel Director, CBE Computers.

"I've heard of sending fortune cookies," you say. "What else can I do?"

Here's a twist. Send the same package of cookies, the card, and whatever else you choose (your resume, curriculum vitae, background sheet, etc.) every day for two weeks. Every day, after the first one, also include a note that says, "Cookies For [Name of person] For Day 2," "Cookies For [Name of Person] For Day 3," and so on. At the end of the two-week period, stop. By now your recipient will probably have called you. If not, he or she will at least be expecting the cookies. If you don't hear from your recipi-

---

Words from the Wise

Make sure cookies are individually wrapped and factory sealed. Otherwise, some people may just toss them.

---

ent, feel free to call the office, identify yourself as the fortune cookie king or queen, and ask for an appointment.

This idea can be expensive, but if it gets you in the door and you can sell yourself or your idea, it will more than pay for itself.

Another great idea that can really grab the attention of a busy executive, or anybody else for that matter, is finding a company that makes gigantic fortune cookies with personalized messages. (You can generally find these companies online.) These cookies are often covered in chocolate, sprinkles, and all kinds of goodies and almost command people to see who sent it. Send these cookies with the same types of messages and supporting material as the others. The only difference is that if you choose to send the gigantic cookies, you probably only need to send one. If you don't get a call within the first week, feel free to call the recipient yourself.

Chocolate Chip Cookies

Chocolate chip cookies are a favorite of most people. Why not use that to your advantage? Go

---

Tip from the Coach

To improve your chances of getting an interview, when possible try to address your letter to the specific person who has hiring authority for the position for which you are applying. In some companies this may be the human resources director. In others it might be the director or manager of the specific department or the owner of a company.

The Inside Scoop

To avoid potential problems with people who have allergies, do not send any food with nuts as an ingredient. Nothing can ruin your chances of getting a job faster than causing an allergic reaction in the person you're trying to impress.

to the cookie kiosk at your local mall and order a gigantic, pizza-sized cookie personalized with a few words asking for what you would like done. For example:

◎ "Please Review My Resume. Stephen Smith"

◎ "Please Call Me For An Interview. Pat Young"

Keep your message short. You want the recipient to read it, not get overwhelmed. Generally, the cookies come boxed. Tape a copy of your resume, or whatever you are sending to the inside of the box.

Write a short cover letter to your recipient stating that you hope he or she enjoys the cookie while reviewing your resume, giving you a call, etc. Put this in an envelope with another copy of your resume, your demo, or other material. On the outside of the box, neatly tape a card with the message, "Getting the attention of a busy person is not easy. Now that I have yours would you please take a moment to review my resume?" Or ask them to give you a call, or whatever you are hoping they will do. Make sure your name and phone number are on the card.

If the cookie company has a mail or delivery service, use it, even if it is more expensive than mailing it yourself. It will be more effective. If there is no mail or delivery service, you can mail or deliver the cookie yourself. You should get a call from the recipient within a few days. If not,

> ### ★ Voice of Experience
>
> Do not try to save money by making the cookies yourself. In today's world, many people won't eat food if they don't know where it came from or if it was not prepared by a commercial eatery.

feel free to call your recipient and identify yourself as the person who sent the large cookie.

Candy Bar

There have been a number of studies that tout chocolate as a food that makes people happy, or at least puts them in a good mood. Keeping this in mind, you might want to use chocolate to grab someone's attention and move them to call you. Most people love chocolate and are happy to see it magically appear in their office. There are a number of different ways you can use chocolate to help your career.

◎ Buy a large, high-quality chocolate bar. Carefully fold your resume or a letter stating what you would like accomplished and slip it into the wrapping of the chocolate bar.

◎ Wrap the chocolate bar with your resume or the letter stating what you would like accomplished.

◎ There are companies that create personalized wrappings for chocolate bars. Use one to deliver your message.

◎ Create a wrapping on your computer. If you do this, make sure you leave the original wrapping intact and cover it with your wrapper.

Whatever method you choose, put the candy bar in an attractive box, and attach a card with the message, "Getting the attention of a busy person is never easy. Now that I have yours could you please take a moment to review my resume?" (or whatever action you are asking your recipient to take). Add a cover letter and send it off.

When was the last time you threw out a mug? If you're like most people, it has probably been a while. How about using this idea to catch the attention of a potential employer? Depending on your career aspiration, have mugs printed with replicas of your business or networking card, key points of your resume, curriculum vitae, or background sheet along with your name and phone number.

Add in a small packet of gourmet or flavored coffee or hot chocolate and perhaps an individually wrapped biscotti or cookie and, of course, a card with the message stating, "Getting the attention of a busy person is never easy. Now that I have yours, could you please take a moment to check out my resume?" (or whatever else you are requesting). Put the mug, a short cover letter, and your resume, background sheet, or other material in a box and mail or deliver it to your recipient. Remember to always put your return address on the box.

Pizza

Want to make sure your resume or background sheet gets attention? Have it delivered to your recipient with a fresh, hot pizza. This technique can be tricky, but it can be effective. Here are the challenges: In order to guarantee the pizza arrives with your information, you really need to be in the same geographic location as the company or organization you're trying to reach. You will need to personally make sure that your information is placed in a good quality Ziploc bag or, better yet, laminated and taped to the inside cover of the pizza box. You also not only have to know the name of the person to whom the pizza will be delivered, but also that he or she will be in the office the day you send the pizza and doesn't have a lunch date. It's difficult to call an office where no one knows you and ask what time the recipient goes to lunch. So you are taking a risk that you will send a pizza to someone who isn't there. One way to get around this is by sending it in the late afternoon instead of at lunchtime.

That way your recipient can have a mid-afternoon "pizza break." And even if your recipient isn't there, his or her employees will probably enjoy the pizza and tell their supervisor about it the next day.

If you use this technique, make sure that you have the pizzeria delivering the pizza tape the card with the message about getting a busy person's attention on the front of the box, so even if the receptionist gets the pizza, he or she will know who it came from.

If you don't get a thank-you call that day, call the recipient the next morning. You probably will speak to the secretary or receptionist first. Just tell whomever you speak to that you were the one who sent the pizza the day before in hopes of getting the attention of the recipient so you might set up a job interview.

Roses

A very effective but pricey way to get your recipient's attention is to have a dozen roses delivered to his or her office. (Once again, do not try to save money by buying roses yourself and bringing them it. It will defeat the purpose.) No matter how many things you have tried with no response, there are very few people who will not place a thank-you call when they receive a dozen roses.

Talk to the florist ahead of time to make sure the roses you send are fragrant. Send the roses to your recipient with a card that simply says something to the effect of, "While you're enjoying the roses, please take a moment to review my resume, sent under separate cover." Sign the card, "Sincerely hoping for an interview," and include your name and phone number.

It is imperative you send your information so it arrives on the same day or at the latest the next day, so the roses you sent are still fresh in the recipient's mind.

It's Who You Know

While, of course, there are some areas of the computer industry that are easier to enter, there generally still is always some amount of competition to get most jobs. There are also individuals who are talented and skilled, yet never get past the front door. Knowing someone who can get you in the door certainly will help.

Before you say, "Me? I don't know anyone," stop and think. Are you sure? Don't you know someone, anyone, even on a peripheral basis, who might be able to give you a recommendation, make a call, or would be willing lend his or her name?

What about your mother's aunt's husband's friend's neighbor's boss? Sure it might be a stretch. But think hard. Who can you think of who might know someone who might be able to help? This is not the time to be shy.

Call your aunt. Explain what you're trying to do with your career. Then ask if she would be willing to talk to her husband's friend about talking to their neighbor about using his name to make an appointment with the neighbor's boss.

"But I don't need any help," you say, "I can do it on my own."

You might be able to and you might not, but why wouldn't you give yourself every edge possible? You're going to have to prove yourself once you get in the door. No one can do that for you.

What if you don't have a relative who has a contact down the line? What about one of your professors? What about someone you met at a chamber of commerce event? What about a neighbor? What about a friend or neighbor who is already working at the company in which you are interested? How about someone on the board of directors?

What about your hair stylist? Your UPS delivery person? Your mail carrier? Your clergy-man or woman? What about one of your physicians? Your pharmacist? Your dentist? The possibilities are endless if you just look.

The trick here is to think outside the box. If you can find someone who knows someone who is willing to help you to get your foot in the door, then all you will have to do is sell yourself.

If someone does agree to lend his or her name, make a call, or help you in any manner, it's important to write thank-you notes immediately. These notes should be written whether or not you actually get an interview or set up a meeting.

If you do go on an interview, it's also a good idea to either call or write another note letting your contact know what happened.

Meeting the Right People

You think and think and you still can't come up with anyone you know with a connection to anyone at all in the area of the computer industry in which you are trying to succeed. What can you do?

Sometimes you have to find your own contacts. You need to meet the right people. How can you do this? The best way to meet the right people in the computer industry is to be around people working in or around computers. There are several possible ways you might do this.

To begin with, consider joining industry organizations and associations. Many of these organizations offer career guidance and support. They also may offer seminars, workshops, and other types of educational symposiums. Best of all, many of these groups host networking events, periodic meetings, and annual conventions and conferences. All of these are treasure troves of possibilities to meet people in the industry. Some of them may be industry experts or insiders. Others may be just like you, people who are trying to get into the industry and succeed. The important thing to remember is, take advantage of every opportunity.

Workshops and seminars are great because not only can you make important contacts, but you also can learn something valuable about the industry. Most of these events have question and answer sessions built into the program. Take advantage of these. Stand up and ask a good question. Make yourself visible. Some seminars and workshops have breakout sessions to encourage people to get to know one another. Use these to your advantage as well.

During breaks, don't run to the corner to check your voice mail. Walk around and talk to people. Don't be afraid to walk up to someone you don't know and start talking. Remember to bring your business or networking cards and network, network, network!

After the session has ended, walk up, shake the moderator's hand, and tell him or her how much you enjoyed the session, how much you learned, and how useful it will be in your career. This gives you the opportunity to ask for his or her business card, so you have the correct spelling of the person's name, as well has his or her company, address, and phone number. This is very valuable information. When you get home,

---

Words from a Pro

Don't just blend in with everyone else at a seminar or workshop. Make yourself visible and memorable in a positive way. Ask questions and participate when possible. During breaks, don't rush to make calls on your cell phone. Instead, try to meet more people and make more contacts.

---

send a short note stating that you were at the session the person moderated, spoke to him or her afterward, and just wanted to mention again how much you enjoyed it.

Depending on the individual's position, you might also ask if it would be possible to set up an informational interview at his or her convenience or if he or she could suggest who you might call to set up an appointment. If you don't hear back within a week, feel free to call up, identify yourself, and ask again. These interviews might just turn into an interview for a job or even a job itself.

Another good way to meet people in the industry is to attend industry annual conventions. These events offer many opportunities you might not normally have to network and meet industry insiders.

There is usually a charge to attend these conventions. Fee structures may vary. Sometimes there is one price for general admission to all events and entry to the trade show floor. Other times there may be one price for entry just to the trade show floor and another price

---

Tip from the Top

When you go to industry events it is important to have a positive attitude and not to have any negative conversation with anyone about anything at the seminar or in the industry. You can never tell who is related to who or what idea someone originated. You want to be remembered as the one who is bright and positive, not a negative sad sack.

The Inside Scoop

Many industry trade organizations offer special prices for students. Make sure you ask ahead of time.

Tip from the Coach

Many industry organization conference managers have begun having mini career fairs at these events to help industry people who have been downsized as well as for companies looking to fill jobs. Check out Web sites of association conferences ahead of time.

if you also want to take part in seminars and other events.

The cost of attending these conventions may be expensive. In addition to the entry or registration fee, if you don't live near the convention location you might have to pay for airfare or other transportation as well as accommodations, meals, and incidentals. Is it worth it? If you can afford it, absolutely! If you want to meet people in a specific area of technology and computers, these gatherings are the places to do it.

How do you find these events? Look in the appendix of this book for industry associations in your area of interest. Find the phone number and call and ask when and where the annual convention will be held. Better yet, go to the organization's Web site. Most groups put information about their conventions online.

If you are making the investment to go to a convention or a conference, take full advantage of every opportunity. As we've discussed throughout this book, network, network, and network some more! Some events to take part in or attend at conventions and conferences might include:

◎ Opening events
◎ Keynote presentations
◎ Educational seminars and workshops
◎ Certification programs
◎ Breakout sessions
◎ Breakfast, lunch, and/or dinner events
◎ Cocktail parties
◎ Trade show exhibit areas
◎ Career fairs

There is an art to attending conventions and using the experience to your best benefit. Remember that the people you meet are potential employers and new business contacts.

This is your chance to make a good first impression. Dress appropriately and neatly.

Do not get inebriated at these events. If you want to have a drink or a glass of wine, that's probably okay, but don't over-drink. You want potential employers or people you want to do business with to know you're a good risk, not someone who drinks at every opportunity.

It is essential to bring business cards with you and give them out to everyone you can. You can never tell when someone might hear about a position, remember meeting you, and want to give you a call. If he or she has your card, they can easily reach you.

Collect business cards as well. Then, when you get home from the convention or trade show, you will have contact names to call or write regarding business or job possibilities.

Walk the trade show floor. Stop and talk to people at booths. They are usually more than willing to talk. This is a time to network and try to make contacts. Ask questions and listen to what people are saying.

Job fairs are another great way to meet industry insiders, especially if you find events

The Inside Scoop

Recruiters and headhunters often attend conferences and conventions in hopes of finding potential employees for their clients.

geared toward computer and technology jobs. Even if there are no jobs available at the job fair that interest you, job fairs can be valuable networking opportunities. The people you meet at these fairs can range from recruiters and headhunters, to human resources directors, department heads, and other company employees.

Always be professional at these events. As you walk around the job fair floor, be pleasant and positive. While the person you meet might not have a job for you today, he or she might know of one tomorrow.

If you have good writing skills, a good way of meeting people within the industry is to interview people for local, regional, or national periodicals or newspapers. We discussed the idea earlier when talking about using your writing skills to help you obtain interviews. It can be just as effective in these situations.

How does this work? A great deal of it depends on your situation, where you live, and the area of the industry you are targeting.

Basically, what you have to do is develop an angle or hook for a story on the segment of the computer industry in which you are interested in meeting people. For example, does the chief information officer of a major health care company go on biking vacations in or out of the country? Perhaps his or her adventures might make a good story. Is the director of human resources from a large technology company appearing on a television game show? Does one of the network security administrators at the local college not only collect art, but also write about it in a major art magazine? Has the owner of a local e-commerce site been asked to speak about her success at a major trade conference? Has someone who graduated from the local high school become one of the top casino video game developers? These are angles or hooks you

might use to entice a local or regional periodical let you do an article.

Your next step is to contact someone who might be interested in the story. If you're still in school, become involved with the school newspaper. If you're not, call your local newspaper or a regional magazine and see if it might be interested in the article or feature story you want to write.

You probably will have to give them some samples of your writing and your background sheet or resume. You might also have to write on "spec" or speculation. What this means is that when you do the story they may or may not use it. If they do, they will pay you. If not, they won't.

Your goal here (unless you want to be a technology reporter) is not to make money (although that is nice). Your goal is to be in situations where you have the opportunity to meet industry insiders. If you're successful, not only will you be meeting these people, you'll be meeting them on a different level than if you were looking for a job. You'll be networking on a different level as well.

Networking Basics

It's not always what you know but who you know. With that in mind, I'm going to once again bring up the importance of networking. You can never tell who knows someone in some area of the industry, so it is essential to share your career dreams and aspirations with those around you. Someone you mention it to might just say, "My cousin is the director of database marketing at one of the casinos in Vegas." Or, "Really, I just heard that the Middleburgh School is looking for a computer sciences teacher." Or, "I just saw an advertisement in the classifieds for a job for a software engineer that you might want to look into."

Think it can't happen? Think again. It has happened to me over the years. It has happened to others, and it can happen to you!

A few years ago I was backstage during a concert of a client. After the show ended, some people from the radio station that presented the event wanted to meet the act, get their CDs autographed, and take some pictures. While I was chatting with them, one of the men told me that he was the Webmaster for the radio station's new Web site. It turned out he was in charge of putting the entire site together as well as developing content and keeping the information fresh and interesting. He said he loved his job, but the pay was just not enough for him.

"Why don't you talk to the guys about me putting together a Web site for them?" he said. I explained that they didn't have their own site, but I would remember him if it ever came up.

We all exchanged cards, they took pictures with the act, and they left. That would have been the end of the story if the next day during a meeting the conversation didn't turn to the act wanting a Web site. I mentioned that the man from the radio station they met the night before developed Web sites. An hour later, he was on the phone. Two weeks later, he was hired to be in charge of the act's Web site.

"But do those things really happen?" you ask. The answer is an unequivocal yes. These are not isolated incidents. Things like this happen all the time. Networking and sharing your dreams can and do work for others and can work for you. But in order for it to happen, you have to be proactive.

Knowing how important networking can be to your career, let's talk about some networking basics.

The first thing you need to do is determine exactly who you know and who is part of your network. Then you need to get out and find more people to add to the list.

When working on your networking list, add the type of contact you consider each person. Primary contacts are those people who you know; your family members, teachers, friends, and neighbors. Secondary contacts are those individuals who are referred to you by others. These would include, for instance, a friend of a friend, your aunt's neighbor, your attorney's sister, and so on.

You might also want to note whether you consider each person as a close, medium, or distant relationship. Close, for example, would be family, friends, employers, and current teachers. Medium would be people you talk to and see frequently, such as your dentist, attorney, or your UPS, FedEx, or mail carrier. Distant would include people you talk to and see infrequently or those you have just met or have met just once or twice.

Here's an example.

It would be great to have a network full of people in the segment of the computer industry in which you hope to have your career. However, that may not be the case. That does not mean, however, that other people can't be helpful. Your network may include a variety of people from all walks of life. These may include:

- ◎ Family members
- ◎ Friends
- ◎ Friends of friends
- ◎ Coworkers and colleagues
- ◎ Teachers or professors
- ◎ Your doctor and dentist
- ◎ Your pharmacist
- ◎ Your mail carrier
- ◎ Your hairstylist
- ◎ Your personal trainer
- ◎ Your priest, pastor, or rabbi

Networking Worksheet

Name	Relationship/ Position	Type of Contact (Primary or Secondary)	Closeness of Contact
John Golden	Former Guidance Counselor	Primary	Medium
Shirley Williams	Bank Teller	Primary	Distant
Bob	UPS Delivery Person	Primary	Medium
William Thomas	Newspaper Reporter	Secondary	Distant
Georgia	Sister-in-law	Primary	Close
Dr. Brenton	Dentist	Primary	Medium
Allen Robertson	Attorney	Primary	Medium
Jeremy Dementri	Technology Reporter	Secondary	Distant
Dr. Williams	College Adviser	Primary	Medium
Morey Albertson	CIO LMR Technology	Secondary	Medium

◎ Members of your congregation
◎ UPS, FedEx, DHL, or other delivery person
◎ Your auto mechanic
◎ Your attorney
◎ The waitress at the local diner
◎ The server at the local coffee shop
◎ Bank tellers from your local bank
◎ Your neighbors
◎ Friends of your relatives
◎ Your college adviser
◎ Business associates of your relatives
◎ People you work with on volunteer, not-for-profit boards and civic groups
◎ Coworkers at your current job

Now look at your list. Do you see how large your network really is? Virtually everyone you come in contact with during the day can be-come part of your network. Just keep adding people to your list.

Expanding Your Network

How can you expand your network? There are a number of ways. Networking events are an excellent way to meet people. Industry networking events are, of course, the best, but don't count out non-industry events too. For example, your local chamber of commerce may have specific networking programs designed to help business people in the community meet and network.

How do you know if the people who are at the event have any possibility of being related to the area of the computer industry in which you're interested? You don't. But as we've discussed, you don't know who people know.

Networking Worksheet

Name	Relationship/ Position	Type of Contact (Primary or Secondary)	Closeness of Contact (Close, Medium, or Distant)

People you meet may know others who are in the part of the industry you want to pursue.

Civic and other not-for-profit groups also have a variety of events that are great for networking. Whether you go to a regular meeting or you attend a charity auction, cocktail party, or large gala to benefit a nonprofit organization you will generally find business people in the community you might not know. As an added bonus, many larger not-for-profit events also have media coverage, meaning that you have the opportunity to add media people to your network.

How do you meet people at these events? You might just walk around and network. Or you might want to volunteer to help with a fundraiser or event so people start to know you and what you can do.

Those who take advantage of every opportunity to meet new people will have the largest networks. The idea in building a network is to go out of your comfort zone. If you just stay with people you know and are comfortable with, you won't have the opportunity to get to know others. You want to continually meet new people; after all, you never know who knows who.

Networking Savvy

You are now learning how to build your network. However, the largest network in the world will be useless unless you know how to take full advantage of it. So let's talk a bit about how you're going to use the network you are building.

Previously we discussed the difference between skills and talents. Networking is a skill. You don't have to be born with it. You can acquire the skill to network, practice, and improve. What that means is that if you practice networking, you can get better at it, and it can pay off big in your career!

Get out. Go to new places. Meet new people. The trick here is when you're in a situation where there are new people, don't be afraid to walk up to them, shake their hand, and talk to them. People can't read your mind, so it's imperative to tell them about your career goals, dreams, and aspirations.

When you meet new people, listen to them. Focus on what they're saying. Ask questions. Be interested in what they are telling you. You can never tell when the next person you talk to is the one who will be able to help you open the door or vice versa.

If you're shy, even the thought of networking may be very difficult for you. However, it is essential to make yourself do it anyway. Successful networking can pay off big in your career. In some situations it can mean the difference between getting a great job and not getting a job at all. It can also mean the difference between success and failure in your career. And that is worth the effort!

Just meeting people isn't enough. When you meet someone that you add to your network the idea is to try to further develop the relationship. Just having a story to tell about who you know or who you met is not enough. Arrange a follow-up meeting, send a note, write a letter, or make a phone call. The more you take advantage of every opportunity, the closer you will be to getting what you want.

A good way to network is to volunteer. We just discussed attending not-for-profit events and civic meetings to expand your network, but how about volunteering to work with a not-for-profit or civic group? A moment ago we discussed volunteering with an event. There are a ton of op-portunities just waiting for you. You just need to take advantage of them.

I can imagine you saying, "When? I'm so busy now, I don't have enough time to do anything."

Make the time. It will be worth it. Why? People will see you on a different level. They won't see you as someone looking for a job or trying to succeed at some level. Generally, people talk about their volunteer work to friends, family, business associates, and other colleagues. What this means is that when someone is speaking to someone else they might mention in passing that one of the people they are working with on their event or project is trying to get a job as a software engineer, trying to locate a position in marketing at a hardware or software company, trying to land a position as a technology report-er or technical writer, or almost anything else.

Anyone these people mention you or your situation to is a potential secondary networking contact. Those people, in turn, may mention you to someone else. Eventually, someone involved in the area of the computer industry you are pursuing might hear about you.

Another reason to volunteer is so people will see that you have a good work ethic. Treat volunteer projects as you would work projects. Do what you say you are going to do and do it in a timely manner. Do your best at all times. Showcase your skills and your talents and do everything you do with a positive attitude and a smile.

⭐ The Inside Scoop

Volunteer to do projects that no one else wants to do and you will immediately become more visible.

Tip from the Coach

While volunteering is good for networking, don't get involved with too many organizations. Depending on your schedule, one, two, or even three is probably fine. Anything more than that, and you're on the road to burnout.

Words from a Pro

Keep a scrapbook of articles, photos, programs, and other supporting material from volunteer events you have worked on or participated in. It will be useful when putting together your career portfolio.

Volunteering also gives you the opportunity to demonstrate skills and talents people might not otherwise know you have. Can you do publicity? Can your write? How about organizing things? Can you design Web sites? Do you get along well with others? Do you have leadership skills? What better way to illustrate your skills than using them by putting together an event, publicizing it, or coordinating other volunteers?

Best of all, you can use these volunteer activities on your resume. While volunteer experiences don't take the place of work experience, they certainly can fill out a resume short of it.

Don't just go to meetings. Participate fully in the organization. That way you'll not only be helping others, you will be adding to your network.

Where can you volunteer? Pretty much any not-for-profit, community group, school, or civic organization is a possibility. The one thing you should remember, however, is that you should only volunteer for organizations in whose cause you believe.

In order to make the most of every networking opportunity it's essential for people to remember you. Keep a supply of your business cards or networking cards with you all the time. Don't be stingy with them. Give them out freely to everyone. That way your name and number will be close at hand if needed. Make sure you ask for cards in return. If people don't have them, be sure to ask for their contact information.

Try to keep in contact with people on your network on a regular basis. Of course, you can't call everyone every day, but try to set up a schedule of sorts to do some positive networking every day. For example, you might decide to call one person every day on your networking list. Depending on the situation you can say you were calling to touch base, say hello, keep in contact, or see how they were doing. Ask how they have been or talk about something you might have in common or that they might think is interesting. You might also decide that once a week you will try to call someone and set up a lunch or coffee date.

Be on the lookout for stories, articles, or other tidbits of information that might be of interest to people in your network. Clip them out and send them with a short note saying you saw the story and thought they might be interested. If you hear of something they might be interested in, call them. The idea is to continue cultivating relationships by keeping in contact with people in your network and staying visible.

Tip from the Top

After you have worked on a volunteer project, ask the executive director or board president if he or she would mind writing you a letter of recommendation for your file.

Keep track of the contacts in your network. You can use the sample sheet provided, a card file using index cards, a database, or contact software program on your computer. Include as much information as you have about each person. People like when you remember them and their interests. It makes you stand out.

Then use your networking contact list. For example, a few days before someone's birthday, send them a card. If you know someone collects old guitars, for example, and you see an article on old guitars, clip it out and send it. Don't be a pest, but keep in contact. People in sales have been using this technique for years. It works for them and it will help you in your career as well.

You might want to use some of the items here and then add more information as it comes up. You don't have to ask people for all this information the first time you meet them. Just add it in when you get it.

Networking and Nerve

Successful networking will give you credibility and a rapport with people in and out of the industry. But networking sometimes takes nerve, especially if you're not naturally outgoing. You have to push yourself to get out and meet people, talk to them, tell them what you are interested in doing, and then stay in contact. On occasion, you may have to ask people if they will help you, ask for recommendations, ask for references, and so on. Don't let the fear of doing what you need to do stop you from doing it. Just remember that the end result of all this effort will be not only be an entrée into a career you want, but a shot at success.

As long as you're pleasant and not rude, there is nothing wrong with asking for help. Just remember that while people can help you get your foot in the door, you are going to have to sell yourself once you open it.

Networking is a two-way street. While it might be hard for you to imagine at this moment, someone might want you to help them in some segment of their career. Reciprocate and reciprocate graciously. As a matter of fact, if you see or know someone you might be able to help, even in a small way, don't wait for them to ask, offer your help.

Finding a Mentor or Advocate

Mentors and advocates can help guide and boost your career. A mentor or advocate in the

Networking Contact Information Sheet

Name
_____

Business Address
_____

Business Phone
_____

Home Address
_____

Home Phone
_____

E-mail Address
_____

Web Address
_____

Birthday
_____

Anniversary
_____

Where and When Met
_____

Spouse or Significant Other's Name
_____

Children's Name(s)
_____

Dog Breed and Name
_____

Cat Breed and Name
_____

Hobbies
_____

Interests
_____

Things Collected
_____

Honors
_____

Awards
_____

Interesting Facts

Tip from the Coach

If someone asks you to be their mentor, or asks for your help, and you can, say yes. As a matter of fact, if you see someone you might be able to help, do just that. You might think that you don't even have your own career on track or you don't have time. You might be tempted to say no. Think again. You are expecting someone to help you. Do the same for someone else. There is no better feeling than helping someone else. And while you shouldn't help someone for the sole purpose of helping yourself, remember that you can often open doors for yourself, while opening them for someone else.

Words from the Wise

It is not uncommon to run into someone who doesn't want to help you. This may be for any number of reasons, ranging from they really don't know how they can help, they don't have the time in their schedule, or they think that if they help you in your career, it puts their position at risk. If you do ask someone to be your mentor and he or she says no, just let it go. Look for someone else. The opposite of the having a great mentor in your life is having someone who is sabotaging your career.

industry often can also provide valuable contacts, which as we now know, are essential to your success. The best mentors and advocates are supportive individuals who help move your career to the next level. While having a mentor in the computer or technology industry would be the ideal, that doesn't mean others from outside the industry might not be helpful.

Can't figure out why anyone would help you? Many people like to help others. It makes them feel good and makes them feel important. How do you find a mentor? Look for someone who is successful and ask. Sound simple? It is simple. The difficult part is finding just the right person or persons.

Sometimes you don't even have to ask. In many cases, a person may see your potential and offer advice and assistance. It is not uncommon for a mentor to be a supervisor or former supervisor. He or she might, for example, hear of a better job or be on a search committee and recommend you. As your career goes on, the individual may follow you and your career, helping you along the way.

Time is a valuable commodity, especially to busy people. Be gracious when someone helps you or even tries to help. Make sure you say thank you to anyone and everyone who shares his or her time, expertise, or advice. And don't forget to ask them if there is any way you can return the favor.

8

THE INTERVIEW

Getting the Interview

You can have the greatest credentials in the world, wonderful references, and a stellar resume, but if you don't know how to interview well, it's often difficult to land the job, especially if you're seeking a job in any aspect of the computer industry. No matter what segment of the industry you dream about pursuing, the first step is always getting the job.

One of the keys to getting most jobs is generally that all-important meeting—the interview. Let's take some time to discuss how to get that meeting. The interview is your chance to shine. During an interview you can show what can't be illustrated on paper. This is the time your personality, charisma, and talents can be showcased. This is where someone can see your demeanor, your energy level, your passion, and your attitude. Obtaining an interview and excelling in that very important meeting can help get you the job you want.

If you do it right, the interview can help make you irresistible. It is your chance to persuade the interviewer to hire you. It is your main shot at showing why you would be better than anyone else—why hiring you would benefit the organization or company and why not hiring you would be a major mistake.

There are many ways to land job interviews. Some of these include:

◎ Responding to advertisements
◎ Posting your resume on job sites
◎ Posting your resume on company Web sites
◎ Recommendations from friends, relatives, or colleagues
◎ Making cold calls
◎ Writing letters
◎ Working with executive search firms, recruiters, or headhunters
◎ Working with employment agencies
◎ Attending job and career fairs
◎ Finding jobs that have not been advertised (the hidden job market)

Responding to an advertisement is probably the most common approach people take to obtaining a job interview. Where can you look for ads for jobs in the computer industry? Depending on the exact type of job you're looking for, here are some possibilities.

◎ Newspapers
◎ Trade journals
◎ Association Web sites
◎ Job posting and career Web sites
◎ Corporate Web sites (various industries)

◎ Technology company Web sites
◎ Computer company Web sites
◎ Software company Web sites
◎ ISP Web sites
◎ Career-oriented Web sites

Let's say you open the newspaper, a trade magazine, or even see advertisements on the Web that look like one of these.

Golden Sun Corporation seeking to fill the following positions: Director of Web site Marketing; Web site Content Editor; IT Systems Manager; Unix Systems Administrator; Technical Writer; Senior Software Engineer; Administrative Assistant to President. For consideration for these positions either fax resume to (888) 000-0000 or mail to P.O. Box 333, Some Town, NY 11111.

General Hospital seeking to fill the following full-time positions: Director of Web site Development; Web site Designer; Computer Graphics Designer; Web site Content Editor. For consideration forward resume and supporting documents to General Hospital; Ms. Diane Hubbard, Director of Human Resources; P.O. Box 911, Some Town, NY 11111.

Once you see the ad you get excited. You have been looking for a job just like one of the positions in the advertisement. You can't wait to send your resume.

Want a reality check? There may be hundreds of other people who can't wait either. Here's the good news. With a little planning, you can increase your chances of getting an interview from the classified or display ad, and as we've just discussed, this is your key to the job.

Your resume and cover letter need to stand out. Your resume needs to generate an interview. Most importantly, in a broad sense, you want your resume to define you as the one-in-a-million candidate an employer can't live without instead of one of the million others that are applying for a job.

In essence, it's essential that your resume and cover letter distinguish you from every other applicant going for the job. Why? Because if yours doesn't, someone else's will and he or she will be the one who gets the job.

Let's look at the journey a resume might take after you send it in response to a classified ad. Where does it go? Who reads it? That depends. In smaller organizations, your resume and cover letter may go directly to the person who will be hiring you. It may also go to that person's receptionist, secretary, administrative assistant, or an office manager.

In larger organizations your resume and cover letter may go to a hiring manager or human resources director. If you are replying to an advertisement placed by an employment agency, your response will generally go to the person at the employment agency responsible for that client and job.

In any of these situations, however, your resume may take other paths. Depending on the specific job and organization, your response may go through executive recruiters, screening services, clerks, secretaries, or receptionists.

⭐ Tip from the Top

Here is what you need to know. The requirements set forth in an advertisement are the ideal requirements that the company would like, not necessarily what they are going to end up with. Yes, it would be great if they could find a candidate with every requirement, but in reality it doesn't always work like that. In many cases, while there may be a candidate who has all the qualifications, someone who is missing one or two stands out and ultimately is the one who lands the job.

Whoever the original screener of resumes turns out to be, he or she will have the initial job of reviewing the information to make sure that it fits the profile of what is needed. But, and I repeat, but, that doesn't mean if you don't have the exact requirements you should not reply to a job.

The trick is to tailor your resume as closely as possible to the specific job and write a great cover letter. For example, let's say the requirements for a job as an online marketing manager look something like this:

ONLINE MARKETING MANAGER— EDIGITAL MUSIC ENTERTAINMENT
Creative, enthusiastic, team player with strong management skills and proven track record in online marketing. Must have strong organizational skills and excellent verbal and writing skills. Minimum requirements include bachelor's degree in marketing or related field and four years experience in online marketing. Experience with e-mail marketing and banner advertising necessary. National media contacts helpful.

Now let's say that while you are creative and enthusiastic and have excellent verbal and writing skills, you don't have four year's experience in online marketing. Instead you have two. You have experience with e-mail marketing, but no experience in banner advertising. You are, however, taking a workshop in banner advertising applications. You have a bachelor's degree, but it is in education, not marketing, or even a related field. You also have a number of national media contacts. Should you not apply for the job? If you want it, go for it.

Here is what you need to know. When you are working on your resume and your cover letter in response to an ad, remember that skills are transferable. Skills for specific areas might need to be fine-tuned; administrative skills are administrative skills, sales skills are sales skills, writing skills are writing skills, publicity and public relations skills are publicity and public relations skills, and communications skills are communication skills. Stress what you have done successfully, not what you haven't done. Use your cover letter to help showcase these accomplishments.

No matter whom your resume and cover letter go to, your goal is to increase your chances of it ending up in the pile of candidates' resumes that ultimately get called for an interview. Whoever the screener of the resumes is, he or she will probably pass over anything that doesn't look neat and well thought out or anything where there are obvious errors.

What can you do? First, go over your resume. Make sure it is perfect. Make sure it is perfectly tailored to the job you are going after. Make sure it is neat, looks clean, and isn't wrinkled, crumpled, or stained. If you are going to mail it, make sure it's printed on good-quality paper.

Human resources and personnel departments often receive hundreds of responses to ads. While most people use white paper, consider using off-white or even a different color such as light blue or light mauve. You want your resume to look sophisticated and classy but still stand out. Of course, the color of the paper will not change what is in your resume, but it will at least help your resume get noticed in the first place.

If the advertisement directs you in a specific method of responding to the ad, then use that method. For example, if the ad instructs applicants to fax their resumes, then fax it. If it says e-mail your resume, then use e-mail and pay attention to whether the ad specifies sending the file as an attachment or in the body of your e-mail. If the ad says to send a scannable resume, make sure you send a scannable resume. The company may have a procedure for screening job applicants.

If given the option of methods of responding, which should you use? Each method has its pros and cons.

◎ E-mail
  ▫ On the pro side, e-mail is one of the quickest methods of responding to ads. Many companies utilize the e-mail method.
  ▫ On the con side, you are never really assured someone gets what you send and even if they do, you're not sure it won't be inadvertently deleted. Another concern is making sure that the resume you send reaches the recipient in the form in which you sent it. If you are using a common word processing program and the same platform (Mac or PC) as the recipient, you probably won't have a problem. If you are using a Mac and the recipient is using a PC or you are using different word processing programs, you might have a problem.
◎ Fax
  ▫ On the pro side, faxing can get your resume where it's going almost instantaneously.

Tip from the Top
Many companies require candidates to apply using online applications. Make sure you follow the directions provided on how to submit your application and any supporting materials and be sure to keep a copy of everything.

  ▫ On the con side, if the recipient is using an old fashioned fax, the paper quality might not be great. The good news is that most companies now are using plain paper faxes.
◎ Mailing or Shipping (United States Postal Service, FedEx, Airborne, United Parcel Service, etc.)
  ▫ On the pro side, you can send your resume on good quality paper so you know what it is going to look like when it arrives. You can also send any supporting materials that might help you get the coveted interview. You can send it with an option to have someone sign for it when it arrives so you definitely know if and when it arrived.
  ▫ On the con side, it may take time to arrive by mail. One of the ways to get past this problem is to send it overnight or two-day express. It will cost more, but you will have control over when your package arrives.

Tip from the Coach
If faxing any documents, remember to use the "fine" or "best" option on your fax machine. While this may take a bit longer to send, the recipients will get a better copy.

When is the best time to send your response to an ad in order to have the best chance at getting an interview? If you send your resume right away, it might arrive with a pile of hundreds of others, yet, if you wait too long, the company might have already "found" the right candidate and stopped seriously looking at new resumes.

Many people procrastinate, so if you can send in your response immediately, such as the day the ad is published or the very next morning, it will probably be one of the first ones in. At that time the screener will be reading through just a few responses. If yours stands out, it stands a good chance of being put into the "initial interview pile."

If you can't respond immediately, then wait two or three days so your resume doesn't arrive with the big pile of other responses. Once again, your goal is to increase your chances of your resume not being passed over.

When you are trying to land an interview through a recommendation from friends or colleagues, cold calls, letters, executive search firms, recruiters, headhunters, employment agencies, people you met at job fairs, through other networking events, or any aspect of the hidden job market, the timing of sending a resume is essential. In these cases you want the people receiving your information to remember that someone said it was coming, so send it as soon as possible. This is not the time to procrastinate. If you do, you might lose the opportunity to set up that all-important meeting.

Persistence is the word to remember when trying to get an interview. If you are responding to an advertisement and you don't hear back within a week or two, call to see what is happening. If, after you call the first time, you don't hear back after another week or so (unless you've been specifically given a time frame) call back again. Don't be obnoxious and don't be a pain, but call.

If you're shy, you're going to have to get over it. Write a script ahead of time to help you. Don't read directly from the script, but practice so it becomes second nature. For example: "Hello, this is Joe Simpson. I replied to an advertisement you placed in the newspaper for a Web developer. I was wondering who I could speak with to find out about the status of the position?"

When you get to the correct person, you might have to reiterate your purpose in calling. Then you might ask, "Do you know when interviewing is starting? Will all applicants be notified one way or the other? Is it possible to tell me whether I'm on the list to be contacted?" Don't be afraid to try to get as much information as possible. Once again make sure you are pleasant.

You want to be friendly with the secretary or receptionist. These people are on the inside and can provide you with a wealth of information.

Be aware that there is a way that you can get your resume looked at, obtain an interview, and beat the competition out of the dream job you want. Remember we discussed the hidden job market?

While many positions are advertised, we know that there are jobs that are not advertised. Following this theory, all you have to do is contact a company and land the job you want before it is advertised.

"How?" you ask. Take a chance. Make a call or write a letter and ask. You might even stop in and talk to the human resources department or one of the department heads. There is nothing that says you have to wait to see an ad in the paper. Call and ask to speak to the human resources department, recruitment services, or hiring manager. Once again, write out a script ahead of time so you know exactly what you want to say. Ask for the hiring manager or human resources department. Ask about job openings. Make sure you have an idea of what you want to do and convey it to the person you are talking to.

If you are told there are no openings or you are told that the company or organization doesn't speak to people regarding employment, unsolicited, be pleasant yet persistent. Ask if you can forward a resume to keep on file. In many cases, they will agree just to get you off the phone. Ask for the name of the person to direct your resume, and then ask for the address and the fax number. Thank the person you spoke with and make sure you get his or her name.

Now here's a neat trick. Fax your resume. Send it with a cover letter that states that a hard copy will be coming via mail. Why fax it?

Did you know that when you fax documents to a company they generally are delivered directly to the desk of the person you are sending it to? They don't go through the mailroom where they might be dumped into a general in-box. They don't sit around for a day. They are generally delivered immediately.

Now that your resume is in the hands of the powers that be, it's your job to call up, make sure they got it, and try as hard as you can to set up an interview. The individual's secretary might try to put you off. Don't be deterred. Thank her or him and say you understand his or her position. Say you're going to call in a week or so after the boss has had a chance to review your material. Send your information out in hard copy immediately. Wait a week or so and call back. Remember that persistence pays off.

Depending on the job, you sometimes might reach someone who tells you, "If I weren't so busy, I would be glad to meet with you." They might tell you when their workload lightens or a project is done, they will schedule an interview. You could say thank you and let it go. Or you could tell them that you understand that they're busy. All you are asking for is 10 minutes and not a minute longer. You'll even bring a stopwatch and coffee if they want. Guarantee them that 10 minutes after you get in the door, you will stand up to leave.

If you're convincing, you might land an interview. If you do, remember to bring that stopwatch. Bring that coffee. Introduce yourself, put the stopwatch down on the desk in front of you, and present your skills. It's essential that you practice this before you get there. Give the highlights of your resume and how hiring you would benefit the company or organization. When your 10 minutes are up, thank the person you are meeting with for his or her time and give him or her your resume, any supporting materials you have brought with you, and your business card. Then leave. If you are asked to stay, by all means, stay and continue the meeting. One way or the other, write a note thanking them for their time.

If you have sold yourself or your idea for a position, someone may get back to you. Once again, remember to follow up with a call after a week or two.

⭐ Tip from the Coach

While the following occurred when I was first trying to enter the music business, I think the concept illustrates how persistence can pay off in any industry. At that time, I met and got to know a young man who was a comedian. He wasn't a very good comedian, but he said he was a comedian and did have a good number of jobs and bookings, so I guess he was a comedian.

During this time, I was trying to land interviews with everyone I could so I could get my own dream job in the music industry.

I made a contact with a booking agent whom I called and then developed a business relationship. Every week I'd call, and every week he would tell me to call him back. It wasn't going anywhere, but at least someone was taking my call. This went on for about three or four months.

One day when I called, the owner got on the phone and said, "Do you know Joe Black? (not his real name). He said he has worked in your area?"

I said, "Yes, he works as a comedian."

"What do you know about him?" he asked.

"He's very nice," I answered.

"But what do you know about him?" the agent asked again. "Is he any good?"

"Well, he's not a great comedian, but he seems to keep getting jobs. He's booking himself," I replied.

"That's interesting," he said. "He has called me over 25 times looking for a job as an agent. What do you think?"

I was wondering why he was asking my opinion, because I had yet to get into his office myself. "If he can book himself, he can probably do a great job for your agency," I said. "You have great clients. I bet he would do a great job."

"Thanks," he said, "I might give him a call."

"What about me?" I asked.

"I still can't think of where you might fit in," he said. "Why don't you give me a call in a couple of weeks."

I waited a couple of weeks, called back, and asked to speak to the owner.

"Hello," he said. "Guess who's standing next to me?"

He had hired Joe Black, the comedian, to work as an agent in his office.

"He had no experience, outside of booking himself," the booking agent said. "But I figured if he is as persistent making calls for our clients as he was trying to get a job, he'd work out for us. Why don't you come in and talk when you have a chance. I don't have anything, but maybe I can give you some ideas."

I immediately said that I had been planning a trip to the booking agent's city the next week. We set up an appointment.

Did the agent ever have a job for me? No, but while in his office, he introduced me to some of the clients he was booking, who introduced me to some other people, who later turned out to be clients of mine when I opened up my public relations company.

No matter what industry you want a job in, the moral of the story is the same. Networking and persistence always pay off.

The Interview Process

You got the call. You landed an interview. Now what? The interview is an integral part of getting the job you want. There are a number of different types of interviews. Depending on the company and the job, you might be asked to go on one or more interviews, ranging from initial or screening interviews to interviews with department heads or supervisors you will be working with.

Things to Bring

Once you get the call for an interview, what's your next step? Let's start with what you should bring with you to the interview.

- ◎ Copies of your resume
  - ▫ While the interviewers probably have copies of your resume, they might have misplaced it or you might want to refer to it. If you are going through a group interview, remember to bring enough copies of your resume so everyone can have one.
- ◎ Letters of reference
  - ▫ Even though people have given you their letters of reference, make sure you let them know you are using them.
- ◎ References
  - ▫ When interviewing for jobs, you often need to fill in job applications that ask for both professional and personal references. Ask before you use people as references. Make sure they are prepared to give you a good reference. Then when you go for an interview, call the people on your reference list and give them the heads up on your job-hunting activities.
- ◎ A portfolio of your achievements and other work
  - ▫ Refer to Chapter 6 to learn how to develop your professional portfolio.
- ◎ Business or networking card
  - ▫ Refer to Chapter 6 to learn more about business cards.
- ◎ Other supporting materials
  - ▫ This might include a variety of materials including copies of certifications, licenses, etc.

You want to look as professional as possible, so don't throw your materials into a paper bag or a sloppy knapsack. A professional-looking briefcase or portfolio is the best way to hold your information. If you don't have that, at the very least put your information into a large envelope or folder to carry into the interview.

Your Interviewing Wardrobe

You've landed an interview, but what do you wear? That depends to a great extent on the specific job for which you're interviewing. However, the rule of thumb is to dress for the job you want.

That doesn't mean that if you're pursuing a career where you will be wearing a uniform you should go to the interview wearing a uniform. What it means is that you want to dress professionally, so interviewers will see you as a professional, no matter what level you currently are in your career.

First let's start with a list of what not to wear.

- ◎ Sneakers
- ◎ Flip-flops
- ◎ Sandals
- ◎ Micro-miniskirts or -dresses
- ◎ Very tight or very low dresses or tops
- ◎ Jeans of any kind

◎ Ripped jeans or T-shirts
◎ Midriff tops
◎ Skin-tight pants or leggings
◎ Very baggy pants
◎ Sweatshirts
◎ Workout clothes
◎ Heavy perfume, men's cologne, or aftershave lotion
◎ Very heavy makeup
◎ Flashy jewelry (This includes nose rings, lip rings, and other flamboyant piercings.)
◎ Tatoos (If you have large, visible tattoos, you may want to cover them with either clothing or some type of cover-up or makeup.)

Now let's talk about what you should wear:

Men
◎ Dark suit
◎ Dark sports jacket, button-down shirt, tie, and trousers
◎ Clean, polished shoes
◎ Socks

Women
◎ Suit
◎ Dress with jacket
◎ Skirt with blouse and jacket
◎ Pumps or other closed-toe shoes
◎ Hosiery

Interview Environments

In most cases interviews are held in office environments. If you are asked if you want coffee, tea, soda, or any type of food, my advice is to abstain. This is not the time you want to accidentally spill coffee, inadvertently make a weird noise drinking soda, or get sugar from a donut on your fingers when you need to shake hands.

In some cases, however, you may be interviewed over a meal. Whether it is breakfast, lunch, or dinner, in these cases it is usually best to order something simple and light. This is not the time to order anything that can slurp, slide, or otherwise mess you up. Soups, messy sauces, lobster, fried chicken, ribs, or anything that you have to eat with your hands would be a bad choice. Nothing can ruin your confidence during an interview faster than a big blob of sauce accidentally dropping on your shirt, except if you cut into something and it splashes onto your interviewer's suit. Eating should be your last priority. Use this time to present your attributes, tell your story, and ask intelligent questions.

This is also not the time to order an alcoholic beverage. Even if the interviewer orders a drink, abstain. You want to be at the top of your game. If, however, the interviewer orders dessert and coffee or tea, do so as well. That way he or she isn't eating alone and you have a few more minutes to make yourself shine.

In some cases, a company may invite you to participate in a meal interview to see how you will act in social situations. They might want to check out your table manners, whether you keep your elbows on the table or talk with your

---

★ Words from the Wise

Never ask for a doggie bag at an interview meal. I don't care how good the meal is, how much you have left over, or how much you've had it drummed into your head that you shouldn't waste food. I don't care if the interviewer asks for a doggie bag. In case you're missing the message, do not ask for a doggie bag. I've seen it happen and I've heard the interviewers talking about it in a negative manner weeks later.

Words from the Wise

In your effort to tell people about your accomplishments, try not to monopolize the conversation by talking solely about you. Before you go to an interview, especially a meal interview, read up on the news of the day in case someone at the table asks your opinion about the day's happenings. You want to appear as well rounded as possible.

The Inside Scoop

If you have been invited to a meal interview, generally the interviewer will pay the tab and tip. At the end of the meal, when you are leaving, thank the person who paid the check and tell him or her how much you enjoyed the meal and the company.

mouth full. They might want to see whether you drink to excess or how you make conversation. They might want to know if you will embarrass them, if you can handle pressure, or how you interact with others. They might want you to get comfortable so they can see the true you. If you are prepared ahead of time, you will do fine. Just remember this isn't a social meal. You are being scrutinized. Be on your toes.

During the meal, pepper the conversation with questions about the company and the job. Don't be afraid to say you're excited about the possibility of working with them, you think you would be an asset to the organization, and you hope they agree. Make eye contact with those at the table.

When the interviewer stands up after the meal, the interview is generally over. Stand up, thank the interviewer or interviewers for the meal, tell them you look forward to hearing from them, shake everyone's hand, and then leave.

Many organizations today pre-interview or do partial interviews on the phone. This might be to pre-screen people without bringing them into the office. This type of interview might also take place if the employer is interested in a candidate and that individual lives in a different geographic location.

Whatever the reason, be prepared. If the company has scheduled a phone interview ahead of time, make sure your "space" is prepared so you can do your best.

Here are some ideas.

◎ Have your phone in a quiet location. People yelling, a loud television, or music in the background is not helpful in this situation.
◎ Have a pad of paper and a few pens to write down the names of the people you are speaking to, notes, and questions as you think of them.
◎ Have a copy of your resume near you. Your interviewer may refer to information on your resume. If it's close you won't have to fumble for words.
◎ Prepare questions to ask in case you are asked if you have any questions.
◎ Prepare answers for questions that you might be asked. Preparing for these questions is essential. While I can't guarantee what an interviewer might ask, I can pretty much guarantee that he or she probably will ask at least one

Tip from the Coach

Everyone has their own opinions on politics and religion. During an interview, stay clear of conversations involving either subject.

of the following questions, or at least something similar.

- Why do you want to work for us?
- What can you bring to the organization or company?
- What would your former coworkers say about you?
- What type of experience do you have?
- Why are you the best candidate?
- Where do you see yourself in five years?
- Why did you leave your last job?
- Did you get along with your last boss?
- What are you best at?
- What is your greatest strength?
- What is your greatest weakness?

Other Types of Interview Scenarios

When you think of an interviewing situation, you generally think of the one-on-one scenario where the interviewer is on one side of the desk and you are on the other. At some time during your career you may be faced with other types of interviews. Two of the more common ones you may run into are group interviews and panel interviews. What's the difference?

Group Interviews

A group interview is a situation where an organization brings a group of people together to tell them about the company and job opportunities. There may be open discussions and a question and answer period. During this time, individual one-on-one interviews may be scheduled.

Companies use these type of situations not only to bring a group of potential employees together, but to screen potential employees. What do you need to know? Remember that while this may not be the traditional interview setting you are used to, this is still an interview.

⭐ The Inside Scoop

I frequently receive calls from individuals who are distraught after going on interviews. It seems that while they prepared for answering every question they can possibly think an interviewer might ask about the job they were applying for, they hadn't prepared for the unexpected.

"I prepared for answering every question," a man told me. "And then the interviewer threw me for a loop. He started asking me all kinds of questions that had nothing to do with the job I was applying for. I just couldn't come up with answers that made sense."

"What did he ask?" I questioned.

"He asked me what my favorite book was when I was a child. He asked me what I wanted to be when I was little. He asked me what my greatest strength was in my last job. Then he asked me what my biggest mistake was in my last job. I couldn't think of anything to say that quick."

Interviewers often come up with questions like this for a variety of reasons. They may want to see how you react to nontraditional questions. They may want to see how well rounded you are. On occasion, they might just be thinking about something else at the time they were interviewing you and the questions just popped out of their mouth.

If this has happened to you in the past, instead of beating yourself up about not coming up with what you consider a good answer, prepare for next time. Know there generally isn't any right or wrong answer. When an interviewer asks you a question, it's okay to take a moment to compose yourself and think about the best answer for you to give.

From the minute you walk in the door in these settings, the potential employer is watching your demeanor and your body language. He or she is listening to what you say and any questions you might ask. He or she is watching you to see how you interact with others and how you might fit into the company.

How can you increase your chances of being asked to a one-on-one interview?

◎ Actively participate in conversations and activities.
◎ Be a leader not a follower.
◎ Ask meaningful questions.

Panel Interviews

Basically, a panel interview is an interview where you are interviewed by a group of people at the same time. While you might run into this type of interview at any time in your career, they are most often utilized more for higher-level positions. You might, for example, go through a panel interview if you are pursuing a position as a chief information officer or as another top administrator for a company. You might even go through a panel interview if you are going for a position as a project manager. It all depends on the company.

Why do employers use panel interviews? Every member of the panel brings something different to the table. Everyone has a different set of skills and experience. Many employers feel that a panel can increase the chance of finding the perfect applicant for the job. It also is sometimes easier to bring everyone involved together for one interview instead of scheduling separate interviews.

The panel interview will rarely be the first interview you go through. Generally, after going on one or more one-on-one interviews, if you become one of the finalists for a position, you will be asked to attend a panel interview.

Tip from the Coach

If the thought of participating in a panel interview stresses you out, think of it this way. You have more than one chance to impress interviewers. While one member of the panel may not be impressed by your credentials, another may think you are the perfect candidate and after the interview be your cheerleader.

Who is there? It can be a mixture of people, depending on the job. If you are pursuing a position as a chief information officer, for example, the panel may include the human resources or personnel director, the president of the company, the chief technology officer, the lead programmer, or the systems administrator. Perhaps members of the search committee will be there. It all depends on the specific job.

How can you succeed in a panel interview? Start by relaxing. Looking or feeling stressed will not help in this situation. When you walk into the interview smile sincerely and make sure you shake each person's hand with a firm handshake. You want each person to feel equally important.

Prepare ahead of time. Know what is on your resume or curriculum vitae. It sounds simple, but believe it or not when you're on the hot seat, it is very easy to get confused. You want to be able to answer every question about your background without skipping a beat.

Research the company for which you are interviewing. Have some questions prepared so you can show a true interest in the position for which you are interviewing. Instead of referring to notes you have written, try to have your questions seem part of the conversation.

One of the important things to remember when participating in a panel interview is to make eye contact with everyone. Start by looking

> ⭐ **Tip from the Coach**
>
> Always prepare a response for the beginning of the interview when someone on an interview panel says, "Tell us about yourself." Have a long and short version of your response. Don't say, "I don't know what to tell you." Or, "Where should I start?" Begin with your short version and ask if they would like you to go into more detail.

at the person who asks you the question. Then as you're answering, glance at the other people sitting around the table, making eye contact with each of them. You want everyone there to feel that you are talking to them.

After the interview, be sure to send a thank-you note. While some suggest just sending one note, I recommend sending a note to each person on the interview panel.

Timing is everything in an interview. Whatever you do, don't be late. If you can't get to an interview on time, the chances are you won't get to a job on time. On the other hand, you don't want to show up an hour early either.

Try to time your arrival so you get there about 15 minutes before your scheduled time. Walk in, tell the receptionist your name, and who your appointment is with. When you are directed to go into the interview, walk in, smile sincerely, and shake hands with the interviewer or interviewers, and sit down. Look around the office. Does the interviewer have a photo on the desk of children? Is there any personalization in the office? Does it look like the interviewer is into golf, fishing, basketball, or some other hobby? Do you have something common? You might say something like:

"What beautiful children."

"Is golf one of your passions, too?"

"Do you go deep-sea fishing?"

"Those are amazing orchids. How long have you had them?"

"What an incredible antique desk. Do you collect antique furniture?"

Try to make the interviewer comfortable with you before his or her questions begin.

What might you be asked? You will probably be asked a slew of general questions and then, depending on the job, some questions specific to your skills and talent.

◎ Why should we hire you?
  ⊡ This is a common question. Think about the answers ahead of time. Practice saying them out loud so you feel comfortable. For example, "I believe I would be an asset to your organization. I have the qualifications. I'm a team player, and this is the type of career I've always wanted to pursue. I'm a hard worker, a quick study, I have a positive attitude, and I get along well everyone. Most of all, I'm passionate about what I do, and I can help you achieve your goals." You can then go on to explain one or two specifics. For example, "In my current position, by introducing new methods of management and production, I turned the project

> ⭐ **Tip from the Top**
>
> If you have an extreme emergency and absolutely must be late, call and try to reschedule your appointment. Do not see if you can get there late and then try to come up with an excuse when you get there.

delivery time from constantly being late to completion seven to 10 days before deadline. This helped increase the company's bottom line. I would love the opportunity and challenge to do the same thing here."

◎ What makes you more qualified than other candidates?
  ▫ This is another common question. Depending on the situation, you might say something like, "I have won over 30 awards for sites I designed. I believe my experience starting off with my own Web design and development business, then working as a Web developer for a small site, and then having a similar position for a larger, better-known site gave me a fuller understanding of everything that needs to be done to design the best sites possible. I was always creative and have been designing Web sites for years, even before I realized that you could be paid for doing something you loved doing. I brought my portfolio so you can actually see some of the projects I've worked on.

◎ Where do you see yourself in five years?
  ▫ Do not say, "Sitting in your chair," or "In your chair." People in every job and every business are paranoid that someone is going to take their job, so don't even joke about it. Instead, think about the question ahead of time. It's meant to find out what your aspirations are and if you have direction? One answer might be, "I hope to be a successful part of the team at this company. I would love to think that I can have a long career here."

◎ What are your strengths?
  ▫ Be confident but not cocky when answering this one. Toot your horn, but don't be boastful. Practice ahead of time speaking about what are your greatest strengths, talents, and skills. "I'm passionate about what I do. I love working at something I'm passionate about. That's one of the main reasons I applied for this position. I am really good at troubleshooting production and development issues and finding solutions. I pride myself in being able to solve problems quickly, efficiently, and successfully."

◎ Where are your weaknesses?
  ▫ We all have weaknesses. This is not the time to share them. Be creative. "My greatest weakness is also one of my strengths. I'm a workaholic. I don't like leaving a project undone. I have a hard time understanding how someone cannot do a great job when they love what they do."

◎ Why did you leave your last job?
  ▫ Be careful answering this one. If you were fired, simply say you were let go. Don't go into the politics. Don't say anything bad about your former job, company, or boss. If you were laid off, simply say you were laid off, or, if it's true, that you were one of the newer employees and, unfortunately, that's how the layoff process worked. You might add that you were very sorry to leave because you really enjoyed working at your former company, but on the positive side, you now were free to apply for this position. If you quit, simply say

the job was not challenging and you wanted to work in a position where you could create a career. Never lie. Don't even try to stretch the truth. I've mentioned it before and I'm going to reiterate it again. This is a transient society. People move around. You can never tell when your former boss knows the person interviewing you. In the same vein, never say anything during an interview that is derogatory about anyone or any other organization or company. The supervisor you had yesterday might just end up moving to your new company and end up being your new boss. It is not unheard of in the industry.

◎ Why do you want to work in technology? (Depending on the specific area of the industry, the question might be, "Why do you want to work as a programmer?" "Why do you want to work in a large organization instead of a small company?" "Why do you be a technical writer?" and so on.)

◎ If you had to pick the most important advancement in technology, what would it be and why?

◎ When did you decide you wanted to work in software development (Web design, systems administration, or whatever your choice of career is)?
  ▫ Think about questions like this ahead of time and come up with answers. There is no right or wrong answer for these types of questions. You just want to be able to come up with answers without saying, "Uh, let me think. Well, I'm not sure."

◎ Are you a team player?
  ▫ Whether you're working at a large or small organization, companies want you to be a team player, so the answer is, "Yes, it's one of my strengths."

◎ Do you need supervision?
  ▫ You want to appear as confident and capable as possible. Depending on the specific job and responsibilities, you might say, "I work well with limited supervision." Or, "No, once I know my responsibilities, I have always been able to fulfill them on my own."

◎ Do you get along well with others?
  ▫ The answer they are looking for is "Yes, I'm a real people person." Do not give any stories about times where you didn't. Do not say anything like, "I get along better with women," or "I relate better to men." Even if it's true, don't make any type of comment that can come back to haunt you later.

Every now and then you get a weird question or a question that you just don't expect. If you could be a car, what type of car would you be and why? If you were an animal, what animal would you be? If you could have dinner with anyone alive or dead, who would it be? These questions generally are just meant to throw you off balance and see how you react. Stay calm and focused. Be creative but try not to come up with any answer that is too weird.

An interviewer might ask what the last book you read, what newspapers you read or what your favorite television shows are. Be honest, but try not to say things like, "I don't have time to read" or "I don't like reading." You want to appear well rounded.

> ### ⭐ Tip from the Top
> Try not to discuss salary at the beginning of the interview. Instead, wait until you hear all the particulars about the job and you have given them a chance to see how great you are.

◎ What type of salary are you looking for?
  ▫ This is going to be discussed in more detail in a moment, but what you should know now is that this is an important matter. You don't want to get locked into a number, before you know exactly what you will be responsible for. You might say something to the effect of, "I'm looking for a fair salary for the job. I really would like to know more about the responsibilities before I come up with a range. What is the range, by the way?" Or, you might turn the tables and say something like, "I was interested in knowing what the salary range was for this position." This turns the question back to the interviewer.

What They Can't Ask You

There are questions that are illegal for interviewers to ask. For example, they aren't permitted to ask you anything about your age, unless they are making sure you are over 18. They aren't supposed to ask you about marriage, children, or relationships. Interviewers are not supposed to ask you about your race, color, religion, national origin, or sexual preference. If an interviewer does ask an illegal question, in most cases it is not on purpose. He or she just might not know that it shouldn't be asked.

Your demeanor in responding to such questions can affect the direction of the interview. If you don't mind answering, then by all means, do so. It is your choice. If answering bothers you, try to point the questions in another direction, like back to your skills and talents. If you are unable to do so, simply indicate in a nonthreatening, nonconfrontational manner that those types of questions are not supposed to be asked in interviews.

What You Might Want to Ask

Just because you're the one being interviewed doesn't mean you shouldn't ask questions. You want to appear confident. You want to portray someone who can fit in with others comfortably. You want to ask great questions. Depending on the specific job, here are some ideas.

◎ What happened to the last person who held this job? Was he or she promoted or did he or she leave the organization?
  ▫ You want to know whose shoes you're filling.
◎ What is the longevity of employees here?
  ▫ Employees who stay for a length of time generally are happy with the organization.
◎ Does the company promote from within as a rule or look outside to fill positions?
  ▫ This is important because companies that promote from within are good companies to build a career with.
◎ Is there a lot of laughing in the workplace? Are people happy here?
  ▫ If there is, it means it is a less stressed environment.
◎ How will I be evaluated? Are there periodic reviews?

⊡ You want to know how and when you will know if you are doing well in your supervisor's eyes.

◎ How do you measure success on the job? By that I mean, how can I do a great job for you?

⊡ You want to know what your employer expects from employees.

◎ What are the options for advancement in this position?

⊡ This illustrates that you are interested in staying with the company.

◎ Who will I report to? What will my general responsibilities be?

⊡ You want to know what your work experience and duties will be like.

Feel free to ask any questions you want answered. While it is perfectly acceptable to ask questions, don't chatter on incessantly. You want to give the interviewer time to ask you questions and see how you shine.

It's normal to be nervous during an interview. Relax as much as you can. If you go in prepared and answer the questions you're asked, you should do fine. Sometime during the interview if things are going well, salary will come up.

Salary and Compensation

No matter how much you want a job, unless you are doing an internship, the good news is, you're not going to be working for free. Compensation may be discussed in a general manner during your interview or may be discussed in full. A lot has to do with the specific job. One way or another, salary will generally come up sometime during your interview. Unless your interviewer brings up salary at the begin-

ning of an interview, you should not. If you feel an interview is close to ending and another interview has not been scheduled, feel free to bring up salary when asked if you have any questions.

A simple question such as, "What is the salary range for the job?" will usually start the ball rolling. Depending on the specific job, your interviewer may tell you exactly what the salary and benefits are or may just give you a range. In many cases, salary and compensation packages are only ironed out after an actual job offer is made.

Let's say you are offered a job and a compensation package. What do you do if you're not happy with the salary? What about the benefits? Can you negotiate? You certainly can try. Sometimes, you can negotiate better terms as far as salary, sometimes better benefits, and sometimes both. A lot of it depends on how much they want you, how much of an asset you will be, and what they can afford.

When negotiating, speak in a calm, well-modulated voice. Do not make threats. State your case and see if you can meet in the middle. If you can't negotiate a higher salary, perhaps you can negotiate extra vacation days. Depending on the company and specific job, compensation may include salary, vacation days, sick days, health insurance, stock options, pension plans, or a variety of other things. When negotiating, look at the whole package.

You might do some research ahead of time to see what similar types of jobs are paying. Depending on the specific job, information on compensation may also have been in the original advertisement you answered.

Over the years I have seen many people who are so desperate to get the job of their dreams that once offered the job, they will take it for almost anything. Often when questioned about salary, they ask for salary requirements far below what might have been offered. Whatever you do, don't undersell yourself.

Accepting a job offer below your perceived salary "comfort level" often results in you resenting your company, coworkers, and even worse, whittles away at your self-worth.

It is perfectly acceptable to ask for a day or two to consider an offer. Simply say something like, "I appreciate your confidence in me. I'd like to think about it over night if that's okay with you. Can I give you a call tomorrow afternoon?"

In some situations, when you are dealing with certain high-level jobs, such as the chief information officer or chief technology officer of a large company, you might have someone like an attorney negotiate your contract including working conditions, earnings, and benefits.

Things to Remember

In order to give yourself every advantage in acing the interview, there are a few things you should know. First of all, practice ahead of time. Ask friends or family members for their help in setting up practice interviews. You want to get comfortable answering questions without sounding like you're reading from a script.

Many people go on real "practice interviews." In essence, this means going on interviews for jobs you might not want in order to get experience in interview situations. Some people think that it isn't right to waste an interviewer's time. On the other hand, you can never tell when you might be offered a job, which you originally didn't plan on taking, but which turns out to be something you want.

Here are some other things to remember to help you land a job offer.

◎ If you don't have confidence in yourself, neither will anyone else. No matter how nervous you are, project a confident and positive attitude.

◎ The one who looks and sounds most qualified has the best chance at getting the job. Don't answer questions in monosyllables. Explain your answers using relevant experiences. Use your experiences in both your work and personal life to reinforce your skills, talents, and abilities when answering questions.

◎ Try to develop a rapport with your interviewer. If your interviewer "likes" you, he or she will often overlook less than perfect skills because you "seem" like a better candidate.

◎ Smile and make sure you have good posture. It makes you look more successful.

◎ Be attentive. Listen to what the interviewer is saying. If he or she asks a question that you don't understand, politely ask for an explanation.

◎ Be pleasant and positive. People will want to be around you.

◎ Turn off your cell phone and beeper before you go into the interview.

◎ When you see the interview coming to a close, make sure you ask when a decision will be made and if you will be contacted either way.

◎ Be sure that the interviewer knows you want the job. Don't be afraid to demonstrate your passion and excitement about the possibility. You might say something like, "This looks like a wonderful organization to work with. I'm so happy you had an opening and hope I will be seriously considered for the position. I would love to work here and be part of the team."

◎ When the interview comes to a close, stand up, thank the interviewer, shake his or her hand, and then leave.
Here are some things you should not do:

◎ Don't smoke before you go into your interview.

◎ Don't chew gum during your interview.

◎ Don't be late.

◎ Don't talk negatively about past bosses, jobs, or companies.

◎ Don't say things like *ain't, heh, uh-huh, don't know, got me*, or other similar things. It doesn't sound professional and suggests that you have poor communication skills.

◎ Don't wear heavy perfume or men's cologne before going on an interview. You can never tell if the interviewer is allergic to various odors.

◎ Don't interrupt the interviewer.

◎ While you certainly can ask questions, don't try to dominate the conversation to try to "look smart."

◎ Don't swear, curse, or use off-color language.

Thank-You Notes

It's always a good idea to send a note thanking the person who interviewed you for his or her time. Think a thank-you note is useless? Think again. Take a look at some of the things a thank-you note can do for you.

A thank-you note after an interview can:

◎ Show that you are courteous and well mannered

◎ Show that you are professional

◎ Give you one more shot at reminding the interviewer who you are

◎ Show that you are truly interested in the job

◎ Illustrate that you have written communication skills

◎ Give you a chance to briefly discuss something that you thought was important, yet forgot to bring up during the interview

◎ Help you stand out from other job applicants who didn't send a thank-you note

Try to send thank-you notes within 24 hours of your interview. You can hand write or type them. While it's acceptable to e-mail or fax them, I suggest mailing.

What should the letter say? It can simply say thank you or it can be longer, touching on a point you discussed in the interview or adding something you may have forgotten.

Waiting for an Answer

You've gone through the interview for the job you want. You've done everything you can. Now what? Well, unfortunately, now you have to wait for an answer. Are you the candidate who was chosen? Hopefully, your are!

If you haven't heard back in a week or so (unless you were given a specific date when an applicant would be chosen), call and ask the status of the job. If you are told that they haven't made a decision, ask when a good time to call back would be.

If you are told that a decision has been made and it's not you, thank them and say how you appreciated the consideration. Request that your resume be kept on file for the future. You might just get a call before you know it. If the

Tip from the Coach
Take every interview seriously. Don't waste any opportunity to sell yourself.

organization is a large one, ask if there are other positions available and how you should go about applying for them, if you are interested.

If your phone rings and you got the job, congratulations! Once you get that call telling you that you are the candidate they want, depending on the situation, they will either make an offer on the phone or you will have to go in to discuss your compensation package. If an offer is made on the phone, as we previously discussed, you have every right to ask if you can think about it and get back to them in 24 hours. If you are satisfied with the offer as it is, you can accept it.

Depending on the job, you may be required to sign an employment contract. Read the agreement thoroughly and make sure that you are comfortable signing it. If there is anything you don't understand, ask. Do not just sign without reading. You want to know what you are agreeing to.

Interviewing for jobs is a skill. Practice until you feel comfortable answering every type of question and being in a variety of situations. The more prepared you are ahead of time, the better you'll usually do. The more you practice interviewing, the more comfortable you'll be going through the process.

Mastering the art of interviewing can make a huge difference in your interviews. Remember the intangible essentials that can help you win the job:

◎ Enthusiasm
◎ Excitement
◎ Passion
◎ Interest
◎ Confidence

> ### ⭐ Tip from the Coach
> Use any connection you have to get an interview. It might be a former teacher or professor, a colleague, a friend or neighbor, or even a supervisor. Often just a phone call from one of these people can land you an interview that can help you get the job of your dreams. You, of course, will be responsible for taking that very important interview and turning it into a job.

Enthusiasm is key when interviewing for a job. You want to be enthusiastic at the interview.

"But I don't want them to think I'm desperate," people always tell me.

My response is always the same. You don't want to appear desperate, but you don't want there to be a question in your interviewer's mind that you want the job.

What else? You want to be excited about the possibility of working at the job for which you are interviewing.

Passion is essential. Make sure you let your passion shine. It can make the difference between you getting the job or someone else getting it.

Anything else? You definitely want to appear interested. What does that mean? You want your interviewer to know without a shadow of a doubt that you are interested not only in the job, but also in the concept of working at that particular job.

And finally, you want to appear confident. As we have already discussed, if you don't believe you are the best, neither will anyone else.

9

MARKETING YOURSELF FOR SUCCESS

What Marketing Can Do for You

Who hasn't heard of Coca-Cola, Pepsi, and Dr Pepper? What about McDonalds, Burger King, and Wendy's? Here's a question. Do you know what those companies have in common with Las Vegas, Disneyworld, the Rolling Stones, and every other successful corporation and person? It's the same thing that hot trends, major sports events, blockbuster movies, top television shows, hot CDs, mega superstars, and even hot new toys have in common. Do you know what it is yet?

Here's the answer. Every one of them utilizes marketing. Do you want to know the inside track on becoming successful and getting what you want no matter what segment of the computer industry you're interested in pursuing? It's simple; all you have to do is utilize marketing yourself.

Many people think that marketing techniques are reserved for businesses, products, or celebrities. Here's something to think about. From the moment you begin your career until you ultimately retire, you are a product. It doesn't matter what direction your career is going, what level you're at, or what area you want to pursue.

There are thousands of people who want to work in various segments of the computer in-

dustry. Some make it, and some don't. Is it all talent? A lot of it has to do with talent, but that is not everything. We all have heard of talented individuals who haven't made it in their chosen field. Is it skills? We have all heard of people who are skilled, yet don't make it either.

So if it isn't just talent or skills, what is the answer? What is the key to success? As we've discussed previously, probably a lot of it may also have to do with luck and being in the right place at the right time. Some of it may be related to working hard and having a strong passion. One of the factors that appears to be related to success is how one individual sets him- or herself apart from another in the way they are marketed or market themselves.

Here's something you should know. When major corporations want to turn a new product into a hot commodity they develop and implement a successful marketing plan. No matter in which segment of the computer industry you want to work and succeed in, marketing can help you become one of the hottest commodities around, too.

While most people can understand how marketing can help a product succeed, or a celebrity become more popular, they often don't think about the possibility of marketing themselves if they are pursuing a career in an industry such as computers.

When I give seminars and we start discussing this area, there are always a number of attendees who inevitably ask, "Does this relate to me? Can't I just look for a job, interview, get it, and forget it?" they ask. "Do I need to go through this extra process? Why do I have to market myself?"

The answer in a nutshell is that if you aren't marketing yourself and someone else is, they will have an advantage over you. One of the tricks to success is taking advantage of every opportunity. Marketing yourself is an opportunity you just can't afford to miss.

What is marketing? On the most basic level, marketing is finding markets and avenues to sell products or services. In this case, you are the product. The buyers are employers.

To be successful, you not only want to be the product, you want to be the brand. Look at Nabisco, Kelloggs, McDonalds, Coke, Pepsi, and Disney. Look at Orange County Choppers, Martha Stewart, NASCAR, American Idol, and Michael Jordan.

Look at Donald Trump. One of the most successful people in branding, Trump, a master marketer, believes so strongly in this concept that he successfully branded himself. While he made his mark in real estate, in addition to successful television shows, Trump has a successful line of hotels, casinos, clothing, water, ice cream, meats, books, seminars, and even Trump University. He continues to illustrate to people how he can fill their needs. Then he finds new needs he can fill. If you're savvy, you can do the same.

If you know or can determine what you can do for an employer or what can help them, you can market yourself to illustrate how you can fill those needs. If you can sell and market your-self effectively, you can succeed in your career, you can push yourself to the next level, and you can get what you want.

Is there a secret to this? No, there really isn't a secret, but it does take some work. In the end, however, the payoff will be worth it.

Do you want to be the one who gets the job? Marketing can help. Want to make yourself visible so potential employers will see you as desirable? Marketing can help. Do you want to set yourself apart from other job candidates? Guess what? Marketing can help. It can also distinguish you from other employees. If you have marketed yourself effectively, when promotions, raises, or in-house openings are on the horizon your name will come up. Marketing can give you credibility and open the door to new opportunities.

And it doesn't matter what segment of the computer or technology industry you are pursuing. Marketing is just as important whether you are pursuing a career as a chief information officer, a software engineer, programmer, technical writer, Webmaster, content editor, help desk technician, or anything in between.

Do you want to stand out from every other network engineer your field? Do you want to set yourself apart from other game developers? Do you want to set yourself apart from other Webmasters? Do you want to set yourself apart from other project managers? You know what you have to do? Market yourself!

Do you want to become more visible or get the attention of the media? Do you want to get the attention of recruiters, headhunters, industry insiders, and other important people? Do you want to open the door to new opportunities? Do you want to catch the eye of board members, human resources directors, or personnel officers of companies whose team you want you to be a part of? Market yourself!

> ### ⭐ Tip from the Top
> Effective marketing focuses on the needs of the customer (in this case the employer). You want to show employers how you can fill their needs, not ask what they can do for you. What does this mean to you? You not only want to show potential employers how good you are, you want to show them how your skills, talents, and other attributes can help them.

"Okay," you're saying, "I get it. I need to market myself. But how?"

That's what we're going to talk about now. To begin with, understand that in order to market yourself effectively you are going to have to do what every good marketer does. You're going to have to develop your product, perform market research, and assess the product and the marketplace.

Are there going to be differences between marketing yourself for a career in the business or administration segments of the industry and a career in a technical area? Are there going to be differences, for example, between marketing yourself for a career as a technical writer and a career as a software engineer? Yes, of course there may be some differences, but in general, you're going to use a lot of the same techniques.

Read over this section and see which techniques and ideas will work best for you. As long as you are marketing yourself in a positive manner you are on the right track.

The 5 Ps of Marketing and How They Relate to Your Career

There are 5 Ps to marketing, whether you're marketing your career, a hot new restaurant, a new product, a school, your talent, or anything else. They are:

◎ Product
◎ Price
◎ Positioning
◎ Promotion
◎ Packaging

Let's look at how these Ps relate to your career.

◎ *Product*: In this case, as we just mentioned, the product is you. "Me," you say. "How am I a product?" You are a package complete with your physical self, skills, ideas, and talents.
◎ *Price*: Price is the compensation you receive for your work. As you are aware, there can be a huge range of possible earnings for any one job. One of your goals in marketing yourself is to sell your talents, skills, and anything else you have to offer for the best possible compensation.
◎ *Positioning*: What positioning means in this context is developing and creating innovative methods to fill the needs of one or more employers or potential clients. It also means differentiating yourself and/or your talents and skills from other competitors. Depending on your career area, this might mean differentiating yourself from other employees, software engineers, programmers, Webmasters, database administrators, online marketing professionals, administrators, business people, journalists, and so on.
◎ *Promotion*: Promotion is the implementation of methods that make you visible in a positive manner.
◎ *Packaging*: Packaging is the way you present yourself.

Putting Together Your Package

Now that you know how the 5 Ps of marketing are related to your career, let's discuss a little more about putting together your package.

The more you know about your product (you), the easier it is to market and sell it. It's also essential to know as much as possible about the markets to which you are trying to sell. What do you have to offer that a potential buyer (employer) needs? If you can illustrate to a market (employer) that you are the package that can fill their needs, you stand a good chance to turn the market into a buyer.

Assess what you have to offer as well as what you think an employer needs. We've already discussed self-assessment in a prior chapter. Now review your skills and talents to help you determine how they can be used to fill the needs of your target markets.

While all the Ps of marketing are important, packaging is one of the easiest to change. It's something you have control over.

How important is packaging? Very! Good packaging can make a product more appealing, more enticing, and make you want it. Not convinced? Think about the last time you went to the store. Did you reach for the name brand products more often then the bargain brand?

Still not convinced? How many times have you been in a bakery or restaurant and chosen the beautifully decorated deserts over the simple un-iced cake? Packaging can make a difference—a big difference—in your career. If you package yourself effectively, people will want your package.

Want to know a secret? Many job candidates in every industry are passed over before they get very far in the process because they simply don't understand how to package themselves. What does this mean to you?

It means that if you can grasp the concept, you're ahead of the game. In a competitive world, this one thing can give you the edge. Knowing that a marketing campaign utilizes packaging to help sell products means that you will want to package yourself as well as you can. You want potential employers, recruiters, headhunters, board members, and others to see you in the most positive manner possible. You want to illustrate that you have what it takes to fill their needs.

So what does your personal package include?

People base their first impression of you largely on your appearance. Whether you are going for an interview for a hot job or currently working and trying to move up the ladder of success, appearance is always important.

It might seem elementary, but let's go over the elements of your appearance. Personal grooming is essential. What does that mean?

- ◎ Your hair should be clean and neatly styled.
- ◎ You should be showered with no body odor.
- ◎ Your nails should be clean. If you polish them, make sure that your polish isn't chipped.
- ◎ If you are a man, you should be freshly shaved. Mustaches and beards should be neatly styled.

- If you are a woman, your makeup should look natural and not overdone.
- Your breath should be clean and fresh.
- Good grooming is important no matter what segment of the industry you are pursuing.

Now let's discuss your attire. Whether you're going on interviews, are in a networking situation, or are already on the job, it's important to dress appropriately. What's appropriate? Good question.

Appropriateness to a great extent depends on what area of the industry in which you're involved and your specific job. If you're working in the business or administrative end of the industry you, of course, want to look professional at all times.

While employees working at some companies often have leeway for casual dressing, it's important to remember that dressing professionally can help your career in a number of ways,

from establishing credibility to maintaining respect to establishing yourself as an authority figure. These things can help you advance your career.

Always dress to impress. Employers want to see that you will not only fit in, but that you will not embarrass them when representing the company. So what should you do? What should you wear?

If you are going on an interview, dress professionally. Men can never go wrong in a suit and tie or a pair of dress slacks with a sports jacket, dress shirt, and tie. Women might wear a suit, a professional looking dress, a skirt and jacket, skirt and blouse, or perhaps a pantsuit. Once you're hired, learn the company dress policy. It's okay to ask. No matter what the policy is, observe what everyone else is wearing. If the policy is casual and everyone is still dressed in business attire, dress in business attire.

"But I'm going for a job as telephone help desk tech," you say, "why would I get dressed up for a job like that? No one will really see me."

> ### ★ Tip from the Top
> Here's a tip for career advancement. Check out what the higher-ups are wearing and emulate them. If you dress like you're already successful, not only you will feel more successful, but you also will set yourself apart in a positive way in your superior's eyes.

> ### ★ Voice of Experience
> If you're not sure if you should say something, don't say it. If you think something might be off color or offend someone, keep it to yourself.

The answer is simple. You want to make a good impression. You want to look like you care and you want to look like you're serious about your career. You want to look professional.

You might also want to think about your image when you're not working. Why is this important? If you project an unprofessional image off the job, it can possibly affect your career in a negative manner.

This isn't to say that you have to wear a suit all the time or even be dressed up. What it means is that you never want to be in a position where you leave home looking sloppy and then run into someone who could be helpful to your career.

Communication Skills

Your communication skills, both verbal and written, are yet another part of your package. What you say and how you say it can mean the difference between success and failure in getting a job or succeeding at one you already have. You want to sound articulate, polished, strong, and confident.

Do you ever wonder how others hear you? Consider using a tape recorder to record yourself speaking, and then play it back.

Is this scary? It can be if you have never heard yourself. Here's what to remember. No matter what you think you sound like, it probably isn't that bad. You generally are your own worst critic.

When you play back your voice, listen to your speech pattern. You might, for example, find that you are constantly saying "uh" or "uh-huh." You might find that your voice sounds nasal or high pitched or that you talk too quickly. If you're not happy with the way you sound, there are exercises you can do to change your pitch, modulation, and speech pattern.

There are even methods to change your accent, if you have one. Do you need to change your accent? Only if you feel it's a hindrance to your career. If, for example, you are an aspiring television or radio technology reporter, you might feel a very heavy accent might limit your career. If you are a corporate software trainer, you want to make sure an accent isn't standing in the way of your success. This is something you have to decide for yourself—no one else can make this decision. If you do feel you need to change your accent, look for a speech therapist, speech coach, or vocal coach.

Because you can't take words back into your mouth after you say them, here are some *don'ts* to follow when speaking.

◎ Don't use off-color language.
◎ Don't swear or curse.
◎ Don't tell jokes or stories that have either sexual, ethnic, or racial undertones or innuendoes.
◎ Don't interrupt others when they are speaking.
◎ Don't use poor grammar or slang.
◎ Don't talk about people.

We've discussed your verbal communication skills. Now let's discuss the importance of your written communication skills. Here's the deal. Written communication skills are important in every industry. If you are pursuing a career in any segment of the computer industry, they are important as well. At the very least, you will need the ability to write letters and reports.

If you are uncomfortable with your writing skills, either pick up a book to help improve them or consider taking some extra writing classes at a local school or college.

Your body language can also tell people a lot about you. The way you carry yourself can show others how you feel about yourself. We've all seen people in passing who were hunched over or who looked uninterested or just looked like they didn't care.

Would you want someone like that representing your company? Would you like someone who looked like that working for you? Well generally, neither do most employers.

What does your body language illustrate? Does it show that you are confident? That you are happy to be where you are? Do you make eye contact when you're speaking to someone? Are you smiling? What about your demeanor? Common courtesy is mandatory in your life and your career. Polite expressions such as *please*, *thank you*, *excuse me*, and *pardon me* will not go unnoticed.

Your personality traits are another part of your package. No one wants to be around a whiner, a sad sack, or someone who complains constantly. You want to illustrate that you are calm, happy, well balanced, and have a positive attitude.

You want to show that you can deal effectively with others, are a team player, and can deal with problems and stress effectively. You might be surprised to know that in many cases employers will lean toward hiring someone with a bubbly, positive, and energetic personality over someone with better skills who seems negative and less well balanced.

We've discussed education in an earlier chapter. The education you have is an important part of your package. Get the best education and training you can. Don't stop at the minimum requirements. Continue learning throughout your career. Education and training, both formal and informal, not only help you increase knowledge and build new skill sets, but help you make new contacts and build your network.

Last but not least in your package are your skills and talents. These are the things that make you special. What's the difference between skills and talents?

Skills can be learned or acquired. Talents are things that you are born with and can be embellished. Your personal package includes both.

What you must do is package the product so the buyer wants it. In this case, as we have discussed, the product is you and the buyer might be a potential employer, recruiter, headhunter, human resources director, and so on.

Now that you know what goes into your package, and you're working on putting together your best possible package, what's next?

Marketing Yourself Like a Pro and Making Yourself Visible

How can you market yourself? If you're like many people, you might be embarrassed to promote yourself, embarrassed to talk about your accomplishments, and embarrassed to bring them to the attention of others. This feeling probably comes from childhood when you were taught, "It isn't nice to brag."

It's time to change your thinking. It's time to toot your own horn! Done correctly, you won't be bragging. Done correctly you are simply taking a step to make yourself visible. You are taking a step to help let potential employers know that you are the one who can fill their needs.

Want to know the payoff to doing this? You can move your career in a positive direction quicker. Career success can be yours, but you need to work at it.

Visibility is important in every aspect of business and the computer industry is no exception. No matter the segment of the industry in which you want to succeed, visibility can help you attain your goals. To start with, it can help set you apart from others who might have similar skills and talents.

How can you make yourself visible?

◎ Tell people what you are doing.
◎ Tell people what you are trying to do.
◎ Share your dreams.
◎ Live your dreams.
◎ Send out press releases.
◎ Toot your own horn.
◎ Make it happen.

When you make yourself visible, you will gain visibility in the workplace, the community, the media, and more. This is essential to get what you want and what you deserve in your career, whether it's the brand new job or a promotion pushing you up the career ladder.

We'll discuss how you can you tell people what you're doing without bragging later, but first, let's discuss when it's appropriate to toot your own horn. Here are some situations.

◎ When you get a new job
◎ When you get a promotion
◎ When you get a good review
◎ When you are giving a speech
◎ When you are giving a presentation
◎ When you are going to be (or have already appeared) on television or radio
◎ When you have a major accomplishment
◎ When you receive an honor or an award
◎ When you chair an event
◎ When you graduate from school, college, or a training program
◎ When you obtain professional certification
◎ When you work with a not-for-profit or charity organization on a project as a volunteer

And the list goes on. The idea isn't only to make people aware of your accomplishments, but to make yourself visible in a positive manner.

How do you do it? Well, you could shout your news from a rooftop or walk around with a sign, but that probably wouldn't be very effective.

One of the best ways to get the most bang for your buck is by utilizing the media.

"I don't have money for an ad," you say.

Here is the good news. You don't have to take out an ad. You can use publicity, and publicity is free. Newspapers, magazines, and periodicals need stories to fill their pages. Similarly, television and radio need to fill airspace as well. If you

Tip from the Top

A press release is not an ad. Ads cost money. There is no charge to send press releases to the media. Press releases are used by the media to develop stories and are either edited slightly or are published as is.

The Inside Scoop

Press releases and news releases are the same thing. The phrases are used interchangeably.

do it right, your story can be one of the ones filling that space and it won't cost you anything.

How do you get your news to the media? The easiest way is by sending out press or news releases.

There are many books, classes, seminars, and workshops that can help you learn how to write news releases effectively. Basically, however, you should know that news releases are developed by answering the five Ws. These are:

◎ Who
   ▫ Who are you writing about?
◎ What
   ▫ What is happening or has happened?
◎ When
   ▫ When did it happen or is it happening?
◎ Where
   ▫ Where is it happening or has it happened?
◎ Why
   ▫ Why is it happening or why is it noteworthy or relevant?

Words from a Pro

Many of the stories you read in newspapers and magazines or hear on the radio or television are the direct result of press releases. Don't make the mistake of not sending out press releases because you think the media won't be interested.

While it would be nice for everyone to have his or her own personal press agent or publicist, this is not generally the case. So, until you have one, you are going to have to be your own publicist. In order to market yourself, you'll have to find opportunities to issue press releases, develop them, and then send them out. You want your name to be visible in a positive manner as often as possible.

Let's look at a possible scenario. Let's say Ryan Dean just graduated from college. He found a job as the Webmaster of a small insurance company. It wasn't as large a company as Ryan had hoped for, but it was a job, and a start.

Ryan was watching the local news one night when he saw a story that caught his eye about a local senior citizens center. It seems someone had donated 10 brand new computers to the center to be used exclusively by the seniors, not for administrative services. The problem was, the majority of the seniors didn't know how to use the computers. The center was looking for someone to volunteer to teach basic computer skills a few hours a week.

"I could do that," said Ryan to himself. The story struck a nerve because his beloved grandmother had died six months ago. He remembered how his entire family had chipped in and bought his grandmother a computer three years ago as a Christmas gift.

He remembered setting it up for her and showing her how to turn it on and turn it off.

By the second day he had shown her how to use the basic software programs and how to send an e-mail. He showed her how to use the Internet and remembered how excited she was when she Googled his name and she found he had made the dean's list. He remembered how she would call in a panic and he would walk her through the steps to getting her computer working again. Yes, he wanted to be the one helping those seniors.

First thing the next morning, Ryan called the senior center and offered his services. He spoke to his supervisor at the insurance company and asked if he could use his lunch hour three times a week to go teach the class at the senior center on a volunteer basis. His supervisor agreed to that and also suggested that he could either come into work an hour early or leave an hour later on days he taught the classes.

The seniors loved the classes Ryan taught almost as much as Ryan loved teaching them.

One day the owner of the insurance company stopped in to see Ryan. It seems his mother was one of the seniors taking Ryan's classes and she loved it.

"Being able to use a computer has made all the difference in the world to my mother," said the owner. "Before, she was always bored and never felt like doing anything. Now she can't wait to get up and see who e-mailed her. She is involved in a number of online senior chat groups. She can't travel much because of her physical limitations, but she now can visit a museum online. We just bought her a new laptop. It just has changed her life. I don't know how to thank you."

"I think most of the seniors like the class," Ryan said. "From what I understand, that is the reaction from a lot of the participants. The class has become so popular, I wish we had more computers."

Within an hour, the owner of the company called Ryan back. While he didn't have brand new computers, he could donate two-dozen year-old computers complete with software.

"What do you think about asking the local business community for donations?" he asked. "I'm the president of the chamber of commerce. We have a meeting tomorrow. I could bring it up."

Ryan suggested a conference call with the senior center director to make sure everyone is on the same page. By the end of the day, he had become the coordinator of the Computers For Seniors program.

The goal of the program was to have a sufficient number of computers donated so there would be enough computers at each of the senior centers in the area so everyone who wanted to could learn and use a computer.

In order to help publicize the program, press releases were written and issued explaining the program. Each press release also contained a small blurb mentioning that Ryan was the coordinator of the program and giving a small bio of his professional career. Ryan participated in media interviews explaining the program. He additionally spoke at civic group and not-for-profit organization luncheon and dinner meetings on a fairly consistent basis.

Within six months the program took off, with over 300 computers being donated. The pilot program continued to expand. Ryan was asked to help put together similar programs in other locations.

Throughout all of this, Ryan continued teaching the seniors how to use computers and continued with his job as a Webmaster.

In this scenario Ryan was gaining visibility in a number of ways. Not only did his supervisor and the owner of the insurance company see him in a different light, but he also was gaining visibility in the community with people who might not have otherwise known him. More importantly, people in various other businesses, corporations, and organizations learned who he was, what he was doing, and some of his capabilities.

During this time other companies were hearing about Ryan, whether through reading stories about the program, seeing him on television news, hearing him on the radio, or hearing him speak at meetings.

It was no surprise then that Ryan began to receive calls from recruiters and others who were interested in setting up interviews. And while Ryan might have taken any of the offers he received, he didn't.

Coincidentally, the small insurance company Ryan worked for was bought out by a much larger company. The former owner spoke so highly of Ryan that the new company offered him a position as the director of Web site development, resulting in increased responsibilities and increased earnings.

And while there are many skilled Webmasters and directors of Web development, Ryan now has something that other candidates wouldn't have on their resume.

Think it can't happen this way? Well, it can! While you might not live this exact scenario, you can potentially create your own scenario

The Inside Scoop
Always be ready for the media. Keep stock paragraphs on your computer so you can turn out press releases quickly when needed. As a matter of fact, you might want to keep stock press releases and bios on hand so you're always ready when the media calls.

with a similar outcome if you are creative and think outside of the box.

On the next page is an example of a press release that Ryan might send out to further market the project. Note that in marketing the project, the press release is also helping market Ryan.

What does this press release do? In addition to publicizing Ryan's radio appearance, it gets his name in the news. It gets his message out. It exposes his career accomplishments and helps keep him in the pubic eye in a positive way. By using this avenue to market himself, Ryan is putting himself in a different light than those who are not doing so.

"Well, that's a nice story," I can hear you saying, "but in the real world does that kind of thing happen?"

You might not hear about it all the time, but those situations do happen and they can happen to you. The key here is that in order for them to occur, you're going to have to start thinking outside of the box.

Tip from the Coach
Contacts are an important part of your career. Once you make them, don't risk losing your relationships. Stay in contact by periodically sending e-mails, cards and letters, making period calls, and arranging to meet for lunch, coffee, or just to get together and talk.

Voice of Experience
It's difficult to proofread your own press releases to catch errors. Always have someone else read them not only for errors but also to make sure they make sense.

NEWS FROM COMPUTERS FOR SENIORS

P.O. Box 491
Some City, NY 11111
For additional information, contact:
Ryan Dean, 111-888-8888

For Immediate Release:

Ryan Dean of Some City, NY, will be a guest on WBIG's popular talk show, *Life Lessons,* on Tuesday, March 10, at 8:00 p.m. He will be discussing a program he is coordinating called Computers For Seniors. The program works to get new and gently used updated computers donated to area senior citizen centers.

These computers are then used to teach senior citizens everything from basic computer usage to putting together simple personal Web sites. After seniors are comfortable using their computers, many then take it home.

Best Computer Repair services all computers free of charge when they are donated, making sure they are all in perfect working order.

Dean graduated in May from State University with a bachelor's degree in computer science and Web design. Soon after graduation he took a job with LMR Insurance as the company's Webmaster.

One night Dean was watching the news when he saw a story that caught his eye about a local senior citizens center where someone had donated 10 brand new computers to be used exclusively by the seniors, not for administrative services. The problem was, the majority of the seniors didn't know how to use the computers. The center was looking for someone to volunteer to teach basic computer skills a few hours a week.

Ryan remembered teaching his grandmother how to use her brand new computer her family bought her as a Christmas gift three years ago. He remembered how excited she was the first time she Googled his name and saw firsthand that he had made the dean's list. He remembered how she would call in a panic and he would walk her through the steps to get her computer working again. Ryan wanted to be the one helping those seniors.

Ryan's classes were popular. So popular, in fact, that more computers were needed. One day, Bill Reynolds, the owner of LMR Insurance stopped in to see Ryan to thank him for teaching his mother how to use a computer. It seems Agnes Reynolds was in one of Ryan's first classes at the senior center.

"Being able to use a computer has made all the difference in the world to my mother," said Reynolds. "Before, she was always bored and never felt like doing anything," he continued. "Now she can't wait to get up and see who e-mailed her. She is involved in a number of online

(continues)

(continued)

senior chat groups. She can't travel much because of her physical limitations, but she now can visit a museum online. We just bought her a new laptop. It just has changed her life."

When Bill asked Ryan if there was anything he could do to thank him, Ryan told him more computers were needed for the program. Within a couple of hours, Ryan and Bill, the president of the Tri-County Chamber of Commerce, put together a plan of action and a program asking for donations of computers.

To date, over 300 computers have been donated by local residents and businesses. The program goal is to have an adequate supply of updated computers so every senior citizen who wants to learn how to use a computer and have one to use, can.

Dean, who became the director of Web development for Country Wide Insurance in 2008 when LMR was purchased, continues to be involved hands on in the program. "I still teach three classes a week at the local senior center," he said. "That is my passion."

"I'm just as excited to see such a positive reaction to the donation program. Giving seniors the opportunity to learn something that can open their world and make it a better place is one of the best gifts you can give. Giving them the tools to do that is the icing on the cake."

-30-

Make sure your press releases look professional by printing them on press or news release stationery. This stationery can easily be created on your computer. Have the words *News* or *News From* or something to that effect someplace on the stationery so the media is aware it is a press release. Also make sure to include your contact information. This is essential in case the media wants to call to ask questions about your release. In many instances, the media just uses the press release as a beginning for an article. Once you pique their interest, they use the press release as background and write their own story.

You've developed a press release. Now what? Whether it's about getting a promotion, being named employee of the month, or anything else, developing and writing a great press release is just the first step. Once that's done, you have to get the releases to the media.

How do you do this? You have a few options. You can print the press releases and then send or fax them to the media or you can e-mail them. Either way it's essential to put together a media list so you can reach the correct people. Look around your area. Get the names of your local media. Then find regional media. If your stories warrant it, national or trade media should also be included. Don't forget any Web or online publications.

★ Tip from the Top

When working on your basic media database, make sure you find out the publication's deadline. The deadline is the day you need to get the information to the publication so your news can be considered for the next issue.

Words from the Wise

Remember that just because you send a press release doesn't mean it will get into the publication. Small, local publications are more likely to eventually use your press releases. Larger publications are more discriminatory. Do not call the media and insist that they use your release. This will make you look like an amateur and they will probably ignore your releases from that day forward.

Tip from the Top

If you're e-mailing press releases, find out what format publications accept ahead of time. If you're sending out printed press releases, you might also call to find out what font is preferred. Many smaller publications just scan in your release and certain fonts scan better.

Call up each media outlet and ask to whom press releases should be directed. Sometimes it may be *News Editor, Technology Editor, Business Editor,* or something to that effect. Sometimes it will be a specific person. Get their contact information. Put together a database of the names of the publications or stations, contact name or names, address, phone and fax numbers, e-mail addresses, and any other pertinent information.

Becoming an Expert

Want another idea to make yourself visible? Become an expert. You probably already are an expert in one or more areas either in or out of the computer or technology industry. Now it's time for you to exploit it.

Many people are used to the things they know well. They don't give enough credence to being great at them. It's time to forget that type of thinking!

One of the wonderful things about being an expert in any given area is that people will seek you out. Everyone knows how to do something better than others. What you have to do is figure out what it is.

"Okay," you say, "you're right. Let's say I'm a gourmet chef. But what does that have to do with computers?"

Well, it might have nothing to do with computers on the surface. However, if it can help you gain some positive attention and visibility, it will give you another avenue to get your story out. This will help you achieve the career success you desire. So with that in mind, it has everything to do with it.

Let's begin by determining where your expertise is. Sit down with a piece of paper and spend some time thinking about what you can do better than anyone else in or out of the computer industry. What subject or area do you know more about than most? Do you volunteer in an interesting area? Are you a gourmet chef? Can you teach almost anyone how to pitch a ball? Can you teach senior citizens how to use a computer? Can you spell words backward?

Need some help? Can't think of what you're expertise is? Here are some ideas to get you started.

◎ Are you a gourmet cook?
◎ Do you bake the best brownies?
◎ Are you a sports trivia expert?
◎ Are you a master gardener?
◎ Do you design jewelry?
◎ Can you speak more than one language, fluently?

⭐ **Words from a Pro**

Make it easier to issue press releases by setting up sheets of labels. That way when you're ready to send out a mailing, you need only to place the labels on envelopes.

Send your press releases to all applicable publications and stations. The idea with press releases is to send them consistently. Keep in mind that while you don't want to write a press release about nothing, anytime you have anything noteworthy to send out a press release, you should.

◎ Do you love to shop?

◎ Do you know how to coordinate just the right outfit?

◎ Do you train dogs to be service animals?

◎ Do you know how to write great songs?

◎ Can you put together events with ease?

◎ Do you know how to write great press releases?

◎ Do you know how to pack a suitcase better than most people?

◎ Are you an expert organizer?

◎ Do you know how to arrange flowers?

◎ Are you an expert in building things?

◎ Are you a great fund-raiser?

◎ Have you set a world record doing something?

◎ Do you volunteer teaching people to read?

◎ Do you know about helping children with special needs?

◎ Do you volunteer reading books for the blind?

◎ Do you have special skills or talents that others don't?

Are you getting the idea? You can be an expert in almost area. It's the way in which you exploit it that can make a difference in your career.

You want to get your name out there. You want to draw positive attention to yourself. You want others to know what you can do. That way you can market yourself in the areas in which you are interested.

Find ways to get your name and your story out there. How? Developing and sending out press releases is one way, but what else can you do? You can become known for your expertise by talking about it. How? Most areas have civic or other not-for-profit groups that hold meetings. These groups often look for people to speak at their meetings. You can contact the president of the board of directors or the executive director to find out who sets up the meeting speakers. In some areas, the chamber of commerce also puts together speaker lists.

You might be asking yourself, "Unless I'm a rocket scientist, why would any group want to hear me speak about anything? Why would anyone want to know about me knowing how to pack a suitcase?" Or, "Why would anyone be interested in my organizing ability?"

They might not, unless you tailor your presentations to their needs. If you create a presentation from which others can learn something useful or interesting, they usually will want to hear it. For example, if you're speaking to a group of business people, you might do a presentation about "The Stress Free Bag: Packing Easily For Business Trips," "Organize Your Career, Organize Your Life," "Helping Children Feel Good About Themselves Through Sports," or "Using Cooking to Build Teamwork."

Whatever your subject matter is, when you speak in front of a group, whether it be 20 or 2,000 people, you will gain visibility. When you are introduced, the host of the event will often mention information about your background to the audience. Make sure you always have a short

---

⭐ The Inside Scoop

Many people are successful at using blogging to help promote themselves as well as promoting their expertise.

⭐ Words from a Pro

The media works on very tight deadlines. If they call you, get back to them immediately or you might lose out.

---

paragraph or two with you to make it easy for the emcee to present the information you want to convey.

For example, based on information you provide, the emcee might introduce you like this: "Good afternoon ladies and gentlemen. Our luncheon speaker today is Scott Peters. Some of you might know him from his weekly technology column in the *Town Times* on making technology easy. Today, he will be discussing how to keep your children safe on the computer. Scott was a graduate of our local high school and then left us to go to college. He just graduated from State University in May with a degree in computer science and is hoping to find a job right here in town utilizing his degree. Please join me in welcoming Scott Peters."

As you can see, Scott is getting exposure that can help him gain career visibility. Someone at the luncheon may know of a job or an upcoming position opening in town. Someone may know someone from another area who might be looking for someone with Scott's skills. Scott

may make contacts and increase his network. The important thing to remember is to use every opportunity to get what you are looking for in your career.

On a local level, you will generally get no fee for most of these types of presentations. The benefit of increased visibility, however, will usually be well worth it. When you are scheduled to do a presentation, make sure you send out press releases announcing your speech. If it was a noteworthy event, you might also send out a release after the event as well. Many organizations will also call the media to promote the occasion. Sometimes the media will call you for an interview before the event. Once again, take advantage of every opportunity.

It's exciting once you start getting publicity. Take advantage of this too. Keep clippings of all the stories from the print media. Make copies. If you have been interviewed on television or radio, get clips. Keep these for your portfolio. Every amount of positive exposure will help set you apart from others and help you market yourself to career success.

I can almost hear some of you saying, "Oh, no! I'm not getting up to speak in public."

Here's the deal: If you don't feel comfortable speaking in public, you don't have to. These ideas are meant to be a springboard to get you thinking outside of the box. Use any of them to get you started and then find ways you are comfortable in marketing yourself.

⭐ Tip from the Coach

If you aren't comfortable speaking in front of large groups, consider joining Toastmasters or the Dale Carnegie Institute. Both will help you gain experience in a nurturing and safe environment.

More Strategies to Market and Promote Yourself

If you aren't comfortable speaking in public, how about writing an article on your area of expertise instead?

What about writing articles or columns on a given subject? The idea, once again, is to keep your name in the public's eye in a positive manner. While it's helpful to write about something in your career area, it is not essential.

For example, you might write an article on what life is like as the content editor for a new dating site or a day in the life of an ISP help desk representative. You might write an article on collecting quilts or cookbooks. You might write articles on organizing your office, your schedule, or your life. You might write an article on stress management or laughter or humor. If you can tailor the articles in some manner to your career area all the better. If not, that's okay as well.

If you look at similar types of articles or stories in newspapers, you will notice that if the article is not written by a staff reporter, after the article there generally is a line or two about the author. For example, "Tom Martin is the Webmaster for the GRS Golf Courses International."

How do you get your articles in print? Call the editor of the publication you are interested in writing for and ask! Tell them what you want to do, and offer to send your background sheet, resume, or bio, and a sample. Small or local publications might not pay very much. Don't get caught up on money. You are not doing this for cash. You are doing it to get your name and your story before the public.

Don't forget to tell media editors about your expertise. You can call them or send a short note. Ask that they put you on their list of experts for your specific area of expertise. Then when they are doing a story on something that relates to your subject area, it will be easy to get in touch with you.

Remember that if you don't make the call or write the note, no one will know what you have to offer. You have to sometimes be assertive (in a nice way) to get things moving.

Consider teaching a class, giving a workshop, or facilitating a seminar in your area of expertise. Everyone wants to learn how to do something new and you might be just the person to give them that chance. Every opportunity for you is an opportunity to become visible and move your career forward. Can you give someone the basics of writing a press release or doing publicity? Offer to teach a class at a local college or school. Can you easily explain how to understand what you see when watching a game on television? Offer to teach a workshop? Do you think you can illustrate the basics of putting together a fund-raiser? Suggest a workshop! Can you easily explain how to put together a MySpace page? Suggest a one or two session workshop. What a great way to get your name out!

There are a plethora of possibilities. You just need to use your imagination.

What can your expertise do for you? It will get your name out there. It will give you credibility and it will give you visibility. Of course, when you're at meetings or speaking to the me-

---

⭐ The Inside Scoop

Don't get caught up in the theory that if you help someone do something or learn how to do something, it will in some way take away opportunities from you. Help others when you can.

dia, it's up to you to network. Tell people what you do. Tell people what you want to do. Give out business cards. This technique works effectively no matter what area of the computer industry in which you want to succeed. As a matter of fact, this technique can help you succeed in any venture.

Join professional associations and volunteer to be on committees or to chair events that they sponsor. Similarly, join civic groups and not-for-profit organizations, volunteering to work on one or two of their projects.

"I don't have time," you say.

Make time. Volunteering, especially when you chair a committee or work on a project, is one of the best ways to get your name out there, obtain visibility, and network.

The radio and television talk show circuit is yet another means to generate important visibility. Offer to be a guest on radio, cable, and television station news, variety, and information shows.

"Who would want me?" you ask.

You can never tell. If you don't ask, no one will even know you exist, in many instances. Check out the programming to see where you might fit. Then send your bio, resume or curriculum vitae with a letter to the producer, indicating that you're available to speak in a specific subject area. Pitch an idea. A producer just might take you up on it.

Here's a sample pitch letter to get you started.

SARAH WALSH, PRODUCER
WTHR Radio
Talk Today Show
P.O. Box 2222
Anytown, NY 44444

Dear Ms Walsh:

I'm not sure how many people have the opportunity to put their passions together and cre-

ate a career they love, but I do know I am one of the lucky ones. I have always loved writing. I love travel. And I enjoy connecting with other people, sharing information, and getting their feedback. That's why I love to blog.

Who knew that I would be able to turn my passions into a great career? Last year I was hired by travelez.com as a professional blogger. As part of my job, I get to travel around the country (and the world on occasion) and then blog about my adventures. I then get to hear about the adventures other people have had in the same location.

I would love to share some of my stories with your listeners. Some are informative, some are funny, and some you'll be happy happened to me instead of you.

I regularly listen to your program and believe that the subject matter fits well into your show's format. We could even blog live on air.

I have included my background sheet for your review. Please let me know if you require additional information.

I look forward to hearing from you.

Sincerely,
David Johnston

Wait a week or so after sending the letter. If you don't hear back in that time, call the producer and ask if he or she is interested. If there is no interest, say thank you, and request that your background sheet can be kept on file.

Remember that people talk to each other so that every person you speak in front of who reads an article about you, who hears you on the radio, or sees you on television has the potential of speaking to other people who might then speak to others.

As we've discussed, networking is one of the best ways to get a job, get a promotion, and advance your career. Even if your expertise is in something totally unrelated to the computer industry, just getting your name out can help boost your career.

> ### ⭐ Tip from the Top
> Many people lose out because they just don't follow up. They either feel like a nuisance or feel like they are being a pain. No matter how awkward and uncomfortable you feel, call and follow up on things you are working on. Be polite, but call to see what's happening.

If your expertise happens to be something related to computers, that's even better. Whatever your expertise, exploit it and it will help your career move forward.

More Ways to Market Yourself

Here's another idea that can get you noticed: A feature story in a newspaper or magazine. How do you get one of these? Well, everyone wants a story about themselves or their product or service, so you have to develop an angle to catch their attention. Then contact a few editors and see if you can get one of them to bite.

Before you call anyone, however, think out your strategy. What is your angle? Why are you the person someone should talk to or do a story on? Why would the story be interesting or unique or entertaining to the reader?

How do you develop an angle? Come up with something unique that you do or are planning to do. What is the unique part of your package? Were you the one who was so afraid to speak in high school that you skipped the class where you had to give a report, yet today you are the spokesperson for a technology company? Were you the one who succeeded despite severe adversities? Do you have a human-interest story?

Send a letter with your idea and a background sheet, bio, curriculum vitae, or resume. Wait a week and then call the editor to whom you sent your information. Ask if he or she

received your information. (There is always a chance it is lost, if only on a reporter's desk.) If the answer is no, offer to send it again and start the process one more time. Sometimes you get lucky. Your angle might be just what an editor is looking for or they might need to fill in a space with a story.

Opening the Door to New Opportunities

If you keep doing the same old thing, things might change on their own, but they probably won't. It's important when trying to create a more successful career to find ways to open the door to new opportunities.

Start to look at events that occur as new opportunities to make other things happen. If you train yourself to think of how you can use opportunities to help you instead of hinder you, things often start looking up.

Do you want to be around negative people who think nothing is going right, people who think they are losers? Probably not. Well neither does anyone else. Market yourself as a winner, even if you are still a winner in training.

The old adage "misery loves company" is true. One problem people often have in their career and life is that they hang around other people who are depressed or think that they're not doing well. Remember that negative energy

> ### ⭐ Tip from the Coach
> If you don't think you're worth something, usually neither will anyone else. In the same vein, if you don't think you're the best, neither will anyone else. Maintain a positive attitude illustrating that you are marketing the best.

attracts negative results, so here's your choice. You can either stay with the negative energy, help change the negative energy, or move yourself near positive energy. Which choice do you want to make?

Work on developing new relationships with positive people. Cultivate new business relationships. When doing that, don't forget to cultivate a business relationship with the media. How? Go to events where the media is present. Go to chamber of commerce meetings, not-for-profit organization events, charity functions, entertainment events, sports events, meetings, and other occasions.

Walk up, extend your hand, and introduce yourself. Give out your business cards. Engage in conversation. If a reporter writes an interesting story about anything, drop him or her a note saying you enjoyed it. If a newscaster does something special, drop a note telling him or her. The media is just like the rest of us. They appreciate validation.

Don't just be a user. One of the best ways to develop a relationship with the media or anybody else is to be a resource. Help them when you can.

Want to close the door to opportunity? Whine, complain, and be a generally negative person who no one wants to be near. Want the doors of opportunity to fly open? Whatever level you are in, more doors will open if you're pleasant, enthusiastic, and professional.

Words from the Wise

Many people go to networking events and social occasions where they meet people and make important contacts. They then proceed to "forget" who they met. It's essential to keep track of business cards, names, people you meet and where you met them. In order to do this, after any event where you make contacts, make it a habit to write notes about who you met, where you met them, and any other pertinent details. Do it quickly. While you think you can't possibly forget meeting someone important to your career, you would be surprised how easy it is to forget details.

Dreams can come true. They can either happen to you or happen to someone else. If you want it bad enough and market yourself effectively, you will be the winner.

It's essential in marketing yourself and your career to move out of your comfort zone, even if it's just a little bit. Take baby steps if you need to, but learn to move out of your comfort zone. Find new places to go, new people to meet, and new things to do

You can be the number-one factor in creating your own success. Don't let yourself down! Market yourself and reap the rewards of a great career.

10

SUCCEEDING IN THE WORKPLACE

Learning As You Go

You got the job! Now what? Are you ready to succeed?

"Well," you say, "I guess so."

No matter what segment of the computer industry you are pursuing, there are things you can do that can help you increase your chances of success—things you can do that can turn your job into the career of your dreams.

"Can't I worry about that later?" you ask.

You don't need to worry about it at all. You need to take action. Lots of people have jobs. You don't just want a job. You want a great career! It doesn't matter what you want to do in the industry. What matters is that you know in order to succeed and move up the career ladder, you sometimes have to do a little extra, do more than is expected of you, and put some effort into getting what you want.

No matter how it looks, there are very few overnight successes. Appearances can be very deceiving. While it may seem that some individuals might just appear to get their foot in the door one day and zoom to the top rung of the career ladder the next, it generally doesn't happen like that.

While there are exceptions, more than likely, the people you think are overnight successes have been working at it and preparing for their dream career for some time. Many of them were probably in the same position you are now.

What looks like someone who became an overnight success, is generally a person who had a well thought out plan, did a lot of work, had some talent, a bit of luck, and was in the right place at the right time.

Unfortunately, just getting your foot in the door is not enough. It's essential once you get in to take positive actions to climb the ladder to success. If you don't take those actions, someone else will.

Once you get your foot in the door you want to create your perfect career. Getting a job is a job in itself. However, just because you've been hired doesn't mean your work is done. It's essential once you get in to learn as you go.

If you look at some of the most successful people, in all aspects of life and business, you'll see that they continue the learning process throughout their life. If you want to succeed you'll do the same.

Learning is a necessary skill for personal and career growth and advancement. Many think that your ability and willingness to learn is linked to your success in life. This doesn't necessarily mean going back to school or taking traditional classes, although for many jobs you are going to have to continue your education or training anyway. In many cases, it means life learning.

What's life learning? Basically, it's learning that occurs through life experiences. It's learning that occurs when you talk to people, watch others do things, work, experience things, go places, watch television, listen to the radio, hear others talking, or almost anything else. Every experience you have is a potential learning experience.

Not only that, but almost everyone you talk to can be a teacher. If you're open to it, you can usually learn something from almost everyone you come in contact with.

"What do you mean?" you ask.

Look for opportunities. Be interested. Everything you learn might not be fascinating, but it might be helpful, maybe not today or tomorrow, but in the future. Sometimes you might learn something work related, sometimes not. It doesn't matter. Use what you can. File the rest away until needed.

How do you learn all these things? Observe what people say or do. Sometimes you might see that someone has a skill you want to master. You might, for example, see someone using a unique method of troubleshooting a computer application. You might see a Web designer lay out Web pages in an interesting way. You might see a computer help desk representative calm an irate customer. You might see someone using more effective sales skills. It could be almost anything.

Tip from the Top

Career progression does not always follow traditional paths. Treat supervisors, colleagues, and subordinates all with the same respect.

Don't be afraid to ask others how to do something. Whether it's simple or complicated, most people are flattered when someone recognizes they're good at something and then asks for their help.

Challenge yourself to learn something new every day. Not only will it help improve your total package, but it also will make you feel better about yourself. Whether it's a new word, new skill, new way to do something, or even a new way to deal better with people, continue to learn as you go.

How else can you continue to learn? Take advantage of internships, formal and informal education, company training programs, in-service programs, and volunteer opportunities. Many companies have formal volunteer programs. If yours does, take advantage of it. If yours doesn't, you might want to see if you can get your company involved in one.

What can you learn by volunteering? The possibilities are endless. You might learn a new skill, or a better way to get along with others, or a more effective way to get things done. You might learn how to coordinate events or run organizations. You might learn almost anything. And as a bonus, if you volunteer effectively you not only will get some experience, you might obtain some important visibility

Don't discount books as a learning tool. As the saying goes, reading is fundamental. Are you a graphic artist who wants to do Web design? Are you a computer science teacher who aspires to be a software engineer? Do you want

Tip from the Coach

While success does sometimes just fly in the window, it always helps to at least open the window.

★ **Tip from the Coach**

Don't assume that because someone is under you on the career ladder they know less than you do.

to learn more about Web design? Do you want to learn how to become a game designer? Are you working as a programmer in the private sector and would rather be working in the governmental sector? Are you working as a project manager and want to find ways to move further up the career ladder? Look for a book. Read more about it.

Are you working in traditional retail, but yearn to have success in some aspect of e-commerce? Look for a book. See if it's a career area you want to pursue. Are you interested in learning more about doing publicity or public relations for a software or hardware company? Find a book. Need help improving your leadership skills? Check out some books for ideas. Want to know more about the life of Steve Jobs or Bill Gates? Do you want to see how You-Tube began? Look for a book! Want to know more about any aspect of the computer industry? There are tons of books on all aspects of the industry. The more you read, the more you'll know. Books often hold the answer to many of your questions. They give you the opportunity to explore opportunities and learn about things you didn't know.

Trade journals offer numerous possibilities as well. They'll keep you up to date on industry trends and let you know about industry problems and solutions. What else can you find in the trades? You might discover advertisements for job openings, notices for trade events, and current news.

How do you find trade journals? You might check with your local library. You can also surf the Internet to check out journals specific to area of the computer industry in which you're interested.

Go to your local newsstand and library to see what's available. If your library doesn't have the periodical you are looking for, try your local community college or university library.

If you are already working in some aspect of the computer industry, these trades may also be available in your workplace. Most companies subscribe to trades related to their specific area of the industry. Ask your supervisor what trades the company receives. Explain that you are interested in learning more about industry trends.

National bookstore chains such as Borders or Barnes and Noble may also often carry some of the more popular trade publications. Be sure to check out the online versions of trade publications. While many require subscriptions to access some areas, they still often carry the latest news and job openings in the free section.

How about workshops, seminars, and other courses? In addition to learning new skills in or out of the area you are pursuing in the computer industry, there are a number of added benefits to going to these. First, you'll have the opportunity to meet other people interested in the same subject area as you are. You also will be able to network. Instructors, facilitators, even other attendees in the class are all potential contacts that might be instrumental in a positive way to your career.

"But," you say, "I'm busy enough without doing extra work. Is this really necessary? Do I have to take classes?"

No one is going to make you do anything, but you should be aware that they can help take your career to a new level. Classes, workshops, and seminars will help give you new ideas and help you to look at things from a different perspective.

Additionally, these classes, seminars, and workshops can help you keep up with changes and advances in your industry. In an ever-changing industry such as computers, this is essential to your success. If you are in an area of the industry where certifications are available, you will want to take continuing education to either get certified or remain certified. Whether or not these are required, they often give you an edge over other employees or job applicants.

Whether you are taking workshops, seminars, or classes, learning new techniques, or honing your existing skills, it will help you in your quest to be the best at what you do. If you continue to navigate your way through formal and informal learning experiences throughout your life and career, you will be rewarded with success and satisfaction.

Workplace Politics

In order to succeed in your career in the computer industry, it is essential to learn how to deal effectively with some of the challenging situations you'll encounter. Workplace politics are a part of life. And depending on the area of the industry in which you are involved, the workplace can be almost anywhere.

The real trick to dealing with workplace politics is trying to stay out of them. No matter which side you take in an office dispute, you're going to be wrong. You can never tell who the winner or loser will be, so try to stay neutral and just worry about doing your job. Is this easy? No. But for your own sake, you have to try.

Will keeping out of it work all the time? Probably not, and therein lies the problem. There's an old adage that says the workplace is a jungle. Unfortunately that's sometimes true.

If you think you're going to encounter workplace politics only in the office, think again. As we just mentioned, the workplace can be almost anyplace. It might be in the computer or electronic store you work. It might be the home or office of a client. It might even be in the community in which you work.

What all this means is that no matter what part of the computer industry you are working, you often may have additional challenges. In many cases, workplace politics will now be expanded to every area of your life, from your personal relationships to your family to your work. With this in mind, let's learn more about them.

Why are there are politics in the workplace? Much of it comes from jealousy. Someone might think you have a better chance at a promotion or are better at your job than they are at theirs. Someone might think you slighted him or her at some time. Believe it not, someone just might not like you. In any business setting there are

⭐ **Words from the Wise**
We've all heard of someone about whom others say, "You know, he (or she) is such a nice man (or woman). He (or she) never says a bad word about anyone. He (or she) stays out of office politics, stays out of office squabbles, and stays out of trouble in the workplace." If you can keep this in mind and try to follow their lead, you will be ahead of the game. It may not be easy, but before you decide to speak about someone, remember that office politics and gossip can be problematic.

people who vie for more recognition, feel the need to prove themselves right all the time, or who just want to get ahead. There really is nothing you can do about workplace politics except to stay out of them to the best of your ability.

In certain segments of the industry, feelings of jealousy might escalate even more. There are many reasons for this. Someone may feel they are more talented than you in their area of the industry.

Often jealousy surfaces when someone doesn't understand why you got the job or the promotion and he or she did not. Some may not understand why you are a department head and they can't get a promotion.

Sometimes people may want to protect themselves from feeling like a failure or may just be frustrated with their career (or lack of a career).

In these situations, many people may lash out and talk about others. Real or not, these words can hurt. Worse than that, your words can come back to haunt you—big time.

Office Gossip

Gossip is a common form of office politics. Anyone who has held a job has probably seen it, and perhaps even participated in it in some form. Have you? Forget the moral or ethical issues. Gossip can hurt your career.

Here's a good rule of thumb. Never, ever say anything about anyone that you wouldn't mind them hearing and knowing it came from you. If you think you can believe someone who says, "Oh, you can tell me, it's confidential," you're wrong.

"But she's my best friend," you say, "I trust her with my life."

It doesn't matter. Your friend might be perfectly trustworthy, but trust is not always the problem. Sometimes people slip and repeat things during a conversation. Other times someone might tell someone else whom they trust what you said and ask him or her to keep it confidential, but then that person tells another person and so it goes down the line. Eventually, the person telling the story doesn't even know it's supposed to be confidential and might even mention it to a good friend or colleague of the person everyone has been gossiping about.

The reason people gossip is because it makes them feel like part of a group. It can make you feel like you're smarter or know something other people don't. Most of the time, however, you don't even know if what you're gossiping about is true, yet once a gossip session gets started, it's difficult to stop.

Most people are good at heart. After gossiping about someone else, they often feel bad. It might just be a twinge of conscience, but it's there. Is it worth it? No. Worse than that, it's safe to assume that if you are gossiping about others, they are gossiping about you.

How do you rise above this? Keep your distance. People generally respect that you don't want to be involved. Don't start any gossip, and if someone starts gossiping around you, just don't get involved.

How do you handle the conversation?

Suppose someone says to you, "Did you hear that Mr. Blair got so drunk that he fell over at a party at the convention? Imagine the CTO (chief technology officer) acting like that."

You respond, "No. Have you tasted that great new flavored coffee at the coffee shop?"

He or she might want to keep the conversation going and say, "Yeah, it's great. But you should have seen Mr. Blair. I don't know how he can show his face around this company."

All you have to do is either change the subject again or say, "I made a decision a long time ago, not to get involved in gossip. It can only get me in trouble."

Every now and then you hear through the grapevine that people are gossiping about you. It's not a good feeling, but you might have to deal with it. What do you do? You have a few options.

- ◎ You can ignore it.
- ◎ You can confront the person or people who are gossiping about you.
- ◎ You can start gossiping about the person or people gossiping about you.

What's your best choice? Well, it's definitely not gossiping about the person who is gossiping about you. Ignoring the gossip might be your best choice except that suppressing your feelings of betrayal and anger can be stressful. So how about confronting the person or people

> ### ⭐ Words from a Pro
>
> Do you like to be around negative people? Probably not. Well, neither does anyone else. We all have bad days when we complain and whine that nothing is going right. The problem comes when it occurs constantly. If you want to succeed in your career, try to limit the negativity, at least around your colleagues. While they say misery loves company, in reality after a while people won't want to be around you. Eventually, they'll start to avoid you. On the other hand, most people like to be around positive people who make them smile and laugh. If you can do this, you'll have an edge over others.

who are gossiping about you? If you're certain about who has been spreading the gossip and you can do this calmly and professionally, it often resolves the situation.

Whatever you do, don't have a public confrontation and don't confront a group. Instead, wait until the person is alone. Calmly approach him or her and say something like this: "John, I didn't want to bring this up in front of anyone else because I didn't want to embarrass you, but I've heard that you've been talking to others here in the office about my performance and discussing my personal life. I've always had respect for you so I really questioned the people who told me it was happening. I'd just like to know if it's true."

At this point, John probably will be embarrassed and claim that he doesn't know what you're talking about. He might ask you who mentioned it.

"Who told you that?" he might say. "I want to straighten them out."

Do not give out any names. It's better to let him start questioning the trust of all the people he's been talking to and gossiping with.

> ### ⭐ Tip from the Top
>
> Use coffee breaks and meetings at the water cooler or in the lounge to your advantage. Instead of gossiping, try using the situations as opportunities. A few pleasant words or a smile can often win over even those with conflicting opinions about you or your work.

Tip from the Coach

Remember the philosophy that on the ladder to success, real successful people pull others up the ladder with them; the ones who try to push others down the ladder will never be real successes themselves.

While he might tell a couple of people you confronted him on the gossip subject, John will probably find someone else to gossip about in the future.

In many situations gossip may lead to bigger problems. Depending on your work environment, you might be privy to private stories about the company's business, company owners, board members, corporate executives, administrators, and so on.

Office gossip is bad enough, but gossiping about your company's business or people is not only in poor taste but may also breech company confidentiality policies. Gossiping about what happens in the workplace, what you hear, or what you know (even if it is true) can ruin your career, especially if it leads to the embarrassment of powerful people.

It's essential to your success and your career, not to spread rumors in the workplace or out. Don't talk about the inside information you have, whether it's good or bad. If anyone pumps you for information, learn to simply say, "Sorry, that's confidential."

Money, Money, Money

How upset would you be if you found out that a coworker who had a job similar to yours was making more money than you? Probably, pretty upset. Whether it's what you're earning, what your coworker is earning, or what someone else is earning, money is often a problem in the workplace, because everyone wants to earn more money. No matter how much money people are paid for a job, they don't think they're getting enough. If they hear someone is getting paid better than them, it understandably upsets them.

Here's the deal: If you know you're earning more than someone else, keep it to yourself. If you're earning less than someone else, keep it to yourself. No matter what your earnings are, keep it to yourself. Don't discuss your earnings with coworkers. The only people in the workplace you should discuss your earnings with are the human resources department and your supervisors.

In some situations, you may land a really good contract, a really good salary, or a really good benefit package. Here's the deal: Even if you've just landed a huge contract it's okay to be happy, it's okay to be ecstatic. But it probably isn't a good idea to walk around gloating—especially around colleagues who may not have negotiated the great salary or benefits package you did.

Why would one person be earning more than another in a similar position? There might be a number of reasons. Compensation for many positions may be negotiated, and the person might be a better negotiator. He or she might have more experience, more education, seniority, different skills, or more responsibilities. Even

Tip from the Top

It is never a good idea to speak badly about your employer, your colleagues, your supervisors, company clients, or customers, no matter what. When you do, people on the outside start doubting your loyalties.

where salary is fixed by statute (such as a job in the governmental sector), an employer may classify two similar employees in different positions that would affect salaries.

Some employees may have skills or attributes that employers feel they need to prosper. A game developer may, for example, have developed a game that became very popular. A software designer may have demonstrated that he or she can develop certain applications more effectively than others. A salesperson may sell more than other sales reps. A graphic artist may be in more demand than other artists with similar skills. There are any number of scenarios that might occur.

"But it's frustrating," you say. I understand, but being frustrated won't help. Worry about your own job. Don't waste time comparing yourself to your coworkers, colleagues, or others in positions you consider similar. Definitely don't whine about it in your workplace. It will get on people's nerves.

What can you do? Make sure you are visible in a positive way. Make sure you're doing a great job. If you're already doing a great job, try to do a better job. Keep notes on projects you've successfully completed, ideas you've suggested that are being used, and things you are doing to increase the bottom line or make things better in the company. Then, when it's

time for a job review, you'll have the ammunition to ask for the compensation you deserve. Use all of your experience and successes to help you land a promotion that will result in increased earnings.

Dealing with Colleagues

Whatever area of the computer industry in which you choose to work, you're going to be dealing with others. Whether they are superiors, subordinates, colleagues, customers, or clients, the way you deal with the people you work with will impact your opportunities, your chances of success, and your future.

Many people treat colleagues and superiors well, yet treat subordinates with less respect. One of the interesting things about many segments of the computer industry is that career progression doesn't always follow a normal pattern. What that means is that with the right set of circumstances someone might jump a number of rungs up the career ladder quicker than expected. The end result could be that someone who is a subordinate might become either a colleague or even a superior. It's essential to treat everyone with whom you come in contact with dignity and respect. Aside from being common courtesy, you can never tell when the person making you coffee today will be at making a decision about your future tomorrow.

Want to know a secret about dealing effectively with people? If you can sincerely make every person you come in contact with feel special, you will have it made. How do you do this? There are a number of ways.

When someone does or says something interesting or comes up with a good idea, mention it to them. For example, "That was a great idea you had at the meeting, Hilary. You always come up with interesting ways to solve problems."

Tip from the Coach
It's very easy to start comparing your earnings with those of others who are making more and start feeling sorry for yourself. Try not to compare yourself, your job, or your earnings to anyone else. Instead of concentrating on what "they're making," try to concentrate on how you can get "there."

Sometimes you might want to send a short note instead. For example:

> Bill,
>
> While I'm sure you're ecstatic that the press conference is over, I hope you know how impressed everyone was with the event. You handled the coordination like a seasoned pro. No one would ever have guessed that this was the first time you had ever put a press conference together.
>
> Everything was perfect. But the real coup was getting the story about the company's new video game on every major television station in the country as well as in every major newspaper. You did a great job. I'm glad we're on the same team.
>
> Debbie

If another employee does something noteworthy, write a note. If a colleague receives an award or an honor, write a note. It doesn't make you any less talented or skill; your words cannot only make someone else's day, but can help you build a good relationship with a colleague.

Everyone likes a cheerleader. At home, you hopefully have your family. In your personal life you have friends. If you can be a cheerleader to others in the workplace, it often helps you excel yourself.

Never be phony and always be sincere. Look for little things that people do or say as well. "That's a great tie, Robert." "Nice suit Amy. You always look so put together." "New semester registration was so busy this morning. We are really lucky to have you coordinating things down there."

Notice that while you're complimenting others, you're not supposed to be self-deprecating. You don't want to make yourself look bad, you want to make others look good. So, for example, you wouldn't say, "Nice suit Amy. You always look so put together. I couldn't coordinate a suite

Tip from the Coach

In an attempt to build up themselves up, many people try to tear others down. Unfortunately, it usually has the opposite effect.

and blouse if I tried." "Great job on the press conference. I never could have coordinated an event like that." Or, "Registration for the software training session was so busy this morning. We are really lucky to have you coordinating things down there. If they left registration solely in my hands, everyone would still would be there."

The idea is to build people up so they feel good about themselves. When you can do that, people like to be around you, they gain self-confidence, and they pass it on to others. One of them might be you. Best of all, you will start to look like a leader. This is a very important image to build when you're attempting to move up the career ladder.

Dealing with Your Superiors

While you are ultimately in charge of your career, superiors are often the people who can help either move it along or hold it back. Depending on the area of the computer industry in which you are involved, your superior might be a supervisor, boss, a director, department head, the chairperson of a company's board of directors, the CEO or president of a company, a client, and so on.

Try to develop a good working relationship with your superiors, whoever they are, throughout your career. A good boss can help you succeed in your present job as well as in your future career.

One of the mistakes many people make in the workplace is looking at their bosses as the enemy. They get a mind-set of us against them. Worse than that, they sit around and boss-bash with other colleagues.

Want to better your chances of success at your job? Make your boss look good. How do you do that?

◎ Don't boss-bash.
◎ Speak positively about your boss to others.
◎ Do your work.
◎ Cooperate in the workplace.
◎ If you see something that needs to be done, offer to do it.
◎ Volunteer to help with projects that aren't done.
◎ Ask if your boss needs help.

"But what if my boss is a jerk?" you ask. It's still in your best interest to make him or her look good. Believe it or not, it will make you look good.

While we're on the subject, let's discuss jerky bosses. With any luck, your boss will be a great person who loves his or her job, but every now and then you just might run into a bad boss. He or she might be a jerk, a fool, or an idiot.

"I could do a better job than him," you say. Well, you might be able to, but not if you can't learn to deal with people so you still have a job. In many cases, your boss has already proven him or herself to the organization and is therefore more of a commodity than you are at this point. So just how do you deal with a bad boss and come out on top?

Let's first go over a list of *don'ts*.

◎ Don't be confrontational. This will usually only infuriate your boss.
◎ Don't shout or curse. Even if you're right, you will look wrong.

◎ Don't talk about your boss to coworkers. You can never tell who is whose best friend or who is telling your boss exactly what you're saying.
◎ Don't send e-mails to people from your office about things your boss does or says.
◎ Don't talk about your boss to colleagues, clients, customers, etc. It's not good business and it's not really ethical.
◎ Don't—and I repeat *don't*—cry in your workplace. No matter how mad your boss or supervisor makes you, no matter what mistake you made, no matter what nasty or obnoxious thing some says about you, keep your composure until you're alone. If you have to, bite your lip, pinch yourself, or do whatever you have to do to keep the tears under control.

Now let's go over a list of *dos* that might help.

◎ Do a good job. It's hard to argue with someone who has done what they are supposed to do.
◎ Be at work when you are scheduled to be there and always be on time.
◎ Attend all scheduled meetings.
◎ Keep a paper trail. Keep notes when your boss asks you to do things and when you've done them. Keep notes regarding calls that have been made, dates, times, etc. Keep a running list of projects you've completed successfully. Do this as a matter of course. Keep it to yourself. Then, if and when you need something to jog your memory, you can refer to it.
◎ Wait until there is no time constraint to finish something and there is no

emergency and ask your supervisor if you can speak to him or her. Then say you'd like to clear the air. Ask what suggestions he or she can give you to do a better job.

- ▫ You might for example say, "Mr. Dalton, I just wanted to clear the air. We're on the same team and if there is something I can be doing to do a better job, just let me know. I'll be glad to try to implement it."
- ◎ Think long and hard before you decide to leave yourself. If your supervisor is as much of a jerk as you think, perhaps he or she will find a new job or be promoted.

No matter what type of boss or supervisor you have, learning to communicate with him or her is essential. Everyone has a different communicating style and it's up to you to determine what his or hers is.

Does your boss like to communicate through e-mail? Some organizations today communicate almost totally through e-mail. Everything from the daily "Good morning" until "See you to-

---

Tip from the Top

Check out your company's policy on private e-mail. Be aware that in many situations private e-mails are not allowed. Whatever you do, don't use your company e-mail address when looking for a new job.

---

morrow" and everything in between will be in your inbox. If this is the way it is at your office, get used to it. E-mail will be your communication style. The good thing about it is you pretty much have a record of everything.

Other bosses communicate mainly on paper. He or she may give you direction, tell you what's happening, or ask for things via typed or handwritten notes. Sometimes communications may be in formal memos; other times informal or even on sticky notes.

It's important to realize that you have a choice in your career. You can sit there and hope things happen or you can make them happen. You can either be passive or pro-active. In order to succeed in your career, being pro-active is usually a better choice.

You can go to work and let your supervisor tell you what to do or you can do that little bit extra, share your dreams and aspirations, and work toward your goals. No matter what seg-

---

Words from the Wise

Do not put anything in e-mail that you wouldn't mind someone else reading. No matter what anyone tells you, e-mail is not confidential. Furthermore, be aware that in many situations your e-mails, private or business, may be classified as company property. What this means is management may have the right to access your e-mail. Additionally, you should be aware that deleting e-mail doesn't necessarily mean it is gone. In many cases, it may still be on the company's e-mail server or the computer hard drive.

Tip from the Coach

If you carry a personal cell phone, set it to the vibrate mode while in the office. Getting constant calls from friends in the office, even on your cell phone, is inappropriate. While we're on the subject, never take a call on your personal cell phone during a business meeting.

ment of the industry you are pursuing, supervisors can help you make it happen.

Ethics, Morals, and More

We all have our own set of ethics and morals. They help guide us on what we think is right and wrong. In your career you may be faced with situations where a person or group of people want you to do something you know or feel is wrong. In return for doing it, you may be promised financial gain or career advancement.

Would you do it? "Well," you might say, "that depends on what I'd have to do and what I'd get." Here's the deal: No matter what anyone wants you to do, if you know it's wrong—even if you only think it might be wrong—it probably is a bad idea.

"But they told me no one would know," you say. Most people are not that good at keeping secrets, and if they get caught, you're going down too. If you're just getting started in your career, you might be looking at ending it for a few dollars. If you're already into your career, are you really prepared to lose everything you worked so hard to get?

"But they told me if I did this or did that, they'd remember me when promotions came up," you say. How do you know someone isn't testing you to see what your morals are? And exactly what are you planning on doing after you do whatever the person asked you to do and he or she doesn't give you the promotion? Report them? Probably not.

It's important to realize that people move around. They move from job to job and location to location. It is not unheard of to hear that someone took a job on the other side of town or the other side of the country.

What this means is that while every supervisor you have may not know every other supervisor, there is a chance that some of them may know other people in the industry. With this in mind, do you really want to take a chance on doing something stupid or unethical? Probably not.

How do you get out of doing something you don't want to do? You might simply say something like, "My dream was to work in this type of job. I am not about to mess it up for something like this." Or, "I've worked so hard to get where I am now, I really don't want to want to lose what I have." What about, "No can do. Sorry." How about, "Sorry, I'm not comfortable with that."

But what do you do if a supervisor wants you to do something unethical? How do you handle that? You can try any of the lines above, but if your job is on the line you have a bigger problem to deal with. In cases like this, document as much as you can. Then, if you have no other choice, go to human resources, a higher-up supervisor, or someone else you think can help.

"What do I do if I see something going on around me?" you say, "what if I'm not involved but I see a supervisor or coworker doing something that I know is wrong? Then what?"

This is a tough one as well. No one likes a tattletale, but if something major is going on, you have a decision to make.

Do you say something? Bring it to the attention of a higher up? Mention it to the alleged

---

⭐ **Words from the Wise**

Never share your company's proprietary information with friends, family, or anyone else. Even if you just happen to mention it in passing, something you say could potentially put your career at risk.

wrongdoer? Or just make sure you're not involved and say nothing?

Hopefully at the time, you'll make the right choice. It generally will depend on the position you hold, your responsibilities, and the alleged crime. It's a difficult decision. If you decide to say something, be very sure that you are absolutely certain about your information.

Accountability

No one is perfect. We all make mistakes. No matter how careful anyone is, things happen. Accept the fact that sometime in your career you are going to make mistakes, too. In many cases it's not the mistake itself that causes the problem, but the way you deal with it.

The best way to deal with a mistake is to take responsibility, apologize, try to fix it, and go on. Be sincere. Simply say something like, "I'm sorry, I made a mistake. I'm going to try to fix it and will make sure it doesn't happen again." With that said, it's very difficult for anyone to argue with you.

If on the other hand you start explaining mitigating circumstances, blame your coworkers, your secretary, your boss, or make excuses, others generally go on the defensive. Similarly, when you're wrong, just admit it and go on. People will respect you, you'll look more professional, and you'll have a lot less turmoil in your life.

For example, "I was wrong about the Web site marketing campaign. You were right. Good thing we're a team." Or, "I am so sorry I was late today. I know we had a client meeting scheduled. I'll make sure it doesn't happen again. Thanks for covering for me."

Okay, you're taking credit for your mistakes, but what happens if someone else makes a mistake and you're blamed or you're the one who looks like you're unprepared. Let's say for example, you are writing a press release for the launch of your company's new Web site. You e-mailed it to your boss, who made some changes. You made the changes, e-mailed it back to him, and the press release was approved. Your assistant was then supposed to e-mail the corrected press releases to the media. Later in the day, however, you find that your assistant e-mailed the wrong version of the press release to the media. What do you do? Ignore it? Blame your assistant? Blame your secretary?

The truth of the matter is, no one really cares if you have an incompetent staff. It isn't their problem. The best thing to do in these types of situations is also to acknowledge the problem, apologize, and see what you can do to fix it quickly.

"I just found out the wrong version of the press release we did today went out. I'm so sorry. I should have triple checked that the correct version of the release went out. I realize we have a problem and I am taking care of it myself. I have already sent out the corrected version with a note and I am personally calling everyone who received it to explain the error."

The result? What could have been a major problem is now just a minor inconvenience that no one will probably even remember a few weeks down the line.

In work, as in life, many people's first thought when there is a problem is to cover themselves. So when things go wrong, most people are busy reacting or coming up with excuses.

Here's something to remember. The most successful people don't come up with excuses. Instead, when something goes wrong, their first thoughts are how to fix the problem, mitigate any damages, and get things back to normal. If you can do this, and remain cool in a crisis, it will enhance your position, whether you are working in the business, administration, creative, or talent areas of the industry.

Time, Time Management, and Organization

Here's a question for you. What is one thing which every person on the planet has the same amount? Do you know what it is?

Here's a hint: I have the same amount you have. Bill Gates has the same amount I have. Oprah Winfrey has the same amount Bill Gates has. William Shakespeare had the same amount as Oprah Winfrey does. Do you know what it is yet?

Every person in this world, no matter who they are or what they do, has the same 24 hours a day. You can't get less and you can't get more, no matter what you do. It doesn't matter who you are or what your job is. You don't get more time during the day if you're young, old, or in-between. You don't get more time if you're a millionaire or you're making minimum wage. You wouldn't even get more time if you were a Nobel Prize winner who had discovered a cure for cancer.

With all this in mind, it's important to manage your time wisely. That way you can fit more of what you need to fit into your day and get the most important things accomplished.

To start with, let's deal with your work day. Try to get to work a little earlier than you're expected. It's easier to get the day started when you're not rushing. On occasion, you might also want to stay late. Why? Because when superiors see you bolting at 5 p.m. (or whenever your work day ends), it looks like you're not really interested in your job.

You also want to be relaxed before dealing with your job, not stressed because you got

The Inside Scoop

The time period before everyone else gets in or after everyone has left the workplace is usually less formal and less stressed. If you make it a habit to come in right before the big brass comes in and leave either when they leave or just afterward, you will generally become visible in a more positive manner to higher ups. More than that however, you will often have the opportunity to ask a question, make a comment, or offer a suggestion. If someone questions you about what you're doing at work so early simply say something like, "Preparing for the day ahead," "Getting some project started before it gets busy," or "Finishing up a few things so I can devote tomorrow to new projects."

stuck in a traffic jam and started worrying that you were going to be late getting to work.

No matter what your career choice in the computer industry, in order to be successful you will need to learn to prioritize your tasks. How do you know what's important?

If your boss or supervisor needs it now, it's important. If it's dealing with a life or death situation, it's important. If you promised to do something for someone, it's important. If something is happening today or tomorrow and you need to get a project done, it's important. If things absolutely need to get done now, they're important.

Generally, what you need to do is determine what is most important and do it first. Then go over your list of things that need to get done and see what takes precedence next.

The more organized you are, the easier it will be for you to manage your time. Make lists of things you need to do. You might want to keep a master list and then a daily list of things

---

⭐ **Words from the Wise**

In prioritizing, don't forget that you must fit in the things you promised others you would do. Don't get so caught up in wanting to be liked or wanting to agree or even wanting to be great at your job that you promise to do something you really don't have time to get done. Doing so will just put you under pressure.

---

you need to do. You might also want a third list of deadlines that need to be met.

It's important to remember that just making lists won't do it. Checking them on a consistent basis to make sure the things that you needed to do actually got done is the key. Here's an example of the beginnings of a master list. Use it to get started on a list of your own.

- ◎ Call Ben Phillips to set up appointment.
- ◎ Develop agenda for meeting.
- ◎ Prepare report for department head meeting Tuesday.
- ◎ Check class schedule for certification program.
- ◎ Make sure errors on Web site are corrected.
- ◎ Dinner with Gina Kennedy, Monday, 7:00 p.m.

Writing things down is essential to being organized. Don't depend on your memory—or anyone else's. Whatever your job within the computer industry, it is sure to be filled with a lot of details, things that need to get done, and just plain stuff in general. The more successful you get, the busier you will be and the more things you'll have to remember. Don't depend on others reminding you. Depend on yourself.

If you want, you can input information into your BlackBerry or another device. However, always keep a backup.

Here's an idea if you want to be really organized. Keep a notebook with you and jot things down as they occur. Date each page so you have a reference point for later. Then make notes. Like what?

- ◎ The dates that people call and the gist of the conversation.
- ◎ The dates you call people and the reason you called.
- ◎ Notes on meetings you attend. Then when someone says something like, "Gee, I don't remember whether we said May 9 or May 10," you have it.
- ◎ Names of people you meet.
- ◎ Things that happened during the day.

After you get used to keeping the notebook it will become a valuable resource. You might, for example, remember someone calling you six months ago. "What was his name?" you ask yourself. "I wish I knew his name." Just look in your notebook.

"It seems like a lot of trouble," I hear you saying.

It is a little extra effort, but I can almost guarantee that once you keep a notebook like this for a while, you won't be able to live without it. You won't be looking for little sheets of paper on which you have jotted down important numbers and then misplaced. You won't have to remember people's names, phone numbers, or what they said. You won't have to remember if you were supposed to call at 3:00 or 4:30. You'll have everything at your fingertips.

A Few Other Things

It's important to realize that while, of course, you want to succeed in your career, everything you do may not be successful. You might not get every job you apply for. You might not get every promotion you want. Every idea you have may not work out. Every project you do may not turn out perfectly. And every job may not be the one you had hoped it would be.

It also is essential to remember that none of these scenarios mean that you are a failure. What they mean simply is that you need to work on them a little bit more. Things take time. Careers take time—especially great careers.

Be aware that success is often built on the back of little failures. If you ask most successful people about their road to success, many will tell you it wasn't always easy. And no matter what it looks like, most people are not overnight successes.

While some may have it easier, others may have had one or more rejections or failures before they got where they were going. What you'll find however, is those who are now successful didn't quit. After keeping at it and plugging away, they landed the jobs they aspired to, got the promotions, received good work reviews, and got where they are today.

You might not get the promotion you wanted right away. You might not have the job of your dreams—yet. That does not mean it won't happen. Keep plugging away and work at it, and success will come to you.

Most successful people have a number of key traits in common. They have a willingness to take risks, a determination that cannot be undone, and usually an amazing amount of confidence in themselves and their ideas.

Can they fail? Sure. But they might also succeed, and they usually do. What does this have to do with you? If you learn from the success of others, you can be successful too. If you emulate successful people, you too can be on the road to success.

Don't be so afraid of getting things right that you don't take a chance at doing it a better way, a different way, or a way that might work better. Don't get so comfortable that you're afraid to take a risk, or you don't work toward a promotion, or don't accept a new job or new responsibilities. Be determined that you know what you want and how to get it, and you will.

If you want to succeed in your career and your life, I urge you to be confident and be willing to take a risk. Success can surprise you at any time.

Take advantage of opportunities that present themselves, but don't stop there. Create opportunities for yourself to help launch your career to a new level by using creativity and innovative ideas.

Whatever your dream career is in the industry, your success is waiting. The more you work toward success, the quicker it will come.

11

SUCCEEDING AS A CONSULTANT, INDEPENDENT CONTRACTOR, OR FREELANCER

Throughout this book we've discussed a multitude of things that can help you in your quest for a great career in the computer industry. We've talked about a variety of jobs and career options in various segments of the industry. We've discussed making your job into a career. We've investigated ways to get past the gatekeeper, some unique ways to obtain interviews and interview tips.

We've discussed developing resumes, cover letters, and putting together action plans. We've talked about job search strategies and tools for success. We've discussed how to market yourself, as well as why marketing is so important.

You may have picked up this book for many reasons. I'm assuming if you're still reading you want to work in some segment of the computer industry. While many choose to work in a traditional job situation as an employee, some choose self-employment as their option.

Only a few short years ago, self-employment was looked at as a way to earn extra money. For many today, however, it is a full-time career choice. Self-employment can take a number of different paths. You might have your own business, be a consultant, a freelancer, or an inde-

pendent contractor. While the terms are often used interchangeably, there can be some slight differences.

What we're going to focus on in this chapter are some of the things that might help you succeed if self-employment is your dream. If your choice is to work in the traditional job setting, you can, of course, skip over the chapter. However, no matter what your career aspirations are right now, down the line you might want to or need to do something else. My suggestion is even if you are currently happily employed, read over the chapter, gather the information, and file it away in case you need it later.

For many in this country (and the world for that matter), being an entrepreneur is the ultimate dream. One of the wonderful things you can do with the specialized computer skills you have is to conceptualize, create, and grow your own successful business. If this is your dream, read on.

What Do You Want to Do?

What are your specialized skills in the computer industry? Are you a software engineer? Do you design applications? Are you a graphic artist? Do you design Web pages? Do you troubleshoot applications? Are you a software trainer? Can you set up systems with ease? Are you a born salesperson? Do you know a variety of programming languages? Do you have other IT skills?

What skills do you have that others need? Once you determine what those skills are, you're on your way to success.

Now, that you have determined the skills you have to offer, you have another decision. In what type of setting do you want to work? Do you want to work on your own? Do you want to have your own business where you have others working for you? Do you want to be a consultant? Do you want to freelance? Do you want to be an independent contractor? There are so many options. You just need to choose exactly what you want to do.

The choices are endless depending on your skills, talents, training, education, and passion. Almost anything you could do as an employee in the computer industry, you can do in your own business, as a consultant, or freelancer.

What are some possibilities?

◎ Desktop publishing
◎ Software development
◎ Data entry
◎ Software engineering
◎ Computer repair
◎ Game development
◎ Hardware support
◎ Software support
◎ IT consulting
◎ Web site design
◎ Computer graphics
◎ Graphic design
◎ Software training
◎ Hardware training
◎ Technology sales

◎ Technology installation and service
◎ Information services
◎ Evaluation of current computer and network technologies
◎ Computer hardware and application software sourcing
◎ Network design
◎ Network implementation
◎ Network maintenance and management
◎ Network cabling
◎ Software setup
◎ On-site computer setup
◎ Computer maintenance
◎ Internet connectivity installation and support
◎ Web development
◎ Computer troubleshooting
◎ Technical support
◎ Web site marketing

Independent Contractors, Freelancers, Consultants, and More: An Overview

As we have just mentioned, while technically there are differences, the terms consultant, freelancer, and independent contractor are often used interchangeably along with the term self-employed. What is important to know is that there are salaried workers or employees and non-salaried workers or free agents who might be referred to as self-employed, consultants, freelancers, or independent contractors.

Employees are hired by a company and paid a salary to do their job. Free agents (self-employed, consultants, freelancers, or independent contractors) offer their services to a person or company and are then paid a fee for those services.

Let's discuss the term independent contractor for a bit. What exactly is an independent contractor? While the Internal Revenue Service has specific regulations for determining what they consider an independent contractor, basically, an independent contractor is someone who runs his or her own business instead of working for an employer. Independent contractors might be consultants or freelancers, although all consultants and freelancers are not independent contractors, at least not according to some of the rules and regulations of the IRS.

As an employee, you generally will work for one employer. As an independent contractor, you may have a number of different clients. One of the major differences between an employee and an independent contractor is the amount of control an employer has over you. As an employee, your employer can control the way you work, your hours, and so on. As an independent contractor, however, the employer (who is generally known as the client) has less control over you and the direction of your work. What that means is that your client may tell you what he or she expects and wants done for the payment or fee you have agreed on, but as a rule, doesn't set your hours or tell you how to get your work done.

Another big difference between being an employee and an independent contractor are finances. As an employee, your employer will pay you a regular salary. You may also get benefits such as health insurance, vacation time, sick days, etc. Your employer is responsible for taking out the appropriate taxes and paying them to the government. As an independent contractor, you are paid a fee. You are responsible for paying your own income taxes and self-employment tax on that fee. Generally, as an independent contractor, you do not receive any fringe benefits such as vacation time, sick days, health insurance, and so on.

Additionally, as an employee, you can usually resign at will. However, as an independent contractor, freelancer, or consultant, you might be contractually obligated to stay until you have completed your assignment or contract.

Why would a company use an independent contractor, or a freelancer or consultant, instead of hiring an employee? There are a number of reasons. Sometimes a company just needs a short-term project completed. Other employers don't want to be responsible for paying an employee's fringe benefits or taking out taxes. In some cases, the company may need someone with specialized skills, yet finds it impractical to keep permanent staff for that specific specialty.

No matter whether you are using the term independent contractor, free agent, freelancer, or consultant to describe your self-employment status, know that in this capacity you hold the key to your success. You control how much you want to work, how hard you want to work, and what you want to do.

Are You Ready to Be Your Own Boss?

You may decide to become your own boss for many reasons. You might just have lost your job and need a way to earn a living. You might want to fulfill your dream of having your own business. Someone may have offered you an opportunity to do some consulting work. Or you may want to control your own destiny. Whatever the reason, the question is, are you ready to be your own boss?

It can be scary to leave the comfort of a job. It can be scary leaving a weekly paycheck behind for the unknown. How do you decide if you want to work as employee or you want to be your own boss? This is a difficult question for many to answer. What you have to do is sit down for a few minutes and ask yourself a few questions.

◎ Are you passionate about starting your new business?
  ▫ You are going to have to put a lot of time, sweat, and energy into making your business successful. If you are passionate about what you are doing, all your hard work will be less of an effort.
◎ Are you committed to your business and your success?
  ▫ Anyone can start a business. However, not everyone can be successful. The path to success has twists and turns. Are you committed? Are you dedicated? If so, you increase your odds for success.
◎ Are you confident? Do you have faith in yourself?
  ▫ If you don't have confidence in yourself, your skills, and your success, neither will anyone else.
◎ Can you sell yourself? Can you sell your services?
  ▫ In order to become successful working for yourself, you are going to have to become the ultimate salesperson. You will continuously have to sell yourself and sell your services to potential clients. You will have to market yourself. You will have to show how you are better than any other employee or consultant.
◎ Are you disciplined enough to get things done on time?
  ▫ When you have your own business, no one is standing over you telling you to get your work done. Do you

have the motivation to get your work finished in a timely basis? Can you set goals? Can you set priorities?
◎ Are you ready to give up the known for the unknown?
  ▫ Are you willing to give up the security of your job for the insecurity of starting your own business?
◎ Are you ready to take the ultimate responsibility?
  ▫ When you are the boss, the buck stops with you. Are you prepared to take this responsibility?
◎ Do you want to have a say in your future?
  ▫ When you are your own boss, you have a say in your future. You have some control over your success. If you're willing to work hard, with a bit of luck you can be successful.
◎ Do you have enough money saved to get you through your business start-up?
  ▫ If you aren't getting a weekly paycheck, do you have enough money saved up to support yourself? Do you have funds to help you start your business?
◎ Are you ready to take on more roles than just that of being an employee?
  ▫ Once you are the boss, you will have to sell your services, market your business, handle the finances, keep track of your expenses, schedule your work, collect fees, negotiate with clients, and more. Are you ready?
◎ Do you see yourself as a problem solver?
  ▫ Are you ready to determine what the needs of potential clients might be and then develop solutions to their needs?

Once you answer these questions you can decide if you are ready to start your own business, become a consultant, and/or freelance.

The Pros and Cons of Self-Employment, Consulting, and Freelancing

There are both benefits and drawbacks to working for yourself, consulting, and freelancing. Let's start with some of the pros.

◎ You are your own boss.
  ▫ To many, this is the ultimate dream. However, you should be aware that as a consultant you do have a boss. As a matter of fact, you might have more than one boss. Every client is in essence your boss. You, however, have the option of choosing who you want your clients to be.
◎ You have a certain amount of freedom.
  ▫ Being the boss gives you freedoms you don't have in traditional job situations.
    ◇ You get to choose who you want your clients to be and whom you don't.
    ◇ You get to choose how you want your business run.
    ◇ You get to choose when you will work.
    ◇ You get to choose how much you will work.
    ◇ You get to love your boss…because it is you!
◎ You have more control over your finances than if you are an employee.
  ▫ As a self-employed freelancer or consultant, you have more control over your finances than if you are working in a traditional job situation. If you want more money you have other options. You can do extra work, find additional clients, or raise your fees. Your finances are therefore related to the amount you work, the number of clients you have and your professional reputation.
    ◇ In many situations you can earn more freelancing than you can working as an employee.
    ◇ Independent contractors, freelancers, and consultants are often paid more than employees for performing similar jobs. That is because employers don't have to pay consultants' or freelancers' Social Security taxes or fringe benefits.
    ◇ Independent contractors, freelancers, consultants, and other self-employed people can take advantage of a great number of tax-related deductions that employees cannot. These might include deducting things such as your office expenses, travel expenses, computers and soft-

★ The Inside Scoop

I often have people tell me that they wish they had their own business so they wouldn't have a boss; so they wouldn't have anyone telling them what to do; so they wouldn't have to answer to anyone. The truth of the matter is, as a consultant, you do have a boss. It is your client. And if you have more than one client, you will have more than one boss.

ware costs, Internet and phone expenses, business insurance, and so on.

◇ Independent contractors, free-lancers, consultants, and other self-employed people don't have to worry about getting fired. In many situations when employees are terminated, freelancers and consultants are brought in to cover the slack.

◇ You can start off consulting and freelancing on a part-time basis. As long as you have the time and you don't have any type of non-compete clause or exclusivity clause with your current employ-er, you can start consulting on a part-time basis.

Then you have the cons of self-employment, freelancing, and consulting:

◎ No benefits

▫ As a consultant or freelancer, you don't get benefits. There is no health insurance, there are no paid vacation days, no paid sick days, no paid personal days, no educational reimbursement, and so on.

◇ This can be solved by finding ways to buy your own health insurance. Many small business or consulting trade associations and organizations as well as local chambers of commerce offer options for buying health insurance.

◇ And while you don't have paid vacation days, sick days, or personal days, as long as you get

your work done, you have more leeway on taking time off.

◎ You don't have any unemployment insurance benefits.

▫ As a freelancer, consultant, or independent contractor you don't have any unemployment insurance benefits, which means that if you aren't working, you cannot apply for unemployment. Even if you are hired by a hiring firm for a consulting assignment, when the assignment ends, that is it. You do not get unemployment and cannot apply for it.

◎ It is often lonely at the top.

▫ As a freelancer or consultant, you won't have the camaraderie you often have when you work in a traditional job situation. Even if you see your clients on a regular basis, you are often looked at as an outsider. Some consultants and freelancers feel lonely.

◇ To counteract the isolation and loneliness, join professional as-sociations and go to meetings. Try to set up business lunch dates one or twice a week with other

---

⭐ **Words from the Wise**

If you are retained by a hiring firm as an independent contractor to do a consulting job and you are injured on the job, as a rule you cannot take any recourse against either the hiring firm or the company for which you are doing the consulting. There is generally no worker's compensation coverage.

consultants so you have some contact with people in the business world.

◎ You may have to advertise your services to get your name out.
  ▫ Unless someone knows you exist, they will hire someone else. Depending on your specialty, you may have to spend money on advertising.
    ◇ Hopefully, the advertising will pay for itself when you get new clients. You can also use publicity and marketing techniques as well as networking to augment advertising costs.

◎ You have to constantly market and sell yourself and your services.
  ▫ No matter how good you are, you have to continually make sure people know that you and your service are available.
    ◇ As you become more successful you might want to hire a marketing firm or publicist to help you with this task.

◎ You will be competing with other consultants, freelancers, etc., who are selling similar services to yours.
  ▫ As more and more people decide that self-employment, consulting, and freelancing are a viable option, you will be competing for clients and assignments.
    ◇ Make sure you are the best. Stay abreast of industry trends. Network to get clients and referrals and market yourself for success.

◎ You will have to negotiate and ask for fees.

Tip from the Coach
You don't have to apologize for charging a fee or be embarrassed to ask for it. You are providing a professional service, not asking for charity.

  ▫ Some people find it very difficult to negotiate their fees. They find it harder to ask others for what they think their time is worth.
    ◇ As you get more experience, asking for fees will be easier.

◎ You have to collect fees.
  ▫ One of the problems many consultants and freelancers have is collecting fees. Some companies pay consultants right away. Others don't.
    ◇ If after sending a bill you do not receive a fee for services rendered within a reasonable amount of time, you will have to ask for it. Often just asking for your fee will get you your check. If you don't get paid on a timely basis, you are going to have to decide how long you will work without payment.

◎ You have to stay motivated.
  ▫ When no one is around to motivate you, it is difficult for many to stay motivated.
    ◇ Find ways to stay positive. Keep your eye on the prize: your great career in computer consulting.

◎ You may have to travel.
  ▫ Depending on your specific area of expertise, you may have to travel in your consulting business. For some people

┌───┐
│ ⭐ **Tip from the Top**   │
│   │
│ Do not start threatening a client if you │
│ bill a company and don't get payment   │
│ right away. Try sending another bill and │
│ asking nicely before taking any further │
│ action. In many companies, consultants   │
│ are just paid last.   │
└───┘

this is a big problem. For others, travel is an advantage, not a drawback.

So now you know some of the pros and cons of self-employment, consulting, and freelancing in the computer industry. You know some of the challenges. Is this still your choice? I'm betting if you are still reading, it is.

Do You Have the Personality To Be a Good Consultant or Freelancer?

We just discussed some of the pros and cons of working as a consultant, freelancer, or other independent contractor. Now let's take a few minutes to see if you have the personality and characteristics to be a good consultant or freelancer? Let's make absolutely sure. Answer the following questions.

◎ Are you ready to give up a regular paycheck?

┌───┐
│ ⭐ **Tip from the Coach**   │
│   │
│ In order to combat the feeling that you │
│ are all alone as a consultant or   │
│ freelancer, be sure to join professional │
│ trade associations, attend their   │
│ meetings, and get involved.   │
└───┘

◎ Do you have a skill that can help others become more successful or fill one of their needs?
◎ Are you ready for success?
◎ Are you a risk taker?
◎ Are you a self-starter?
◎ Are you respected in your community?
◎ Are you respected by your peers?
◎ Are you confident?
◎ Are you an expert in your field?
◎ Are you ready to keep learning and updating your skills?
◎ Are you ready to work long hours to build up your business?
◎ Are you a leader?
◎ Are you passionate?
◎ Are you creative?
◎ Do you have good sales skills?
◎ Do you look for solutions instead of dwelling on problems?
◎ Are you motivated?
◎ Can you set goals?
◎ Do you have good written and verbal communications skills?
◎ Are you comfortable around others?

If you have answered yes to a good portion of the questions, you have the personality and characteristics to help you succeed as a consultant or freelancer in the area of the computer industry in which you aspire.

A Little About Fees

No matter what type of consulting or freelancing you do in the computer industry, you are going to have to set your fees for payment. For many people this can be a difficult task in itself. How do you figure out what to charge clients? How do you determine what your time and expertise is worth?

There are many variables that can affect your fee. These include your specific area of expertise, the uniqueness of your skills, your professional reputation, the level of your education and/or training, and your geographic area, to name a few. Other variables include what you perceive is your self-worth as well as what a potential clients sees as your worth. Another additional factor is what other similar consultants are charging for similar services.

While it is not your client's responsibility to pay your bills, your expenses, and your overhead, you need your fee to adequately compensate you for your time, your expertise, and your services. You also want your fee to be enough to provide a profit after expenses. One of the ways to at least come up with a starting number is to see what other consultants doing similar work are getting in your area. You can get this information by simply speaking to other consultants, checking with trade associations, or by doing some research online.

Some individuals decide to charge substantially less than other consultants who do the same type of work in order to try to snag a contract. The problem with this is that some clients might

⭐ **Tip from the Coach**
    It is essential that you feel comfortable with your pricing. While you don't want to overprice your services, you certainly don't want to underprice them either. While many don't agree, I am a firm believer that if you think your work is worth more, you should ask for more. Once you set a price, you can always go down, but it is very difficult to go up. In order to ask for a higher fee, you must be the best in your field and your professional reputation needs to be exemplary.

⭐ **Tip from the Coach**
    Did you ever wonder why one consultant can command thousands of dollars for his or time and services while another similar consultant can hardly give his or her time and services away? Sometimes it is because one individual had enough confidence in his or her work to ask for that high price. Don't undervalue your talent, your skills, or your time.

take your lower fee to mean that you are doing inferior work compared to those charging more.

Conversely, some individuals decide to charge more than others who do similar work. The problem with this is that in some situations, clients may tell you that they can get someone else to do the work for a lower fee.

If you can effectively illustrate to a client that your work is better, that you are more skilled, more talented, and can do a better job than other similar consultants, you will have a better chance at landing a higher fee.

In addition to setting your fee, you also have to decide how you want to be reimbursed for your services. By that I mean, do you want to be paid by the project? Do you want a flat fee? Do you want to be paid an hourly rate? Do you want to be paid a daily rate? What about a monthly retainer?

You need to know approximately how much time a project will take before coming up with your fee. Additionally, you want to make sure you don't undervalue your worth.

Be sure you think about your fee and how you want to be reimbursed before you meet with a potential client. You don't want to start hemming and hawing while you are in a meeting. You want to appear confident and illustrate that you know what you are doing and have done it before (even if it is your very first time).

Contracts, Agreements, and Protecting Yourself

Once you determine your fee, you will want to make sure you have a written agreement between you and your client spelling out exactly what you are expected to do, when the project needs to be completed, and what you will receive in return. Many people ask me if they really need this written agreement. The answer is an unequivocal yes!

A written agreement protects both you and your client. A written agreement means that neither party can say, "That's not what you said you wanted." Or, "We never agreed on that fee."

I've given you a lot of advice in this book. We've covered a lot of different areas. Here is one of the most important things I have to tell you. No matter what you want to do in the computer industry, whether you want a traditional job, or you want to be self-employed, an independent contractor, a consultant, or a freelancer, what you have to sell is you. You are the product. If you don't protect yourself, you will have nothing! Do not get so caught up in what you want, that you forget this fact.

If you take nothing else from this book, I hope you'll take this: I want you to protect yourself. Before you sign a contact, any contract, I want you to not only read it, but know and understand what you're reading. If you don't understand something, no matter how small, ask. Don't be embarrassed, don't feel stupid, and don't feel like someone will laugh at you. Ask and get an explanation of what you don't understand. Clarify points.

If you're thinking, "Isn't that what lawyers are for?" the simple answer is yes. But that

doesn't mean you should leave your career to chance. Just because a lawyer reads over your contract, doesn't mean you shouldn't too.

In some cases your client might have a written agreement that he or she wants you to sign. Be sure to read the contract carefully before signing it. If you don't understand something or you don't agree with something, ask about it when you see it. Don't just sign and hope you won't have a problem.

In other cases, you may be the one responsible for providing your client with an agreement. While you can write one yourself, you might want to contact an attorney to develop a basic agreement that you can then customize for each client.

At some point during your career—especially if you are freelancing or doing consulting work—I can almost guarantee someone will give you something to sign and say something to the effect of: "You can read it over if you want, but it's a standard contract. You're really wasting your time."

Should you take their word? No! Read everything. They probably are telling the truth, but perhaps their version of standard is not your version. Read every line. Be aware that a contract is a legally binding agreement. Both parties must live up to the terms of the contract. If you don't read the contract, you don't know what you're signing on to do.

I can also guarantee you that sometime in your career someone will say to you one or more of the following.

◎ "We don't need a contract, we trust each other."
  ▫ You need a contract.
◎ "We're friends, we don't need a contract."
  ▫ A contract will assure you will stay friends.

◎ "You were an employee here. We always paid you before. We don't really need a contract do we?"

  ▫ Yes. A contract will assure that you both parties are protected.

◎ "It's a simple project. Don't worry about a contract. All you have to do is finish the project and you'll get paid."

  ▫ You will have little recourse if you don't get paid. You need a contract or an agreement of sorts.

◎ "A verbal contract is as good as a written one."

  ▫ Not really. You can produce a written contract. Even if you have a witness to what was said, a written contract is better.

◎ "A contract is as only as good as the paper it's written on."

  ▫ While written contracts can be broken, they are still contracts.

★ Tip from the Top

Whether you are an IT consultant, a Web design consultant, or any type of consultant in between, one of the most important things you need to do before your first meeting with a client is find out as much as possible about them. You want to know what the company does, how long it has been in existence, what type of goods or services they provide, and so on. Do your homework. Some companies have Web sites. Others may have articles about them in newspapers or periodicals. Sometimes you can just Google the company name and get a wealth of information. Research as much as you can. Your potential clients will appreciate that you took the time to learn about them and it will better prepare you to be able to develop solutions to your client's needs.

◎ "Let's just shake on it."

  ▫ You can shake on it, after you sign a contract.

Are you getting the idea? You need to protect yourself. Do you always need a complicated contract? No, a simple agreement can suffice sometimes, but you should always have some sort of dated agreement signed by both parties stating what is expected of you, when it is expected, and what is expected in return. The best person to give you advice in this area is an attorney.

Succeeding as a Consultant

How many times have you wished you could quit your job and become a successful consultant? How many times have you wished you had your own business? How many times have you wished you had more control over your career?

There is certainly nothing wrong with wishing. It definitely can't hurt, and as a matter of fact it sometimes helps you focus more clearly on what you want. But wishing alone can't make something happen. In order to succeed as a consultant it's essential to take some positive actions.

Have you ever wondered why some people struggle with their own business while others succeed? Is it that some have more talent? Or is it something else? While, of course, talent in your specific area of the computer industry can have a lot to do with your ultimate success, as we've discussed throughout this book, talent alone doesn't really guarantee success. It's no secret that the computer industry is competitive, but why shouldn't you be the one on top?

It's crucial to your success to understand that no matter what area of the computer industry you are pursuing as a consultant, it needs to be treated as a business. Hopefully starting your own business will be fun, it will be exciting, it will be something you have a passion for and something that you love to do. But in the end, it is still a business. In order to succeed you need to act in a professional manner in every situation.

How can you be professional? Present yourself professionally. If you say you're going to be someplace, be there. If you say you're going to call somebody, call them. If someone calls you and leaves a message, call them back on a timely basis. If you say you're going to do something, do it. Most importantly, be on time for everything. There is nothing worse for your career than being known as the individual who is always late.

Professionalism doesn't only mean the way you act. It also encompasses how you present yourself. Are you ready to make it? Are you prepared?

"I have the expertise, the skills, and I'm talented," you say. "Isn't that all anyone is really interested in anyway?"

It is true that expertise, talent, and skills are what industry professionals are looking for, but it's not always that simple. Here's the deal. There are a lot of talented and skilled consultants in a variety of fields. You want to give yourself the best possible chance at success. You don't want someone to say, "What a great software engineer, but I hear he shows up to meetings late." Or, "He's a great Web designer, but he doesn't complete anything on time."

Tip from the Top

The more you know about the industry, the less chance there will be that someone will try to take advantage of you. Learn something new every opportunity you get.

The Inside Scoop

Learn the lingo of the industry. Every industry has its own set of words, jargon, terms, and acronyms. If you don't know the lingo of the industry, you can make crucial mistakes doing business.

You want everything about you and your work to stand out from others in a positive manner.

What else should you know? To give yourself the best chance at success, learn as much as possible about the business end of the industry. Knowledge is power. The more you know, the more you can help yourself in your quest for success.

You've already started by reading this book. Don't stop here. Read everything you can about the specific area of the computer industry in which you are consulting. Read everything you can about the industry in general. Find books on people who have made it. Look for books on ways to become successful.

Look for books on improving your skills. Seek out books on marketing, public relations, and publicity. Look for books on selling and creating a brand. Read trade publications. Scour the Internet for information.

"But I'm busy," you say, "I spend every spare moment working and trying to build up my business. I don't have time to continually read books and magazines and surf the Internet."

Make time. If you just find one thing in a book, or magazine, or on the Internet that you can relate to your career, it will be worth it.

And don't stop there. Take classes, workshops, and seminars, both in the specific technical area of the industry in which you are involved and in the business segment of the industry. Why? You will gain valuable information, learn new skills, and have the opportunity to network and make important contacts. And that is what can help you when building a consulting business.

Moving Up and Taking the Next Step

As a professional consultant what you want to do is continually work toward building success in your given area. You need a strategy and a plan.

Have you decided that you're ready to commit to your career as a consultant? Are you ready to put in the hard work and perseverance that's necessary? Do you have the passion? Are you ready to pursue your dream? If your answer is a definitive yes, let's take some time to discuss some additional actions that can help you get where you want to go.

What's your next move if you are ready to take the next step toward success? How can you get attention of potential clients?

Whatever segment of the industry in which you choose to consult, you need to take stock of where you are in your career now and determine where you want to be. You need to get ready for your journey to success. You have a lot of work ahead of you, but you can do it successfully if you have a plan.

Start thinking now about a marketing campaign. Find ways to get your name out to companies and people who might be able to use your services. Get involved with one or two not-for-profit organizations. Consider sending out letters or brochures to potential clients. Check out the newspaper help wanted section for jobs that match your area of consulting. Send letters offering to handle the position on a consulting basis. You just might be surprised with a new client.

One of the most exciting things about deciding to start your own business or become a consultant or freelancer is that you can do it at any age and any stage of your career. There are some people who decide to consult right after college. There are others who start their own business or consult after they have retired. And of course, there are those at every stage in between. While I've discussed it before, I want to reiterate that whatever your age and whatever stage you are in your career, it is never too late to pursue your dream.

It also bears repeating that no matter what you think you want to do and how far you have gone in your career, you are allowed to change your mind. As long as you keep pursuing your dreams, you are going in the right direction.

In order to succeed you have to do everything you can to get an edge over others. While no one can guarantee success, a combination of education and training, hard work, good business sense, being in the right place at the right time, talent, and, of course, a bit of luck will stack the deck in your favor.

Taking Care of Business

No matter what area of the computer industry in which you want to consult or freelance, there are certain things you need to do to take care of business in a professional manner. One of the first things you may want to do is select your business name. It might be as simple as, "John Jones Consulting" or "Sandra Bennet Web Design." And while your business name can just be your actual name or have your name in it, it doesn't have to. For example, "Web's Best Graphics" or "Complete Computer Repair" would be fine.

You might also want to think about your business structure. There are a lot of questions you need to answer. Are you going to be a sole proprietor? Are you going to incorporate? Are you going to have a legal partnership with one or more other people?

What should you do? Do some research. You might want to speak to an attorney to decide what is the best path for you to take. Each option has its pros and cons.

Many cities and/or counties also require businesses to have business permits or business licenses. Contact your city and county government offices to see if this is necessary and what you need to do to get the required licenses and permits.

Once you decide upon your business name and set up your business, you are probably also going to want to open a separate bank account for your business.

You might also consider business insurance. The type of insurance you need will depend on the type of consulting you are doing and the business set up you have decided on. Do you need it? I recommend it, but once again, only you can make the final decision. You might want to speak to your insurance agent to get some feedback. Then make your decision. Your agent might also be able to tell you if you need any other type of insurance for your particular consulting business as well.

Keeping Records

Keeping records of finances related to your business is important for tax purposes as well as to accurately determine how your business is doing financially.

Keep records of all expenses incurred on behalf of your business, including equipment, supplies, travel, advertising, marketing, and so on. You also need to keep accurate records of all monies you bring in on behalf of your consulting business. Additionally, it is essential

> **Tip from the Top**
> Be sure to check to see if the area in which you are interested in consulting requires certification or special licensing. For example, if you are interested in consulting as a computer networking specialist, in many situations you are required to pass the Microsoft Certified Systems Engineer certification.

to keep track of all clients who still owe you money.

As time is money to a consultant, it is crucial for you to keep track of the time it actually takes for you to do each project. In this manner, you will be able to see if you underestimated or overestimated the time a project would take. This information can be very important when setting your fees.

Building Your Business: Getting Clients

How do you build your business? Basically, what you need to do is make people aware of your consulting business. You need to get clients. There are a number of methods you might use to do this.

◎ Networking.
  ▫ We've discussed networking in depth throughout the book. We've discussed its importance in your career. Networking can be a very positive force in helping you get new clients as well. The more people who know what you do and the more contacts you have, the better your chances are of finding people who need your services.

- Networking with people in your specific industry such as former bosses, supervisors, and colleagues can be especially helpful. Don't discount networking opportunities with those outside of your industry. You can never tell who might know someone who needs the services you provide.
- Word-of-mouth referrals.
  - Word-of-mouth advertising is one of the best ways to get clients. Generally, a satisfied client will be happy to recommend you to someone else. It is perfectly acceptable to ask satisfied clients for referrals and recommendations.
- Advertising.
  - Depending on the specific area in which you are planning to consult, you may want to put advertisements in local newspapers, periodicals, or trade magazines. Only advertise in publications that you feel will reach your potential clients.
- Direct mail campaign.
  - Developing a direct mail campaign directed to your target audience can be an effective way to let people know about your consulting services. Direct mail marketing pieces might include sales letters, brochures, or postcards, among other things. With direct mail you need to design eye-catching pieces with copy that grabs the eye of the reader while illustrating what your services are and how the reader can benefit from them.
  - You should be aware that in order for direct mail to be effective, as a rule, you normally will have to send out your mailings a number of times.
- Join professional trade associations.
  - Professional trade associations can be a wealth of information and support for those seeking to grow their business. The Independent Computer Consultants Association for example, provides business support programs and professional support to their members. Check them out at http://www.icca.org.
- Join your local chamber of commerce, Rotary, Kiwanis, and other business organizations and get involved.
  - Make sure people in the business community are aware of your consulting business and the services you provide. You can never tell who might need your skills.
- Present yourself as an expert.
  - As a consultant, one of the best ways to get new clients is by presenting yourself as an expert in your field. What you need to do is find ways to get out word of your expertise. Once that is accomplished, when a company needs someone with your expertise, they will hopefully think of you first. How can you present yourself as an expert? There are a number of ways.
    - ◇ Do public speaking. If you are comfortable speaking in front of groups of people, giving speeches, facilitating workshops, and leading seminars are an excellent way to help position you as an expert. Where can you speak? Civic group meetings, indus-

try and business meetings and events, conferences and conventions, colleges and universities, and so on.

◇ Get published. If you really want to establish yourself as an expert, find a way to get published. Whether you write a book on your area of expertise, an article for the newspaper, a monthly column for a trade magazine, or an online article, getting published gives you credibility. How do you get started? Contact editors and pitch ideas or write on spec and submit your article for consideration. Some individuals also develop and publish their own newsletter to help bring their name and expertise to the eyes of potential clients. Many people today also use blogging as a way to let others know of their expertise and to help build their credibility.

◎ Cold call.

    ▫ Cold calling can be another effective method of finding new clients. We've discussed cold calling earlier in the book. What is it? Basically, in this situation cold calling is when you call potential clients who don't expect you to be contacting them. In order to be successful with cold calling you need to prepare and perfect your sales pitch explaining what you do and how your services can be useful to the potential client you are targeting.

What else? Do you have literature that looks professional? It's imperative you have some-

thing to give or send to potential clients so they remember who you are. What do you absolutely need? Among other things, you need a brochure or color flyer and business cards.

Marketing Your Business

We discussed marketing and its importance in your career in Chapter 9. What you need to know here is that as an independent contractor or freelancer, marketing can help advance your career as well. Use every opportunity to market yourself and your product.

What can marketing do for you? Depending on where you are in your career, marketing can help establish you as a new consultant, help enhance your reputation, help you introduce new consulting services, and most of all, increase your bottom line.

Before you embark on a marketing program, its essential for you to determine whom your potential customers are. Will you be targeting tech companies, health care facilities, financial institutions, or retail companies? Will you be targeting computer companies? What about software firms?

Once you know who your potential customers are, you can determine how to market yourself and your business. Will television exposure help? What about guest appearances on radio shows? Will sending out postcards with some of your key consulting services be of value? What about sending out press releases on your company? What about sending e-mail blasts out to your mailing list to tell people who have expressed an interest in using your services? There are a ton of ideas.

In Chapter 9 we discussed the 5 Ps of marketing and how they relate to your career. Let's briefly look at how the 5 Ps of marketing relate to your consulting business.

⭐ **Tip from the Coach**
There are hundreds of opportunities between the point where you might currently be in your career and where you want to be. Becoming a successful consultant or freelancer is a journey. Some people get there faster than others. Whatever your final destination, you can have a successful and fun career getting there. The important thing to remember is to look at every opportunity as a way to get where you want to go.

⭐ **The Inside Scoop**
You might be able to get another opportunity, but you can never get back the opportunity you missed.

- Product
  - This is you and your specific consulting service.
- Price
  - This relates to the price you have determined is best for your services. One of your goals in marketing is getting the best price possible for your time.
- Positioning
  - This relates to how you can fill the needs of potential clients with your services. It also relates to how you and services are different or better than your competitors.
- Promotion
  - Promotion relates to the way you promote your services to gain visibility in a positive manner. Promotional methods might include a variety of things, including

advertising, publicity, marketing, public relations, and so on.
- Packaging
  - Packaging in this context refers to the way you package your services or your business. It refers to the way you package yourself as an expert. Are your services unique? Are you professional? Your package spotlights what you and your services can do for a client. Just as your packaging in the way you look and dress and the way you conduct yourself can affect your career, the packing of your services can affect your bottom line.

Finding and taking a class or seminar in marketing methods can be very useful to your consulting career. A seminar or workshop geared specifically toward marketing for consultants in the computer industry can be especially helpful too.

Don't discount the power of marketing in your success as a consultant. Use it every opportunity you can. Done correctly and used together with your talent, skills, and expertise, marketing can assist you in creating a presence in the area of computer consulting in which you work and can help catapult you to success.

No matter what type consultant you are or you aspire to be, you can have a long and successful career. Continue working toward your goals. You will be rewarded with an exciting and fulfilling career that many only dream of.

⭐ **Tip from the Coach**
Believe in yourself. No one will believe in you, unless you do so first.

12

SUCCESS IS YOURS FOR THE TAKING

Imagine working in an industry that has an impact on each and every one of us on a daily basis. Imagine working in an industry that really makes a difference in every aspect of our lives. Imagine not only living your dream, but also succeeding. If you are reading this book, you don't have to imagine one more second. You are closer than ever to your dream career in the computer industry.

Computers are used in just about every aspect of our lives. Whether in this country or on the other side of the world, computers and computer technology make a tremendous difference in the way people live, work, and exist.

Depending on your interests, passions, skills, talents, education, and dreams, the career possibilities in this wonderful industry are endless. Not only that, the choice of working within the computer industry can also encompass almost any other industry you choose in some manner.

This book was written for every person who aspires to work and succeed in any aspect of the computer industry. If this is you, and you know who you are, I need to ask you a very important question.

Do you have what it takes?

"What do you mean, do I have what it takes?" you ask.

Do you have what it takes to be successful in this industry?

"Well, I think so," you say.

You think so? That's not good enough. You have to know so! Why? Because if you don't believe in yourself, no one else will either.

"Okay," you say, "I get it. I know I can be successful."

That's good. That's the attitude you need to succeed!

With that out of the way, let's go over a couple of other facts that can help you in your quest for success in the computer industry. You have to remember that no matter what comes your way, you can't give up. Whatever you have to deal with, when you achieve your goals, you most likely will feel it was worth it. There may be stumbling blocks. You may have to take detours. There may even be times you have to choose at a fork in the road. But if you give up, it's over.

Here's something else you should know: When you share your dreams and goals with others about working in any aspect of the computer industry, there will always be some people who insist on telling you their version of the statistics of the industry.

They may try to tell you how technology is changing, how no matter what you know you will have to keep updating your skills. They may tell you that you won't really be able to get a good job, because all the good jobs are taken by people who are more skilled, more educated, or better trained than you. They may tell you that once anyone hears you know anything about computers, you're going to be barraged with calls from friends and family who want you to help them fix their computers free.

They may tell you that a great deal of technology and computer jobs are being outsourced out of the country, and eventually you might not even be able to get a job.

They may tell you that the successes you hear about in the industry are successes that other people have. "Chances are," they may say, "it won't be you." They may tell you that as talented as you are, you probably will never be able to create the next hottest video game or that you will probably not be the one to create the next popular social networking site.

There might be people who insist on quoting you statistics on everything from burnout to high stress to failures within the industry, and the list will go on. It probably doesn't matter what area of the computer industry (or any other industry for that matter) in which you are trying to create a career—there will be people who will try to make you feel that if you go for your dreams, statistically, you will stand absolutely no chance of success.

If you listen to those people and start believing them, you probably will become one of their statistics. If you pay attention to them, a career in any aspect of the computer industry probably isn't for you. I'm willing to bet that no matter what career you choose and in what industry, they will probably have something negative to say about it.

However, if you have gotten to this section of the book, I'm guessing you aren't going to

let anyone negatively influence you. I am also betting that you are still going to go after your dream.

Here's something to think about. Let's look at a few analogies. Statistically, it's difficult for most people to lose weight, yet there are many people who do. Statistically, most people who play the lottery don't win, yet there are always winners. Statistically, the chances of winning the Publishers Clearing House Sweepstakes aren't great, yet someone always wins. Will it be you? Not if you don't enter.

With those analogies in mind, I stand behind what I have said throughout this book. No matter what the statistics are, someone has to succeed. Why shouldn't it be you? Someone has to be at the top. Why shouldn't it be you? If you give up your dream, someone else will be there. You will be standing on the outside looking in and watching someone doing what you want. I don't think that is your dream.

Will it be easy? Not always. But the industry is full of programmers, software engineers, software testers, and network administrators. It's full of computer designers, computer product design engineers, and computer scientists. It's full of hardware designers and software developers, and people who develop, design, produce, and publish video games.

It's full of applications developers, information systems developers, systems analysts and IT analysts, wholesale hardware and software sales representatives, retail hardware and software sales people, technical sales representatives, and more. It's full of computer and software retail store managers, assistant managers, and support people.

It's full of data security specialists and information security directors, computer service technicians, computer support representatives and ISP support representatives, and call center operators and managers.

It is full of data entry keyers, typesetters, and compositors, computer operators, statisticians, accountants, auditors, and actuaries. It's full of people working in the business and administrative segment of the industry, and people working in the public relations, advertising, and marketing area of the industry.

The industry is full of technical writers; newspaper, periodical and Web technology reporters; journalists; columnists; and authors. It's full of television and radio technology reporters and journalists, and people working as communications specialists, technical support specialists, and software specialists. It is full of people doing research and more.

It's full of project managers, systems technical managers, operations research specialists, network administrators, database administrators, information managers, IT directors and administrators, chief technology officers, and chief information officers. It is full of teachers, professors, and trainers who teach in schools, colleges, universities, and situations outside of the traditional classroom environment, as well as people who do corporate and business training in a wide array of hardware and software applications.

It's full of CIOs, people working in various computer oriented organizations and trade associations, Web designers, Webmasters, Web content developers, Web site editors, graphic artists, and graphic designers, as well as those who sell Web advertising, develop and implement Web promotions, handle Web site marketing, work in e-commerce, customer service, technical support, and so on.

It's full of full-time workers, part-time workers, freelancers, consultants, and more. The industry is huge. It is jam packed with wonderful

and fulfilling opportunities. Why shouldn't you live your dream and be part of it?

Many are concerned about their chances for success. Often they are concerned that there are too many variables. Will there be jobs? Will you have to move to a different geographic location? Will you be good enough? Will you get burned out? Will you be able to actually make a difference? Will your job be outsourced overseas? Will you be able to climb the ladder? Will this? Will that? What happens if this? What happens if that? And the list goes on.

Many are concerned that in certain parts of the industry, success (or failure) is too dependent on other people. What you need to know is that while it is true that others can affect your career, they can't stop it, unless you let it happen. You are in the driver's seat. You can make it happen! What I am saying, in essence, is the decision to keep on working toward your goal is yours.

You have the power. Are you going to quit?

Here's what I want you to remember. Whether you want to be in the forefront of the industry, behind the scenes, or somewhere in between, know this. Whatever area of the industry in which you are dreaming of success, you can do it and do it successfully as long as you don't give up.

Throughout your journey, always keep your eye on the prize: the great career you are working toward in the computer industry.

Sometimes your dream may change. That's okay. As long as you are following your dreams, not those of others, you usually are on the right road.

Whatever segment of the computer industry in which you are interested, your choices are huge. What is going to be your contribution to this important industry?

> ## ⭐ Words from the Wise
>
> Throughout all history, the great wise men and teachers, philosophers, and prophets have disagreed with one another on many different things. It is only on this one point that they are in complete and unanimous agreement. We become what we think about.
>
> —Earl Nightingale

What path do you want to follow? Where do you envision yourself? What do you see yourself doing? Seize your opportunity. It's there for you. Grab onto your dream to start the ball rolling.

Over the years, I've talked to many people who are extremely successful in a variety of careers. One of the most interesting things about them is that most were not surprised at all that they were successful. As a matter of fact, they expected it.

I want to share a story with you, and while it isn't about someone in the computer field, it does help illustrate the point of just how important a positive focus can be in your career.

One night I was on the road with one of the acts I represented. We were sitting backstage before the concert while the opening act was on. I was talking to one of the singers and we were discussing some of the other hot artists in the industry. The singer was telling me a story of another artist who was on the charts.

"We knew he was going to be a star," he said about the other artist. "When he was still in school, he told everyone he was going to be a star, and that's all he talked about."

"Doesn't everyone say that?" I asked.

"Sometimes they do," he continued, "but what made him different was he was so specific about what he was going to do and when. He told everyone he was going to have a hit record before he graduated. [At the time, the man hadn't even recorded anything yet.] He started acting like a star and then dressing the part of a star. He went on and on about it so much that he almost had to become a star to save face. Funny thing was, he did have a hit before he graduated and he did turn into a huge star."

This is not an isolated story. There are probably hundreds like it in every industry. Stories like this help prove the point of just how important a positive focus and believing in yourself can be to your career. What's really interesting is that in many cases, way before successful people even plan their success, they expect it.

Is it the planning and the work that creates the reality or is it the dream that puts them on the road to success? I think it's a combination.

And in case you're thinking that you're only supposed to expect success in the computer industry if your career aspirations are to be a chief technology officer, chief information officer, or other top administrator, think again. You are supposed to expect success in whatever area of the industry you pursue and at whatever level. Every job is important. Every job can make a difference in some manner.

Are you ready for success? Are you really ready?

Do you know what you're going to say when you're being interviewed by the media the day you are named CIO of the Year? Can you imagine the feeling you will have as you stand on stage and accept the award?

Can you imagine how wonderful you will feel as the marketing director of a new e-commerce Web site the day it is voted one of the top 10 new sites? Can you almost feel the excitement you will experience when you get the job as Webmaster of the site for your favorite sports team? Can you imagine the feeling you will have when you get your first patent for software you've developed?

Can you imagine the exhilaration you will experience when you see the video game you helped develop on the shelves in the store? Can you almost see your first byline on a story you wrote for a major technology trade?

Have you chosen the perfect suit you're going to wear to the meeting when you are named project manager? Can you almost see the press release in the newspaper when you are named the chief technology officer of the local college?

Can you hear the introduction you are given when you are presenting a paper at a major technology conference? Can you imagine what your first class as the computer science teacher in the high school will be like?

Can you almost see what are wearing when you sign an employment contract for that hot job you wanted? Can you picture what your office will look like? Do you know what you're going to say?

If not, you should—at least in your mind. Why? Because if you claim something, you're often closer to making it happen.

Over the years, I have heard many similar stories from people who are successful in their careers of choice. Was it that they knew what they wanted to do and focused on it more than others? Was it that they had a premonition and things just worked out? Were they just lucky? Were they more talented than others? Was it visualization? Or was it that a positive attitude helped create a positive situation? No one really knows. The only thing that seems evident is that those who expect to be successful usually have a better chance of achieving success. Those who

> ## Tip from the Coach
> Before writing my first book, I mentioned to a number of people that I wanted to write a book and was looking for a publisher. Their response was always the same. "It is very difficult to get a publisher. It's very hard to write a book. Don't get your hopes up." While my book wasn't yet written, I had already seen it in my mind. I knew what it would look like; I knew what it was going to say.
>
> I had a plan and told everyone the same story. I was going to send out queries to publishers whose names started with A and go through the alphabet until I reached Z and I knew I would find a publisher. The book would be a reality no matter what anyone thought.
>
> By the time I got to the Fs, I had sold my book idea. I wasn't surprised, because I not only knew it would happen, I also expected it. That first book, *Career Opportunities in the Music Industry*, is now in its fifth edition. Shortly after that, I sold other book ideas. The rest is history. Over 25 books later, my dream has turned into reality.

have a positive attitude usually have a better chance of positive things happening.

We've covered visualization earlier in the book. Whether you believe this theory or not, one thing is for sure: visualization can't hurt. So start planning your acceptance speech for becoming CIO of the Year. Start planning the party you are going to have when your book on social networking Web sites is published.

Plan on what you will say at the press conference when you sell the social networking site you created for one billion dollars. Plan your own celebration for your new promotion. Plan your celebration for getting the career that you've been dreaming about. Plan for your own success and then get ready for it to happen.

Creating a Career You Love

While working toward your perfect career, it's important to combine your goals with your life objectives. The trick to success in any industry is not only following your interests but also following your heart. If you're working toward your dream, going that extra mile and doing that extra task won't be a chore.

And when you run into obstacles along the way, they won't be problems, just stepping-stones to get you where you're going.

By now, you have read some (if not all) of this book. You've learned that there are certain things you need to do to stack the deck in your favor, no matter in which segment of the computer industry you want success.

You know how to develop and write your resume and/or curriculum vitae. You know how to write captivating cover letters, develop career portfolios, business cards, and other tools. You know how to get past the gatekeeper. You know what to do in interviews—and what not to do.

You know how important it is to develop a plan and how essential it is to have a good attitude.

You know that it is crucial to read everything before signing it so you can protect yourself, and you know how important good communications skills are no matter what segment of the computer industry you are pursuing.

You know a bit about freelancing, self-employment, and consulting. You've learned how to network and how to market yourself. You've learned some neat little tips and tricks to get your foot in the door. You've learned that you need to find ways to stand out from the crowd.

Most of all, you've learned that it's essential to create a career you love. You've learned that

you don't ever want to settle and wonder "what if?"

Creating the career you want and love is not always the easiest thing in the world to accomplish, but it is definitely worth it. In order to help you focus on what you want, you might find it helpful to create a personal mission statement.

Your Personal Mission Statement

There are many people who want a career in various areas of the computer industry. Some will make it and some will not. I want you to be the one who makes it. I want you to be the one who succeeds.

Throughout the book, I've tried to give you tips, tricks, and techniques that can help you succeed. I've tried to give you the inspiration and motivation to know you can do it. Here's one more thing that might make your journey easier.

Create your personal mission statement. Why? Because your mission statement can help you define your visions clearly. It will give you a path, a purpose, and something to follow. Most importantly, putting your mission statement in writing can help you bring your mission to fruition.

What's a mission statement? Basically, it's a statement declaring what your mission is in your life and/or your career. How do you do it? As with all the other exercises you've done, sit down, get comfortable, take out a pen and a piece of paper, and start writing. What is your mission? What do you want in your career?

Remember that your mission statement is for you. You're not writing it for your family, your friends, or your employer. It can be changed or modified at any time.

Think about it for a moment. What do you want to do? Where do you want be? What's the path you want to take? What are your dreams? What is your mission?

There is no right way to write your mission statement. Some people like to write it in paragraph form. Others like to use bullets or numbers. Your mission statement might be one sentence, one paragraph, or even fill two or three pages. It's totally up to you. It really doesn't matter as long as you get it down in writing. The main thing to remember is to make your statement a clear and concise declaration of your goals and your mission.

Here are some examples of simple mission statements.

◎ A Computer graphics designer
  ▫ My mission once I get my degree is a job designing the graphics for a record label in the music industry. I want to design the graphics for CD covers, T-shirts, and other merchandise. After I get some experience, one of my goals is to eventually start my own computer graphics business, handling the graphics needs of clients in the music industry.

◎ Game developer
  ▫ My mission is to use my education, skills, talents, and love of games to develop games for the biggest gaming companies in the world. I want to develop games that everyone not only want to play, but can't stop playing. And while most people just focus on only one or two parts of a game's development, it is my mission to have input in as many pieces of the process as I can. I want to be involved in the concept, the program, the graphics, the design, the music, the production, and the testing. As a matter of fact, I want to be the publisher. It is my goal to develop games that are the classics of our time.

◎ A Computer science teacher
  ▫ My mission is to use my education, skills, talent, patience, and love of computers and technology to become an elementary school computer science teacher. I want to provide new experiences to children in my classroom. I want to help maximize the success of every child and give them confidence in themselves. I want to be instrumental in every child being computer and technology savvy.
  ▫ It is also my mission to eventually write a book about innovative methods of teaching older people who have no experience with computer technology to become comfortably computer literate.

◎ An Online marketing director
  ▫ My goal is to finish college and get my bachelor's degree with a double major in business and marketing. My mission is to use my education, talents, and skills to first get a job as an assistant online marketing director for an established site. After obtaining some experience, my mission is to find a position as a full-fledged marketing director of a large, prestigious retail site. It is my goal, through my efforts, to help the site create a huge online presence.

- I eventually want to start my own online marketing agency with a large roster of prestigious sites.
◎ CTO
  - I want to be the chief technology officer of a large, prestigious entertainment company. I want to develop and define an IT architecture that will maximize revenue for the company so the company becomes the most profitable and respected entertainment company in the world.
◎ Professional blogger
  - My mission is to become a professional blogger. I want to work in the marketing department of a large corporation and, through blogging, help them build their brand.
  - I want to write a best-selling business book on using professional blogging to help build brands.
◎ Technology reporter
  - My mission is to get my bachelor's degree in journalism with a minor in computer science. After completing my education I want to become a technology reporter for a major newspaper. I eventually want a syndicated column focusing on all aspects of computers and technology. I further want to have my own satellite radio show where listeners can call in to discuss technology issues.
◎ Web site Owner
  - I want to use my education, training, skills, experiences, and passion for

---

⭐ Tip from the Coach

Put your personal mission statement on post-it notes and stick them up all around you to keep focused on your goals.

---

providing women with the most comprehensive information on health, work, and family issues to develop and create the best Web site for women ever.
  - I expect to build the Web site into such a great resource that five years after its launch, I want to sell it to one of the major Internet companies for $100 million dollars! (I still want to stay on as a consultant.)

What do you do with your mission statement? Use it! Review it to remember the goals you are working toward. Use it as motivation. Use it to help you move in the right direction.

You would be surprised at how many successful people have their personal mission statement hanging on their wall, taped to their computer, or in their pocket. I know individuals who keep a copy of their mission statement in their wallet, taped to their bathroom mirror, stuck on their computer monitor, placed in the inside of a desk drawer, or in another location where they can regularly glance at it.

Where ever you decide to place your mission statement, be sure to look at it daily so you can always keep your mission in mind. It makes it easier to keep focused on your ultimate goal.

Success Strategies

We have discussed marketing, promotion, and publicity. Used effectively, they can help your career tremendously. Here's what you have to remember: Don't wait for someone else to recognize your skills, accomplishments, and talents; promote yourself. There are many keys to success. Self-promotion is another important one.

Don't toot your own horn in an annoying or obnoxious manner, but make sure people notice you. You want to stand out in a positive way. Don't keep your accomplishments a secret. Instead claim them proudly.

We've all been taught to be modest. "Don't boast," your mother might have said as you were growing up. But if your goal is success in your career, sometimes you can just be too quiet for your own good.

Your ultimate challenge is to create buzz. You need to create spin. You need others to know what you've done and what you're doing in the future. Some people aren't willing or able to do what it takes. If you want to succeed, it's imperative that you get started. Buzz doesn't usually happen overnight, but every day you wait is another day you're behind in the job.

Begin to think like a publicist. Whatever segment of the industry you're working in and whatever level you are in your career, you need to constantly promote yourself or no one will know you exist. While others may help, the responsibility is on you to make your career work and make your career successful.

It's essential to continuously look for opportunities of all kinds and then grab hold of them. You need to be aware that in your life and career, on occasion, there may be doors that close. The trick here is not to let a door close without looking for the window of opportunity that is always there. If you see an opportunity, jump on it immediately. It is usually there just waiting for you!

Throughout the book we've discussed the importance of networking. Once you become successful, it doesn't mean it is over.

If you've landed a new job, keep networking. Continue meeting people. Continue getting your name out there. You can never tell who knows who and what someone might need. There are always new opportunities ahead and if you don't keep networking you might miss some of them. Keep nurturing your network and developing contacts. This is also true as your career progresses. Keep networking, meeting people, and making contacts. It is essential to the success of your career.

Don't be afraid to ask for help. If you know someone who can help you in your career, ask. The worst they can say is no. The best that can happen is you might get some assistance. Of course, if you can help someone else, do that as well.

Always be prepared for success. It might be just around the corner. Whatever segment of the industry you are pursuing, continue honing your skills. Keep taking classes, attending seminars, and going to workshops.

Technology continues to change and evolve. Keep up with the trends, read the trades, and make sure you know what is happening today.

Don't get caught into the thought pattern, of "that's not how they did it in the old days." Or, "My way is the only way." Get used to the idea that in our ever-changing world, there will be change. Instead of pushing it away or making believe it doesn't exist, embrace it. You might just come up with a better or more effective way to do things.

Stay as fit and healthy as you can. Try to eat right, get sleep, exercise, and take care of yourself. After all your hard work, you don't want to finally succeed and be too sick or tired to enjoy it.

Whatever facet of the industry you are involved with, you are going to be selling yourself or ideas. You might, for example, be selling yourself to a hiring committee or a human resources manager. You might be selling yourself to partners of a consulting group. You might be selling yourself when you are going after a project or a promotion. You might be selling your

---

Tip from the Coach

They say it takes approximately 21 days to break one habit and form a new one. With that in mind, if there is any habit you have that bothers you, is detrimental to your career, or any part of your life for that matter, know that you can not only change it, but do so fairly quickly. If, for example, you find yourself speaking over others when they are talking, begin today by consciously making an effort to listen, and then speak. You will find that if you continue to do that on a daily basis, soon it will become a habit.

Similarly, if you are told that you are negative at work, start today by consciously making an effort to be positive. Before you make a comment about something, stop, think about what you are saying, and try to put a positive spin on it. Continue doing this and a few weeks later, you will find that not only will your attitude be perceived more positively, it will be more positive.

Words from the Wise

Keep all professional conversations professional and positive. Don't complain. Don't whine. Don't be negative.

---

services to clients. You might be selling your ideas to the director of your department.

What else? You might be selling or pitching your story for publicity. You might be selling an idea for a weekly newspaper column. There are any number of situations in which you may be selling yourself or your ideas. Take a lesson from others who have made it to the top and prepare ahead of time. That way when you're in a situation where you need to say something, you'll be ready.

Sales skills are essential. Know that you are the best and know how to sell yourself the best way possible. Come up with a pitch and practice it until you're comfortable.

Always be positive. A good attitude is essential to your life and your professional success. Here's the deal. We've discussed this before. People want to be around other people who are positive. If there is a choice between two people with similar talents and skills and you have a better outlook than anyone else, a more positive type of personality, and passion, you're going to be chosen. You're going to get the job. You're going to succeed.

Change the way you look at situations and the situations you look at will change. What does that mean? If you look at a situation as a problem, it will be a problem. If, on the other hand, you look at a situation as an opportunity, it becomes one.

If, when looking at the computer industry, all you see are the trials and tribulations of trying to succeed, all you will have are trials and tribulations. If, on the other hand, you look at the road to success in this industry as a wonderful and exciting journey, it will be.

Keeping Things Confidential

Privacy and confidentiality are crucial when working in many parts of the computer and technology industry. What this means is that it is your responsibility to keep insider information private and confidential when required.

Climbing the Career Ladder

Generally, whatever you want to do in life, you most likely are going to have to pay your dues. Whatever segment of the computer industry you've chosen to pursue, most likely you're going to have to pay your dues as well. Now that you've accepted that fact, the question is, how do you climb the career ladder? How do you succeed?

How do you go, for example, from a job as a junior programmer to a senior programmer? How do you go from a position as a coordinator to a job as the assistant director of a department? How do you move up to become a department head? How do you make sure, you're the one to get the promotion? How do you go from the technology reporter for a local weekly newspaper to becoming a successful technology reporter for a major publication?

How do you move up to the position of project manager? How do you go from being the new computer science professor to one of the most sought out professors on campus? How do you go from a job as a publicity assistant at a software company to their director of public relations? How do you go from a database manager at a small company to a database administrator at a large, prestigious company? How do

you go from a computer technical support representative at an ISP to the shift manager?

There are many things you're going to have to do to climb the career ladder, but it can be done. We've covered a lot of them throughout the book. Work hard, keep a positive attitude, and act professionally at all times. Stay abreast of the business, network, and hone your skills and talents so you can back up your claims of accomplishments.

Look for a mentor who can help you move your career in the right direction and propel you to the top of your field. Join trade associations and the unions. Read the trades, take seminars, classes, and workshops, and take part in other learning opportunities. Continue your education when you can. Be the best at what you do. Keep your goal in mind.

Look at every opportunity with an open mind. When you're offered something, ask yourself:

◎ Is this what I want to be doing?
◎ Is this part of my dream?
◎ Is this part of my plan for success?
◎ Is this opportunity a stepping-stone to advancing my career?
◎ Will this experience be valuable to me?

Fortunately or unfortunately, job progression doesn't always follow the normal career path. A coordinator in the marketing department of a software company may come up with a great idea or get a break and end up in the position of director of public relations. An unknown author may get a mention on *Oprah* about his book using the Web to find the perfect mate and be catapulted to the bestseller list and tremendous success.

An innovative software program that can stop identity theft in its tracks, mentioned in a number of media stories, might catapult the career of a new program developer. It all depends. If it can happen to someone else, it might happen to you. That is one of the greatest things about your career. You just never know what tomorrow might bring.

You never know when a chance meeting is going to land you a great job. You never know when someone passing through town might read about one of your accomplishments in a local newspaper and recruit you for a position in a larger company or a more prestigious job. You never know who will tell a headhunter, recruiter, or human resources director about you and you will get an unexpected call. You really never know when success will come your way. It can happen at any time.

It should be noted that success means different things to different people. There are many people who work in the computer industry who are not chief information officers or chief technology officers. There are many who don't work for the biggest or most prestigious companies. Many who never become an administrator or the director of a department. Yet these people are all still successful. They are earning a living, doing what they love, and living their dream.

And it's like that in all segments of the industry. There are thousands of individuals working in various areas of the computer industry and the peripheral fields who may not be the ones you hear of, might not be the ones winning the awards, or may not be the ones you read the stories about in the newspaper. They may not be the ones developing the games that become popular or the Webmasters of the largest, most prestigious sites. That doesn't preclude them from having a successful career. To the contrary, one of the best things about working in the computer industry is that almost every job has some impact on others. Every job can make a differ-

ence—even if it's just a little one. And that little difference can make a big difference in the lives of others.

Risk Taking—Overcoming Your Fears

Everyone has a comfort zone from which they operate. What's a comfort zone? It's the area where you feel comfortable both physically and psychologically. Most of the time you try to stay within this zone. It's predictable, it's safe, and you generally know what's coming.

Many people get jobs, stay in them for years, and then retire. They know what's expected of them. They know what they're going to be doing. They know what they're going to be getting. The problem is that it can get boring, there's little challenge, and your creativity can suffer.

Stepping out of your comfort zone is especially important to your career if you want to climb the career ladder. Wanting to step out of your comfort zone is often easier said than done, but every now and then you're going to have to push yourself.

The key to career success in the computer industry as well as your own personal growth is the willingness to step outside of your comfort zone. Throughout your career you're going to be faced with decisions. Each decision can impact your career. Be willing to take risks. Be willing to step out of your comfort zone.

⭐ **Tip from the Coach**

If you're starting to feel comfortable in your career or starting to feel bored, it's time to step out of your comfort zone and look for new challenges.

Is it scary? Of course, but if you don't take risks you stand the chance of your career stagnating. You take the chance of missing wonderful opportunities.

Should you take a promotion? Should you stay at the same job? Should you go to a different company? Should you go back to school? Should you move? Should you strike out on your own? Should you take a chance?

How do you make the right decision? Try to think about the pros and cons of your choices. Get the facts, think about them, and make your decision.

"What if I'm wrong?" you ask.

Here's the good news. Usually you will make the right decision. If by chance you don't, it's generally not a life and death situation. If you stay at the same job and find you should have left, for example, all you need to do is look for a new job. If you change jobs and you're not happy, you can usually find a new job as well. Most things ultimately work out. Do the best you can and then go on.

If your career is stagnant, do something. Don't just stay where you are because of the fear of leaving your comfort zone and the fear of the unknown.

Some Final Thoughts

No matter where you are in your career, don't get stagnant. Always keep your career moving. Once you reach one of your goals, your journey

---

★ Words from the Wise

Persevere. The reason most people fail is because they gave up one day too soon.

–Shelly Field

---

isn't over. You have to keep setting new goals and move forward to reach them.

Keep working toward your goal. It can happen. Don't settle for less than what you want. Every goal you meet is another stepping-stone toward an even better career, no matter what segment of the computer industry you are pursuing.

While I would love to promise you that after reading this book you will become a the CIO of the year, owner of the most prestigious Web site in the world, the developer of one of the most popular games ever, the director of your department, the CTO of a well-known company, or the recipient of $10 million for selling your social networking site, unfortunately I can't.

What I can tell you is that the advice in this book can help you move ahead and stack the deck in your favor in this industry. I've given you the information. You have to put it into action.

There are numerous factors that are essential to your success. You need to be prepared. There's no question that preparation is necessary. Talent in your field is critical as well. Being in the right place at the right time is essential, and good luck doesn't hurt. Perseverance is vital to success, no matter what you want to do, what area of the industry you want to enter, and what career level you want to achieve.

Do you want to know why most people don't find their perfect job? It's because they gave up looking before they found it. Do you want to know why some people are on the brink of success, yet never really get there? It's because they gave up.

★ Tip from the Top

Try to treat everyone from subordinates to colleagues to superiors to customers to clients the way you want to be treated—with respect and dignity.

Do you want to know what single factor can increase your chances of success? It's perseverance! Don't give up.

Have fun reading this book. Use it to jump-start your career and inspire you to greater success and accomplishments. Draw on it to achieve your goals so you can have the career of your dreams. Use it so you don't have to look back and say, "I wish I had." Use it instead so you can say, "I'm glad I did."

I can't wait to hear about your success stories. Be sure to let us know how this book has helped your career by logging on to http://www.shellyfield.com.

I would also love to hear about any of your own tips or techniques for succeeding in any aspect of the computer industry. You can never tell. Your successes might be part of our next edition!

APPENDIX I

TRADE ASSOCIATIONS, UNIONS, AND OTHER ORGANIZATIONS

Trade associations, unions, and other organizations can be valuable resources for career guidance as well as professional support. This list includes many of the organizations related to the computer industry. Names, addresses, phone numbers, e-mail addresses, and Web sites (when available) have been included to make it easier for you to obtain information. Check out the Web sites in Appendix II to learn more about various organizations and what they offer.

Academy of Security Educators and Trainers (ASET)
PO Box 802
Berryville, VA 22611-0802
(540) 554-2540
http://www.asetcse.org

Accrediting Commission of Career Schools and Colleges of Technology (ACCSCT)
2101 Wilson Boulevard, Suite 302
Arlington, VA 22201-3062
(703) 247-4212
info@accsct.org
http://www.accsct.org

Advanced Computer Engineers Society (ACES)
1325 Las Villas Way
Escondido, CA 92026-1946
(760) 747-8766
hyrotkel1@cox.net

Alliance for Telecommunications Industry Solutions (ATIS)
1200 G Street, NW, Suite 500
Washington, DC 20005-6706
(202) 628-6380 (202) 393-5453 (fax)
atispr@atis.org
http://www.atis.org

American Association for Adult and Continuing Education (AAACE)
10111 Martin Luther King Jr. Highway
Suite 200C
Bowie, MD 20720-4200
(301) 459-6261
aaace10@aol.com
http://www.aaace.org

American Association of Webmasters (AAWM)
124 South 107th Drive

Avondale, AZ 85323-3307
(623) 202-5613
info@aawebmasters.com
http://www.aawebmasters.com

American Computer Science League (ACSL)

PO Box 521
West Warwick, RI 02893-0521
(401) 822-4312
info@acsl.org
http://www.acsl.org

American Design Drafting Association

105 East Main Street
Newbern, TN 38059-1526
(731) 627-0802
(731) 627-9321 (fax)
corporate@adda.org
http://www.adda.org

American Electronics Associations (AeA)

601 Pennsylvania Avenue, NW, Suite 600
Washington, DC 20004-2601
(202) 682-9110
(202) 682-9111 (fax)
csc@aeanet.org
http://www.aeanet.org

American Federation of Government Employees, AFL-CIO

80 F Street, NW
Washington, DC 20001-1528
(202) 737-8700
(202) 639-6441 (fax)
comments@afge.org
http://www.afge.org

American Management Association (AMA)

1601 Broadway

New York, NY 10019-7420
(212) 586-8100
(212) 903-8168 (fax)
customerservice@amanet.org
http://www.amanet.org

American Society for Information Science and Technology

1320 Fenwick Lane, Suite 510
Silver Spring, MD 20910-3560
(301) 495-0900
(301)495-0810 (fax)
asis@asis.org
http://www.asis.org

American Society for Training and Development (ASTD)

1640 King Street
PO Box 1443
Alexandria, VA 22313-2043
(703) 683-8100
memberservices@astd.org
http://www.astd.org

American Training International

12638 Beatrice Street
Los Angeles, CA 90066-7312
(310) 823-1129
(310)827-1636 (fax)

Applied Computer Research

PO Box 41730
Phoenix, AZ 85080-1730
(602) 216-9100
alan@acrhq.com
http://www.acrhq.com/

Association for Career and Technical Education (ACTE)

1410 King Street
Alexandria, VA 22314-2749

(703) 683-3111
acte@acteonline.org
http://www.acteonline.org

Association for Computational Linguistics (ACL)

209 North Eighth Street
East Stroudsburg, PA 18360-1721
(570) 476-8006
(570) 476-0860 (fax)
acl@aclweb.org
http://www.aclweb.org

Association for Computer Aided Design in Architecture (ACADIA)

PO Box 218171
Columbus, OH 43221-8171
(973) 596-6095
president@acadia.org
http://www.acadia.org

Association for Computer Professionals in Education (ACPE)

c/o Blair Loudat
14211 SE Johnson Road
Milwaukie, OR 97267-2336
(503) 353-6105
loudat@nclack.k12.or.us
http://www.acpenw.org

Association for Computing Machinery

Two Penn Plaza, Suite 701
New York, NY 10121-0701
(212) 626-0500
(212)944-1318 (fax)
acmhelp@acm.org
http://www.acm.org

Association for Educational Communications and Technology (AECT)

1800 North Stonelake Drive, Suite 2

Bloomington, IN 47404-1517
(812) 335-7675
aect@aect.org
aect@aect.org
http://www.aect.org

Association for Information Systems (AIS)

PO Box 2712
Atlanta, GA 30301-2712
(404) 413-7444
office@aisnet.org
http://www.aisnet.org

Association for Machine Translation in the Americas (AMTA)

c/o Priscilla Rasmussen
209 North Eighth Street
Stroudsburg, PA 18360-1721
(570) 476-8006
(570) 476-0860 (fax)
business@amtaweb.org
http://www.amtaweb.org

Association for Retail Technology Standards (ARTS)

325 Seventh Street, NW, Suite 1100
Washington, DC 20004-2818
(202) 626-8140
(202) 626-8145 (fax)
arts@nrf.com
http://www.nrf-arts.org

Association for Technology in Music Instruction (ATMI)

312 East Pine Street
Missoula, MT 59802-4624
(406) 721-1152
atmi@music.org
http://www.atmionline.org

Association for Women in Computing (AWC)

41 Sutter Street, Suite 1006
San Francisco, CA 94104-4905
(415) 905-4663
(415) 358-4667 (fax)
info@awc-hq.org
http://www.awc-hq.org

Association for Work Process Improvement (TAWPI)

75 Federal Street, Suite 901
Boston, MA 02110
(617) 426-1167
(617) 521-8675 (fax)
info@tawpi.org
http://www.tawpi.org

Association of Computer Support Specialists (ACSS)

c/o Edward J. Weinberg, President
333 Mamaroneck Avenue
White Plains, NY 10605-1440
(917) 438-0865
(914) 713-7227 (fax)
edw@acss.org
http://www.acss.org

Association of Information Technology Professionals

401 North Michigan Avenue, Suite 2400
Chicago, IL 60611-4267
(312) 245-1070
aitp_hq@aitp.org
http://www.aitp.org/

Association of Records Managers and Administrators (ARMA)

13725 West 109th Street, Suite 101
Lenexa, KS 66215-4200
(913) 341-3808
(913)341-3742 (fax)
hq@arma.org
http://www.arma.org

Association of Shareware Professionals (ASP)

PO Box 1522
Martinsville, IN 46151-0522
(765) 349-4740
(765) 349-4744 (fax)
http://www.asp-shareware.org

Association of Support Professionals (ASP)

122 Barnard Avenue
Watertown, MA 02472-3414
(617) 924-3944
(617) 924-7288 (fax)
jfarber@asponline.com
http://www.asponline.com

Business Technology Association (BTA)

12411 Wornall Road, Suite 200
Kansas City, MO 64145-1212
(816) 941-3100
(816) 941-2829 (fax)
info@bta.org
http://www.bta.org

Computer and Automated Systems Association of Society of Manufacturing Engineers (CASA/SME)

PO Box 930
One SME Drive
Dearborn, MI 48121
(313) 271-1500
(313) 425-3400 (fax)
techcommunities@sme.org
http://www.sme.org/cgi-bin/communities.pl?/
communities/casa/casahome.htm

Computer Measurement Group (CMG)

PO Box 1124

151 Fries Mill Road

Turnersville, NJ 08012-0894

(856) 401-1700

cmghq@cmg.org

http://www.cmg.org

DVD Association (DVDA)

2250 East Tropicana Avenue, Suite 19-435

Las Vegas, NV 89119-6541

(702) 948-0443

president@dvda.org http://www.dvda.org

Entertainment Merchants Association

16530 Ventura Boulevard, Suite 400

Encino, CA 91436-4551

(818) 385-1500

emaoffice@entmerch.org

http://www.iema.org

Entertainment Software Association (ESA)

575 Seventh Street, NW, Suite 300

Washington, DC 20004-1611

(202) 223-2400

esa@theesa.com

http://www.theesa.com

Graphic Arts Education and Research Foundation (GAERF)

1899 Preston White Drive

Reston, VA 20191-4326

(703) 264-7200

(703) 620-3165 (fax)

gaerf@npes.org

http://www.gaerf.org

High Technology Crime Investigation Association (HTCIA)

7441 Foothills Boulevard, Suite 175

PMB 41

Roseville, CA 95747-6597

(916) 408-1751

(916) 408-7543 (fax)

exec_secty@htcia.org

http://www.htcia.org

IEEE Communications Society (COMSOC)

Three Park Avenue, 17th Floor

New York, NY 10016-5902

(212) 705-8900

society@comsoc.org

http://www.comsoc.org

Independent Computer Consultants Association

11131 South Towne Square, Suite F

St. Louis, MO 63123-7817

(314) 892-1675

(314)487-1345 (fax)

execdirector@icca.org

http://www.icca.org

Information Systems Security Association (ISSA)

9220 SW Barbur Boulevard, Suite 119-333

Portland, OR 97219-5428

(866) 349-5818

http://www.issa.org

Information Technology Association of America (ITAA)

1401 Wilson Boulevard, Suite 1100

Arlington, VA 22209-2318

(703) 522-5055

http://www.itaa.org

Institute for Certification of Computing Professionals

2350 East Devon Avenue, Suite 115

Des Plaines, IL 60018-4610

(847) 299-4227
office@iccp.org
http://www.iccp.org

Institute of Electrical and Electronic Engineers (IEEE)
Three Park Avenue, 17th Floor
New York, NY 10016-5902
(800) 701-4333
http://www.ieee.org

International Association of Webmasters and Designers (IAWMD)
11924 Forest Hill Boulevard
Executive Suite 22-276
Wellington, FL 33414-3256
(561) 248-5507
(561) 828-0495 (fax)
http://www.iawmd.com

International Computer Music Association (ICMA)
1819 Polk Street, Suite 330
San Francisco, CA 94109-3003
(734) 878-3031 (fax)
icma@umich.edu
http://www.computermusic.org

International Computer Science Institute (ICSI)
1947 Center Street, Suite 600
Berkeley, CA 94704-1159
(510) 666-2900
(510)666-2956 (fax)
info@icsi.berkeley.edu
http://www.icsi.berkeley.edu

International Game Developers Association (IGDA)
19 Mantua Road
Mount Royal, NJ 08061-1006

(856) 423-2990
contact@igda.org
http://www.igda.org

International Intellectual Property Alliance (IIPA)
2101 L Street, NW, Suite 1000
Washington, DC 20037-1526
(202) 833-4198
info@iipa.com
http://www.iipa.com

International Microcomputer Software Inc.
100 Rowland Way, Suite 300
Novato, CA 94945-5041
(415) 878-4000
http://www.imsisoft.com

International Society for Technology in Education
180 West Eighth Avenue, Suite 300
Eugene, OR 97401-2916
(800) 336-5191
iste@iste.org
http://www.iste.org

International Systems Security Engineering Association (ISSEA)
c/o Dana McCulloch
13873 Park Center Road
Herndon, VA 20171-3223
(703) 478-7615
dmcculloch@ewa.com
http://www.issea.org

International Training and Simulation Alliance (ITSA)
2111 Wilson Boulevard, Suite 400
Arlington, VA 22201-3061
(703) 247-9471

prowe@ndia.org
http://itsalliance.org

International Webmasters Association (IWA)

119 East Union Street, Suite F
Pasadena, CA 91103-3952
(626) 449-3709
richardb@iwanet.org
http://www.iwanet.org

Internet Society

1775 Wiehle Avenue, Suite 102
Reston, VA 20190-5108
(703) 439-2120
isoc@isoc.org
http://www.isoc.org

Internet Systems Consortium (ISC)

950 Charter Street
Redwood City, CA 94063-3110
(650) 423-1300
info@isc.org
http://www.isc.org

ITTE: Education Technology

National School Boards Association
1680 Duke Street
Alexandria, VA 22314
(703) 838-6722
(703) 683-7590 (fax)
info@nsba.org
http://www.nsba.org/MainMenu/Conferences
Training/EducationTechnologySiteVisits.aspx

National Association of Computer Consultant Businesses (NACCB)

1420 King Street, Suite 610
Alexandria, VA 22314-2750
(703) 838-2050
(703) 838-3610 (fax)

staff@naccb.org
http://www.naccb.org

National Society of Professional Engineers (NSPE)

1420 King Street
Alexandria, VA 22314-2794
(703) 684-2800
(703) 836-4875 (fax)
memserv@nspe.org
http://www.nspe.org

Network Professional Association (NPA)

1401 Hermes Lane
San Diego, CA 92154-2721
(888) 672-6720
http://www.npanet.org

Professional and Technical Consultants Association

PO Box 2261
Santa Clara, CA 95055-2261
(408) 971-5902
info@patca.org
http://www.patca.org

Public Relations Society of America (PRSA)

33 Maiden Lane, 11th Floor
New York, NY 10038-5150
(212) 460-1400
(212) 995-0757 (fax)
exec@prsa.org
http://www.prsa.org

Recreational and Educational Computing (REC)

Dr. Michael Ecker
Penn State University W-B Campus
Lehman, PA 18627
DrMWEcker@aol.com
http://members.aol.com/DrMWEcker/REC.html

Search Engine Marketing Professional Organization (SEMPO)
401 Edgewater Place, Suite 600
Wakefield, MA 01880-6200
(781) 876-8866
http://www.sempo.org

Society for Computers in Psychology (SCiP)
c/o Kay Livesay
Department of Psychology
Linfield College
900 SE Baker Street
McMinnville, OR 97128
(503) 883-2708
(503) 883-2566 (fax)
info@scip.ws
http://home.scip.ws

Society for Information Display (SID)
610 South Second Street
San Jose, CA 95112-4006
(408) 977-1013
(408) 977-1531 (fax)
office@sid.org
http://www.sid.org

Society for Software Quality (SSQ)
PO Box 86958
San Diego, CA 92138-6958
pete.miller@baesystems.com
http://www.ssq.org

Society for Technical Communication (STC)
901 North Stuart Street, Suite 904
Arlington, VA 22203-1821
(703) 522-4114
(703) 522-2075 (fax)

stc@stc.org
http://www.stc.org

Society of Manufacturing Engineers
One SME Dive
Dearborn, MI 48121-2408
(313) 425-3000
service@sme.org
http://www.sme.org

Software and Information Industry Association (SIIA)
1090 Vermont Avenue, NW, 6th Floor
Washington, DC 20005-4095
(202) 289-7442
(202) 289-7097 (fax)
industrydaily@siia.net
http://www.siia.net

Software in the Public Interest (SPI)
PO Box 501248
Indianapolis, IN 46250-6248
officers@spi-inc.org
http://www.spi-inc.org

Web Analytics Association (WAA)
401 Edgewater Place, Suite 600
Wakefield, MA 01880-6200
(781) 876-8933
info@webanalyticsassociation.org
http://www.webanalyticsassociation.org

World Organization of Webmasters
PO Box 1743
Folsom, CA 95630-1743
(916) 989-2933
info@joinwow.org
http://www.joinwow.org

APPENDIX II
CAREER WEB SITES

The Internet is a premier resource for information, no matter what you need. Surfing the Web can help you locate almost anything you want, from information to services and everything in between.

This list contains an assortment of both general and computer industry specific career-related Web sites. Use this list as a start. The author is not responsible for any site content. Inclusion or exclusion in this list does not imply that any one site is endorsed or recommended over another by the author.

ActiveWin.4jobs
http://activewin.4jobs.com

America's Job Bank
http://www.jobbankinfo.org

Association For Computers and the Humanities
http://www.ach.org/jobs

Best Jobs USA
http://www.bestjobsusa.com

Career.com
http://www.career.com

Career Age/Information Technology
http://www.careerage.com/infotech/index.shtml

Careerbuilder.com
http://www.careerbuilder.com

Career Exchange
http://www.careerxchange.com

Careers.computers.org
http://www2.computer.org/portal/web/careers

CareerShop
http://www.careershop.com

Computerjobs.com
http://www.computerjobs.com/homepage.aspx

Computer Professionals For Social Responsibility
http://cpsr.org/

ComputerWork.com
http://www.computerwork.com

Computing Research Association
http://www.cra.org

Contract Job Hunter
http://www.ceweekly.com

Cram Session.com
http://www.cramsession.com

Dice
http://www.dice.com

DZone Jobs
http://jobs.dzone.com

E-Commerce Jobs
http://ecommerce.computerwork.com

E-Commerce Tech Jobs
http://www.ecommerce.computerjobs.com

E-consultancy.com
http://www.e-consultancy.com/jobs

EngineeringJobs.com
http://www.engineeringjobs.com

IEEE Job Site
http://www.ieee.org/web/careers/home/index.html

International Game Developers Association
http://www.igda.org

ITJobs.org
http://www.itjobs.com/search.shtml

JobBank USA
http://www.jobbankusa.com

Job Openings.net/Internet
http://www.jobopenings.net/jobs.
php?industry=internet

JobServe
http://www.jobserve.us

Jobs For Programmers
http://www.prgjobs.com

Jobster.com
http://www.jobster.com

Just e-Commerce Jobs
http://www.juste-commercejobs.com

JustWindowsJobs.com
http://www.justwindowsjobs.com

Monster.com
http://www.monster.com

MySpace Jobs
http://jobs.myspace.com/a/ms-jobs/list

National Technical Employment Services
http://www.ntes.com

OnlineJobs
http://www.online-jobs.com

SiliconValleyCareers
http://www.siliconvalleycareers.com/index.php

SiliconValley.com
http://www.siliconvalley.com/jobs

Simply Hired
http://www.simplyhired.com

Tech Careers
http://www.techcareers.com

Tech_centric
http://www.tech-centric.net

Technical Employment Services
http://www.techemp.com

Vault.com
http://www.vault.com

Write Jobs
http://www.writejobs.com

Yahoohotjobs.com
http://hotjobs.yahoo.com

BIBLIOGRAPHY

A. Books

There are thousands of books about all aspects of the computer industry. Books can be a treasure trove of information if you want to learn about a particular aspect of a career or gain more knowledge about how something in the industry works.

Sometimes just reading about someone else's success inspires you, motivates you, or simply helps you come up with ideas to help attain your own dreams.

The books listed below are separated into general categories. Subjects often overlap. Use this list as a beginning. Check out your local library, bookstore, or online retailer for other books that might interest you about the industry.

Apple MacIntosh

McMurdie, William F. *Hey, Mac!: A Combat Infantryman's Story*. Gig Harbor, Wash.: Red Apple Publishing, 2000.

Regan, Schoun. *Mac Os X System Administration Reference*. Berkeley, CA: Peachpit Press, 2008.

Simon, Lois. *Mac (the Story of a Happy Apple)*. New York: Vantage Press Incorporated, 2008.

Smithe, G. W. *Macintosh Basics: All the Essential Stuff You Need to Know about Macs*. North Charleston, NC: BookSurge, LLC, 2008.

White, Kevin. *Mac OS X Support Essentials*. Berkeley, CA: Peachpit Press, 2008.

Blogging

Brown, Bruce C. *The Secret Power of Blogging: How to Promote and Market Your Business, Organization, or Cause with Free Blogs*. Ocala, FL: Atlantic Publishing Company, 2008.

Day-MacLeod, Deirdre. *Career Building Through Blogging*. New York: Rosen, 2007.

Demopoulos, Ted. *Secrets of Successful Blogging System: 101+ Tips for Blogging More Efficiently, Effectively, and Profitably*. Durham, NH: Demopoulos Associates, 2007.

Krakoff, Patsi. *Better Business Blogging: The simple four-point system to attract, sell and profit through smart blogging*. San Diego, CA: Customized Newsletter Services, 2008.

Rowse, Darren. *ProBlogger: Secrets for Blogging Your Way to a Six-Figure Income*. Hoboken, NJ: John Wiley & Sons, 2008.

Computer Graphics

Chung, Yongkuk. *Processing Web Ads: The Effects of Animation and Arousing Content*. Youngstown, NY: Cambria Press, 2007.

Shirley, Peter. *Fundamentals of Computer Graphics*. Wellesley, MA: A K Peters, Limited, 2005.

Sung, Kelvin. *Essentials of Interactive Computer Graphics: Concepts and Implementation*. Wellesley, MA: A K Peters, Limited, 2008.

E-Commerce

Collier, Marsha. *Ebay Powerseller Business Practices*. Hoboken, NJ: John Wiley & Sons, 2008.

Ennico, Cliff. *The eBay Business Answer Book: The 350 Most Frequently Asked Questions about Making Big Money on eBay*. New York: Amacom, 2008.

Miller, Michael. *Absolute Beginner's Guide to eBay*. Indianapolis, IN: Que, 2008.

Traver, Carol. *E-commerce: Business, Technology, Society*. East Rutherford, NJ: Prentice Hall, 2007.

Game Development

Bancroft, Tom. *Creating Characters with Personality: For Film, TV, Animation, Video Games, and Graphic Novels*. New York: Watson-Guptill Publications, 2006.

Darby, Jason. *Going to War: Creating Computer Wargames*. Boston: Course Technology, 2008.

———. *Picture Yourself Creating Video Games*. Boston: Course Technology, 2008.

Grootjans, Riemer. *XNA 2.0 Game Programming Recipes: A Problem-Solution Approach*. Berkeley, CA: Apress L. P., 2008.

Hohmann, Luke. *Innovation Games: Creating Breakthrough Products Through Collaborative Play*. Boston: Addison Wesley Professional, 2007.

Information Systems

Laudon, Jane. *Essentials of Management Information Systems*. Boston: Prentice Hall Higher Education, 2007.

———. *Management Information Systems: Managing the Digital Firm*. Moorpark, CA: Academic Internet Publishers, 2006.

Laudon, Kenneth. *Essentials of Business Information Systems*. East Rutherford, N.J.: Prentice Hall PTR, 2006.

Internet and Data Security

Calder, Alan. *IT Governance: A Manager's Guide to Data Security and ISO 27001/ISO 27002*. London, UK: Kogan Page Limited, 2008.

Periorellis, Panos. *Securing Web Services: Practical Usage of Standards and Specifications*. Hershey, PA: Idea Group Publishing, 2007.

Vacca, John R. *Practical Internet Security*. New York: Springer, 2006.

Warren, Paul. *ICT Futures: Delivering Pervasive, Real-time and Secure Services*. Hoboken, N.J.: John Wiley & Sons, 2008.

Marketing and E-Marketing

Clarke, Irvine. *Advances in Electronic Marketing*. Hershey, PA: Idea Group Publishing, 2005.

Scott, David Meerman. *Cashing in with Content: How Innovative Marketers Use Digital Information to Turn Browsers into Buyers*. Medford, NJ: Information Today, 2005.

Wiley Editors. *Wiley Pathways E-Marketing*. Hoboken, NJ: John Wiley & Sons, 2008.

Programming

Deitel & Associates Staff. *Simply Visual Basic 2008*. Boston: Prentice Hall Higher Education, 2008.

Deloura, Mark. *Best of Game Programming Gems*. Boston: Charles River Media, 2008.

McGrath, Mike. *C++ Programming in Easy Steps*. Southam, UK: Computer Step, 2008.

Speiregen, Paul. *Programming, Planning and Practice 2009*. New York: Kaplan Publishing, 2008.

Wagner, Richard. *Building Facebook Applications*. Hoboken, NJ: John Wiley & Sons, 2008.

Wang, Wallace. *Beginning Programming All-in-One Desk Reference for Dummies*. Hoboken, NJ: John Wiley & Sons, 2008.

Wolf, Wayne. *Computers as Components: Principles of Embedded Computing System* Design. Burlington, MA: Elsevier Science & Technology Books, 2008.

Social Networking

Rutledge, Patrice-Anne. *The Truth about Profiting from Social Networking*. Paramus, NJ: Financial Times/Prentice Hall, 2008.

Success Stories

Biographiq. *Bill Gates - Software Billionaire*. Minneapolis, MN: Filiquarian Publishing, 2008.

Corrigan, Jim. *Business Leaders: Steve Jobs*. Greensboro, NC: Morgan Reynolds, 2008.

Dell, Michael. *Direct from Dell: Strategies That Revolutionized an Industry*. New York: HarperCollins, 2006.

Friedman, Lauri S. *Business Leaders: Michael Dell*. Greensboro, NC: Morgan Reynolds, 2008.

Gillam, Scott. *Steve Jobs: Apple and iPod Wizard*. Edina, MN: ABDO Publishing, 2008.

Lemke, Donald B. *Steve Jobs, Steven Wozniak and the Personal Computer*. Jacksonville, IL: Perma-Bound Books, 2007.

Lockwood, Brad. *Bill Gates: Profile of a Digital Entrepreneur*. New York: Rosen, 2007.

Paik, Karen. *To Infinity and Beyond!: The Story of Pixar Animation Studios*. San Francisco, CA: Chronicle Books, 2007.

Web Advertising

Borelli, Anthony. *Affiliate Millions: Make a Fortune Using Search Marketing on Google and Beyond*. Hoboken, NJ: John Wiley & Sons, 2008.

BottleTree Books Editors. *Google Advertising Guerrilla Tactics: Go.* Collierville, TN: BottleTree Books, 2006.

Brown, Bruce. *The Complete Guide to Google Advertising: Including Tips, Tricks, and Strategies to Create a Winning Advertising Plan*. Ocala, Fla.: Atlantic Publishing, 2008.

Davis, Harold. *Google Advertising Tools: Cashing in with Adsense, Adwords, and the Google APIs*. Cambridge, MA: O'Reilly Media, 2006.

Taylor, Vickie. *The Complete Guide to Writing Web-Based Advertising Copy to Get the Sale: What You Need to Know Explained Simply*. Ocala, FL: Atlantic Publishing, 2008.

Web and Internet

Clarke, Andy. *Inspired CSS: Styling for a Beautiful Web*. Berkeley, CA: New Riders Publishing, 2008.

Gray, Michael. *Create Your Own Website: Learn to Design, Build and Publish on the Internet*. London, UK: HarperCollins, 2008.

Huddleston, Rob. *HTML, XHTML, and CSS: Your Visual Blueprint for Designing Effective Web Pages*. Hoboken, NJ: John Wiley & Sons, 2008.

Kent, Peter. *Search Engine Optimization*. Hoboken, NJ: John Wiley & Sons, 2008.

Peters, Paula. *The Quick-and-Easy Web Site: Build a Web Presence for Your Business in One Day*. Avon, MA: Adams, 2008.

Wiley, William B. Sanders. *Web Design and Information Architecture Bible*. Hoboken, NJ: John Wiley & Sons, 2008.

Miscellaneous

Lacy, Sarah. *Once You're Lucky, Twice You're Good: The Rebirth of Silicon Valley and the Rise of Web 2*. East Rutherford, NJ: Penguin Group, 2008.

Levy, Frederick. *15 Minutes of Fame: Becoming a Star in the YouTube Revolution*. East Rutherford, NJ: Penguin Group, 2008.

B. Periodicals

Magazines, newspapers, membership bulletins, and newsletters may be helpful for finding information about a specific job category, finding a job in a specific field, or providing insight into what certain jobs entail.

This list should serve as a beginning. Many periodicals could not be listed because of space limitations. The subject matter of some periodicals may overlap with others. Look in your local library, in a newspaper/magazine shop, and online for other periodicals that might interest you.

Names, addresses, phone numbers, Web sites, and e-mail addresses have been included when available.

BUSINESS TECHNOLOGY

BIZ – Excite
Game Group
50 Beale
San Francisco, CA 94105-1813
(415) 547-8000
http://www.excite.com/bizexcite

BTA Solutions
12411 Wornall Road, Suite 200
Kansas City, MO 64145-1212
(816) 941-3100
info@bta.org
http://www.bta.org

Business Solutions
5539 Peach Street
Erie, PA 16509-2683
(814) 868-9935

corrypub@corrypub.com
http://www.corrypub.com

COMPUTERS IN RETAIL

Software Distribution in Retail-Workbook
Association for Retail Technology Standards
325 Seventh Street, NW, Suite 1100
Washington, DC 20004-2818
(202) 626-8140
arts@nrf.com
http://www.nrf-arts.org

COMPUTER SCIENCE

Journal of Organizational Computing
Association for Information Systems (AIS)
PO Box 2712
Atlanta, GA 30301-2712
(404) 413-7444
office@aisnet.orghttp://www.aisnet.org

COMPUTER SUPPORT

The Floppy Desk
Association of Computer Support Specialists
333 Mamaroneck Avenue
White Plains, NY 10605
(917) 438-0865
edw@acss.org
http://www.acss.org

COMPUTING

ACM Journal of Data and Information Quality
Association for Computing Machinery, Inc.
Two Penn Plaza, Suite 701
New York, NY 10121-0701

(212) 869-0481
http://www.acm.org

ACM Queue
Association for Computing Machinery, Inc.
Two Penn Plaza, Suite 701
New York, NY 10121-0701
(212) 869-0481
http://www.acm.org

CRN
600 Community Drive
Manhasset, NY 11030-3825
(516) 562-5000
feedback@cmp.com
http://www.cmp.com

The Information Executive
Association of Information Technology Professionals
401 North Michigan Avenue, Suite 2400
Chicago, IL 60611-4267
(312) 245-1070
http://www.aitp.org

Management Information Systems Quarterly
Association For Information Systems
PO Box 2712
Atlanta, GA 30301-2712
(404) 413-7444
office@aisnet.org
http://www.aisnet.org

CONSULTING

Professional and Technical Consultants Association
543 Vista Mar Avenue
Pacifica, CA 94044
(408) 971-5902
http://www.patca.org

CORPORATE MANAGEMENT/ADMINISTRATION

CIO Decisions
117 Kendrick Street, Suite 800
Needham, MA 02494-2728
(781) 657-1000
info@techtarget.com
http://www.techtarget.com

CIO Insights
28 East 28th Street
New York, NY 10016-7939
(212) 503-3500
info@ziffdavis.com
http://www.ziffdavis.com

CIO Today
21700 Oxnard Street, Suite 2040
Woodland Hills, CA 91367-3662
(818) 713-2500
http://www.newsfactor.com

CTO Magazine
501 Second Street
San Francisco, CA 94107
(415) 978-3120

EWEEK
28 East 28th Street
New York, NY 10016-7939
(212) 503-3500
info@ziffdavis.com
http://www.ziffdavis.com

DATABASES

Database Trends and Applications
500 Madison Avenue
Morristown, NJ 07960
(973) -285-3305

DESIGN

Design Drafting News
American Design Drafting Association
105 East Main Street
Newbern, TN 38059-1526
(731) 627-0802
corporate@adda.org
http://www.adda.org

E-COMMERCE

E-Commerce Market Reporter
1913 Atlantic Avenue
Manasquan, NJ 08736
(732) 292-1100
ecic@thecic.com
http://www.theecic.com

E-Business Strategies and Solutions
PO Box 290565
Boston, MA 02129-0210
(617) 742-5200
info@psgroup.com
http://www.psgroup.com

ELECTRONICS DESIGNERS

EDN World
275 Washington Street
Newton, MA 02458
(617) 558-4454
http://www.reedbusiness.com

ENGINEERING

IEEE Design & Test of Computer
445 Hoes Lane
Piscataway, NJ 08854-4141
(732) 981-0060
http://www.ieee.org

Engineering Times
National Society of Professional Engineers
(NSPE)
1420 King Street
Alexandria, VA 22314-2794
(703) 684-2800
memserv@nspe.org
http://www.nspe.org

GAME DEVELOPMENT

CCGDA Report
International Game Developers Association
(IGDA)
19 Mantua Road
Mount Royal, NJ 08061-1006
(856) 423-2990
contact@igda.org
http://www.igda.org

INFORMATION MANAGEMENT

Academy of Information and Management Sciences Journal
145 Travis Road
PO Box 2689
Cullowhee, NC 28723

INTERNET

1st Steps in the Hunt
PO Box 637
Mill Valley, CA 94941-0637
(415) 377-2255
staff@interbiznet.com
http://www.interbiznet.com

Inter@ctive Week
100 Quentin Roosevelt Boulevard
Garden City, NY 11530-4874

(212) 503-3999
http://www.zdnet.com/intweek/

Net Developer's Journal
SYS-CON Media, Inc.
135 Chestnut Ridge Road
Montvale, NJ 07645-1152
(201) 802-3040
info@sys-con.com
http://www.sys-con.com

INTERNET TECHNOLOGY

Baseline
28 East 28th Street
New York, NY 10016-7939
(212) 503-3500
info@ziffdavis.com
http://www.ziffdavis.com

OFFICE TECHNOLOGY

Office Technology
12411 Wornall Road, Suite 200
Kansas City, MO 64145-1212
(816) 941-3100
info@bta.org
http://www.bta.org

PROGRAMMING AND SOFTWARE

C/C++ Users Journal
2800 Campus Drive
San Mateo, CA 94403
(650) 650-513-4300
http://www.cmp.com

SECURITY

Business Security Advisor
4849 Viewridge Avenue
San Diego, CA 92123-1643
(858) 278-5600
subscribe@advisor.com
http://www.advisor.com

SOFTWARE DEVELOPMENT

Dr. Dobb's Journal
600 Harrison Street.
San Francisco, CA 94107
(415) 947-6746
http://www.cmp.com

Software Engineering Technical Committee Newsletter
Software Engineering Technical Committee
IEEE Computer Society
Institute of Electrical & Electronics Engineers Inc.
1730 Massachusetts Ave., NW
Washington, DC 20036-1992
http://www.ieee.org

TECHNOLOGY MARKETING

Customer Inter@ction Solutions
One Technology Plaza
Norwalk, CT 06854-1924
(203) 852-6800
tmc@tmcnet.com
http://www.tmcnet.com

INDEX